The

Leopard

Hat

PANTHEON BOOKS
60 YEARS OF PUBLISHING

Valerie Steiker

Pantheon Books, New York

The Leopard Hat

A Daughter's Story

Pantheon Books and colophon are registered trademarks
of Random House, Inc.

Library of Congress Cataloging-in-Publication Data
Steiker, Valerie.
The leopard hat : a daughter's story / Valerie Steiker.
p.   cm.
ISBN 0-375-42101-7 (hard : alk. paper)
1. Steiker, Valerie.   2. Mothers and daughters—New
York (State)—New York—Biography.   3. Daughters—
New York (State)—New York—Biography.   I. Title.
HQ755.85 .S739 2002   306.874'3'092747—dc21
2001133047

www.pantheonbooks.com

Book design by Johanna S. Roebas

Printed in the United States of America

9   8   7   6   5   4   3   2

For Stephanie,
with love and gratitude
for all the yous in you

Contents

Contents

The

Leopard

Hat

Ladybug, Ladybug

Two, three afternoons a week, I find my mother at the beauty parlor. She uses it like an office, talking on the telephone while her hair is being combed out, her nails painted. She doesn't call it a hairdresser's or a beauty salon, like American mothers. She is Belgian and, with throaty *R*s, she says "beauty parlor," the words repeated together so often in our household that they almost become one word. The place doesn't exist anymore. The main hairdresser died of AIDS while my mother was still with him; the other stylist went on to make movies. I have no idea what happened to the soft-spoken women in white nurses' dresses, all those mysterious bottles of potions, the dated equipment, the peach-painted walls. An entire world has vanished.

In my mother's address book, though, a treasurebook filled with her musical handwriting, it is still there, impossible to find unless you know to turn to "Beautyparlor"—the way you can't get the number for the drugstore, the garage, the carpenter, the curtain store, unless you look under "Pharmacy," "Parking," "Handyman," "Draperies." My mother, speaker of nine languages, has her own way of saying things, which I unconsciously adopt. Later my sister and I will cherish these linguistic oddities, the way we always get an adage just slightly wrong—*Will wonders never seize!*, my mother writes to me my sophomore year in college—and will jokingly refer to it as European Mother Syndrome. But for now friends tease me because I say "valise" instead of "suitcase," or they try to imitate her French accent when she calls for me or my sister from the other end of the apartment, *Valérie! Stéphanie!* It is always urgent when she calls us, she has to tell us something, wants us to do something right away. She is a woman of the moment.

The beauty parlor is called Davir. I can hear my mother say it, her resonant voice bearing down on the "eeer." We don't have to cross the street to get there. It's right on our block, and like our apartment, it, too, is on the second floor, which is low enough for my mother, who has a fear of heights. Walking into the peach enclave, its floor-to-ceiling windows overlooking Madison Avenue, one is quickly embraced by the pungent blend of hair spray and nail polish remover, laced with an assortment of women's perfumes, the barest trace of men's sweat. Under the spinning chairs, there are mouselike heaps of dead hair on the floor, which are continually swept away. Aside from the hairdressers, there are no men, mother laughs whenever she tells us this, maybe in relief that it remained just talk, that he never made her actually do it.

Once her head is a mass of ringlets, Norberto does one of two things, depending on the mood she's in. Either her hair goes up, teased into a seductive pile of curls on top of her head and held with pins and a couple of well-placed combs, or down, a more "natural" style, with spray-stiffened waves softly reaching to her shoulders. Whichever one she picks, when she gets home that day and looks in the mirror, she likes it better than the way she had it before. If it's up, she gets mad at us for having liked it down, why were we trying to keep her away from her true look. If it's down, she says we must have wanted her to look old by having it up all the time, it's "younger" this way. She is not really mad, though, just reasoning out loud.

I myself prefer it up. This is what I'm used to, how I think of her, the curls when she first comes home so perfectly arranged. No other mother I have ever seen has her hair that way. As the hours wear on, after the first night of sleeping on it, the upsweep becomes a little lopsided, my mother adding combs and bobby pins haphazardly to keep it upright. She's less coiffed, but maybe more charming that second day. By the third morning, the curls are quite matted down, my mother vainly pulling at them to make them come back to life. No matter what she tries to do, her hair resists her, as if it senses that this is an area where she is not in control. This is why she loves hats. Placing one right on top of her now collapsed do, she is ready—for lunch, for walking up Madison Avenue, for her next appointment at the beauty parlor.

After a hat day, my mother's hair sticks closely to her head, like a little cap. In her bathrobe, she hugs us, her face slick with moisturizer. This is her private side, not the one of lunches at

Le Relais with the girls, dinners out with my father. Hair in disarray, pins protruding in odd ways, this is when she organizes our lives, scheduling doctors' appointments, planning trips, keeping up with her family in Belgium. No one else sees her this way. She is ours, not "on." This is how she keeps the whole thing moving, and somewhere here I learn that you can't work unless you're willing to get down and dirty. On a trip with my father, my mother once walked with a friend, talking about the dinner party she was hosting the night after they got back to New York. "How do you do it, Gisèle?" her friend asked, marveling at the abundance of plans. My mother answered right away. "With this," she said, raising up her right pointer finger, her dialing finger, revealing her favored mode of making things happen.

My mother's hands are very shapely. She has square palms, long, elegant fingers, gently curving nails. Her two aunts, my *tantes*, instruct me from an early age on how nails are supposed to grow, with a roundness from side to side as well as a small curve as the nail leaves the tip of the finger. My nails will never curve as well as theirs—perhaps it's the American air. My mother gets her nails done at the beauty parlor, although in a pinch she will do her hands herself. She always wears the same color, a bright red, so that I almost don't recognize her hands on the few occasions I see them bare. She gestures a lot as she talks, her cherry-tipped fingers moving about like wands, enhancing every story.

My mother's toes are different. From childhood her mother made her wear too-small shoes, to be ladylike. (When my mother married my father, he encouraged her to buy larger shoes, so her feet wouldn't hurt her all the time. Overnight, she went from a six to a seven and a half.) After her painful experiences, she is very vigilant about making sure that my sister's and my toes have enough room in our shoes. My *tantes,* come to New York from Antwerp on a short visit, gaze with disapproval at the sneakers we wear all the time. It is summer, we are out in our country house on Long Island running around. They cluck and say that our feet will spread in those sneakers, just get bigger and bigger without any proper leather to keep them reined in. We are glad to wear sneakers, scared that our feet will turn out like our mother's, which are highly sensitive and have strange contours. Her toes overlap, coming together even without shoes to a kind of point. When she gets a pedicure, she makes sure to tell the woman to be careful, it hurts to have her toes manipulated too much. We can't tell whether her toes are misshapen as a result of wearing shoes that are too tight for her, or because she inherited them—her mother's toes, my *tantes'* toes, are all in the same condition. Growing up, we will constantly look down to check that our toes are straight, praying for them to stay that way and not start to cross over one another. But they never do, so we learn that the plight was environmental, not genetic.

According to my mother, it's good for you to wear shoes of different heights, but she herself wears only high heels, including the satin slippers in which she traipses around the house. After years and years of nothing but high-heel wearing, her hips have been realigned. Anything flat makes her whole body hurt. A woman who was once on a sailing trip with her was amazed to see that even my mother's canvas boat shoes had a small heel. "But do you always wear high heels?" the friend asked my mother with disbelief. "Always," my mother said. "What about at night?" her friend asked, trying to trip her up. My mother thought about it for a moment, and then answered, "I kick them off!"

From the tips of her toes to the crown of her head, my mother gets dressed as if it were a military operation, every detail fine-tuned to ensure a successful mission. But the final ensemble is not a protective shield or a weapon. It just instinctively becomes part of the way she disarms people, wins them over with her warmth, her charm. She has the European habit of wearing the same outfit several days in a row, especially if it is new or she feels particularly good in it. We have to remind her she is in America, where people wear something different every day.

There is a huge contrast between my mother, fitted out in her finery, and the fury of activity that precedes any outing. The whole house is in a fracas until she finishes getting dressed, especially if it is night and she is going out with my father. (Once, when they were off to the theater, she was in such a hurry that she forgot to bring their tickets, and offered up her diamond earrings for the evening to the man at the box office as proof she wasn't lying.) After her bath, she sits on her bed, pulling on her stockings, demanding her silver-tipped shoes, her beaded handbag, a glass of club soda from the kitchen. She is quick-tempered. My sister and I, the housekeeper, all scurry about, trying to keep up with her impatience. We are allowed to vote on what she's wearing, putting in a plea for a certain bracelet, shoes whose shape or color we feel will work better than the ones she has out. As we grow older, she listens to our suggestions more and more. My sister and I learn how an outfit is constructed, the disparate pieces fitting together just so until she is no longer a woman but a vision. We watch in the bathroom as she blackens her lashes, applies different lipsticks, one on top of the next, until she hits on her own inimitable shade of red. My father has safely removed himself to the library by this point, where we hear him fooling around on the piano, waiting for her. He plays one of several standards, ranging from his and my mother's song, "All of Me," to his own anthem, "The Sunny Side of the Street." The minute my mother's ready, jewels and eyes sparkling, an invisible garland of perfume sparking the air around her, she goes and stands in the library door. "What are you doing, Jerry?" she asks. "We have to leave, we're late." My father, laughing a little because he's been ready all along, puts an early end to his song and stands up to join her. It is a sight we are used to, him handsome in his hat, her enveloped in one of her furs, their attention already out the door, my parents, dressed up and going out for the evening. Then they're gone, the scent of my mother's Opium lingering in the foyer air.

We are not the only ones to notice how regularly she glitters. On March 8, 1983, two men with pistols break into our apartment. They don't even break in, they just put a gun to our superintendent's head and have him ring our back door. They know exactly where they want to go. When our housekeeper asks who it is and then hears the super's voice, she lets them in. It is 9 A.M. on a Tuesday morning. My sister and I are at school. My father is at work. The two men tie up the housekeeper, the super, the back elevator man. They tie up my mother. For shackles they use a motley selection of belts, busting into my closet and grabbing them from where they hang neatly on brass hooks. We will throw them all out afterward, disgusted, the innocent pink grosgrain become tainted, the rainbow stripes no longer happy to the eye.

My mother tries not to tell the men where she keeps her jewelry. She tries to pretend that whatever they see, that's all there is. But they know better. They put a gun to her head and say, *We don't want to hurt you, Mrs. Steiker. We're only doing our job.* She gives in.

A few things are at the bank, in a safe-deposit box, but everything else is stashed in her gleaming Biedermeier desk, in a secret drawer you can open only if you press a button hidden in its depths. ("In case we have to go into hiding, we'll have these diamonds," she told my aunt once, prepared to repeat history.) We learn never to store everything in one place, that it is a mistake to keep the sentimental tokens with the serious pieces.

As they walk with her through the rooms, they compliment her on the apartment, then ask if her children are home. When she replies no, they say, *Good, we don't like to do this with kids around.* The thieves stick things in their pockets like pirates looting a ship, first whatever she's wearing—her gold wedding band, her mother's onyx-and-diamond ring, her favorite bracelet, with its fat ruby-studded clasp—and then whatever's lying about, an old watch, a monogrammed compact I gave her for Mother's Day. (Later this makes us laugh, that they took the compact, thinking they were taking something real.) They have brought sacks, into which they pour the contents of the secret drawer. They take all her fur coats, the fox-trimmed mink, the astrakhan jacket, the raccoon cape, cramming them in. They don't touch the silver, or anything else in the house. They only take what's distinctly hers.

When I come home from school that day I am tired, in a teenage bad mood. My sister meets me at the door and tells me we were robbed. I get annoyed, thinking it's a joke, but she persists with her story until I have to believe her. I start crying, hugging my mother again and again, the notion that there was a gun to her head making me crazy, the thought of losing her unthinkable. The police are there, interrogating. We are sent to stay with friends. I stare at people on the street differently, any one of them could have done it. The world is no longer a safe place. Something ugly has come into our home, tried to wreck it. For a long time, my mother won't wear any jewelry. We pester her about it, wanting her to resume being her usual self. Eventually she relents, buying herself a matching bracelet and earrings. Only years later do we realize they are fake, that she bought them just to mollify us.

Out of a noir film, a few days later my parents get a phone call from a man they've never met. He says he will tell my father who the thieves are for a ten-thousand-dollar reward. They agree to meet in the lobby of the Hilton, my father promising to wear a raincoat and carry an umbrella. Our apartment has turned into a kind of police headquarters. There are men in the kitchen drinking coffee. My mother, in her bedroom, gets hysterical. Crying, she absolutely forbids my father to go, she has lost enough without worrying about her husband's life. In the end my father agrees with her (perhaps he is a little relieved after all), and the police chief of our precinct, who is about the same size and also wears a moustache, goes in his place, wired up.

At first the man is suspicious, saying my father's voice sounds different. The police chief mumbles something about having a cold, and finally the man is convinced. He pulls out a photograph of the two robbers and our back elevator man, the three of them smiling with their arms around one another, standing in front of a booth on Coney Island, literally thick as thieves. The photograph, we can see from the date printed on its bottom, was taken the day we were robbed, the thieves so happy with themselves they went there to celebrate. We learn that it was an inside job, that our anonymous caller wasn't cut in on the deal. Even we get that this makes him a rat. The police raid one of the robbers' houses. They recover whatever was put into pockets, nothing of what was put into sacks. But this means that my mother has her wedding ring back, her mother's ring, her bracelet. Gone are innumerable treasures, our baby trinkets, my mother's pearls, the ruby-and-diamond parure my father had just given her as an anniversary gift, the necklace, bracelet, and earrings designed like lush sprays of asymmetrical flowers. My mother likes only old jewelry, Deco pieces like her mother wore.

The *New York Post* headline will read BIG E. SIDE JEWEL HEIST: BANDITS TIE UP RICH WOMAN AND MAID. A policeman is quoted in the article, his only comment "She is a wealthy woman." I am embarrassed that all my friends see this printed in the paper. I hate that the articles name dollar amounts, both because it reveals too much about our family and because it gives a value to the stolen jewelry when what was taken, things of my mother's, my grandmother's, was beyond counting. There will be a trial. It will emerge that my mother gave that same back elevator man money on a regular basis, a hundred dollars here, fifty dollars there, to help him out with his family. He is someone who was always around, coming into the apartment to fix something, operating the back elevator to relieve someone else's shift. We know this man only slightly, but it is still hard to reconcile that he knew my mother and could want to hurt her.

For months my sister and I go with our mother on trips to 47th Street, scanning shop windows for her stolen pieces. We half expect to see one of her coats walking by on Madison Avenue. My mother goes to see a psychiatrist, to discuss the trauma of the event. She explains that she feels lucky to be alive, that she is aware it's only material things that were lost, nothing that really matters. She is concerned about rebuilding the sanctity of our home, making sure that we all feel safe there, that we can all move on. He tells her he has never met anyone with such a healthy outlook on life.

Afterward my mother puts heavy locks on our doors. An alarm system is installed, holes drilled into every window for thin nails, which will block them from opening wide. Before we leave the house for the weekend, my mother makes us check every window to be sure that the nails are in place. We grow adept at snaking our hands behind curtains, feeling for them. At night I have dreams that men I don't know are coming in through the windows, into my room—the classic nightmare of an overprotected child.

After it is all done with, and the shock, the fear for my mother's life, has somewhat subsided, we are grateful to have those few pieces that were stored safely at the bank, for the history they embody that no new jewelry ever will. This is especially true of the diamond-and-platinum set that belonged to my mother's mother. My grandmother was a chameleon, looking like a Spanish matron in a rose-covered shawl in one photograph, a Hollywood diva with turban and sunglasses in another, and like her, her jewels are complicated and changeable. The necklace breaks down into two bracelets, the insectlike brooches, one large and one small, become pendants. There are a seemingly infinite number of ways the elements can be combined. At her wedding, my mother wore the necklace as a tiara, an anchor for the lace veil floating from her dark hair.

I come from a long line of small, elegant, dark-haired women who are somewhat excitable and look good in red. Before I am old enough to speak, I see my mother in a bright red coat, a ring of fur at her neck and hem, a shiny black belt around her waist. She is the most beautiful woman in the world. Her poise, her presence, her easy glamour—these are all things she inherited from her own mother. My grandmother, of ivory skin, dark hair and eyes, apple cheeks, was a coquette. She had three husbands in all: the first and most important was my grandfather, who died in Auschwitz; the second was impossible, and eventually became one of the reasons my mother left Belgium; the third was sweet, but perhaps slightly inconsequential after the purity of the first and the pettiness of the second.

Whatever the occasion, my grandmother was always decked out, as a woman had to be in those days. It was from her that my mother got her sense of vogue, so that during my childhood in the seventies, my mother will look back to the thirties and forties, to the memory of my grandmother in fox stoles, clip earrings, crocodile handbags, a jeweled pin ever present on her lapel. My mother even collects vintage evening dresses from those decades, one-of-a-kind beaded gowns that my sister and I help her put on so as not to muss her hair. But whereas my mother will be overly generous with us, lavishing my sister and me with affection, with loving words, with presents, my mother and her mother were rivals. When my mother, age eighteen, came home one day in Antwerp and told her mother about a pretty coat she had seen in a boutique— *Will you go look at it for me?* she asked. *To see if you like it?*—my grandmother came back the next day with the coat in a shopping bag, having bought it for herself. *It's too old for you,* she said, as she hung it up in her closet. My mother reacts to this minor cruelty, this dashing of her feminine hopes, by going too far in the other direction. If my sister and I ever compliment something of hers, it is ours. *No, no, I don't want it,* we have to say, *it's yours, I was only saying I liked it, that it looks good on you.* She always offers us the first cut of an apple—the best piece, with its sweet flesh preserved under a shiny red back—even though we know she likes it too. We repeatedly have to stop her from trying to give us too much.

Despite all her womanly ways, I learn that my mother was mortified at becoming a woman, a momentous event that took place in Antwerp, after her father had died in the camps, after she and her mother and her brother had come out of hiding. Within months of my grandmother's somewhat precipitous second marriage, it became clear that her new husband was a mean-spirited man. He took pleasure in thwarting my mother and her brother at every turn. He ordered them to do the dishes after dinner, but if he sensed they were having fun while doing so, he would make them stop. Whenever he noticed they were enjoying a song on the radio, he changed the station. To amuse themselves, and to stay out of trouble, my mother and her brother lay on the floor and read the dictionary, starting from the first page, teaching themselves each word in a project they would never finish.

The day my mother got her first period she told her mother in the morning. Her mother and stepfather were having a dinner party later that evening, and as the guests all settled in the living room, her stepfather called for her to come out. She came, uncomfortable, not feeling well, not wanting to be there. He announced to all the adults what had happened to her that day, embarrassing her in front of everyone under the guise of celebrating the fact. She stood there, shamed, not wanting to believe it was happening, hoping that she could crawl back into bed and this news, this horrible man, would all go away.

My mother suffered from her periods, often spending the day

in bed. When, to her dismay, her breasts started to develop, she bound them with scarves, which she pulled tightly around her chest so she could keep it absolutely flat. Perhaps she didn't want to change from the little girl her father had known, felt no desire to become as complex as she felt her own mother to be. Whatever the reasons, her ruse came to an end the day my grandmother put her hand on my mother's back and felt a bump in the middle of it, where the knot was tied. She made her remove it at once, forbidding her to ever do something so ridiculous again.

Years later I will feel the same disbelief when my body starts to change without my consent. When I wake up one morning with one of my nipples protruding from my wall-flat chest, I am very upset. I figure I must have bumped into something without realizing it, or else I have some unusual and deadly disease. I call my mother into my room and we examine my chest closely. One side is level, same as it's always been. The other is slightly poufed out and feels a little sore. We call the doctor. I turn crimson as he begins to explain puberty to me over the phone. How could this be happening to me already?

A couple of years later, when I become a woman, I am fourteen. I am on the coast of Italy, staying in a house with a friend and her mother. My mother brings me there, spends a few days with us, and then leaves to join my father at a spa. I can't believe she is going. I love the friend I'm with, but we are just at that age where one does and the other one copies. I am the doer. It infuriates me unreasonably whenever I see she has done the exact same thing I have—pierced her ears, chosen the same kind of ice-cream cone, bought the same color espadrilles. I can't see that it is out of love. I am mad at my mother for leaving me. My friend's mother is more strict, less fun. Before my mother goes, she asks me to keep a box of feminine pads for her. The box is unwieldy, she doesn't want to carry it with her. Puzzled, I comply.

The day after she leaves, I develop severe cramps. I don't know what they're from, all I know is that I'm in pain and have to spend a lot of time in the bathroom. Every time I pull down my underwear, I see brown stains. I don't make the connection with blood. I just think that something has gone terribly wrong. I confess to my friend and her mother that I'm not well. I feel hot, I can't get away from my physical self. We all decide it's a stomach flu, and her mother promises to feed me nothing but rice, which will make me better in no time. The beach is a rocky challenge, the water wonderfully cool, but I no longer feel like going. I don't trust my body anymore. At night, I cry in bed for my mother, wondering what is happening to me. After three days, I finally figure out what it is, alone in the green-tiled bathroom, my abdomen killing me, the blood streaming from between my legs. I use the pads my mother left for me. Later, stumbling to get the words out, I tell my friend. Her mother slaps me. It is a Jewish tradition, to ward off the evil eye. When my mother returns, I tell her, too, making her swear not to tell my father. She slaps me again, hard, then cries with happiness.

Weaving the Web

My mother attracted a varied group of women to her, from the ones who were strong and funny and emotional, like she was, to the assorted odd ducks, those who hadn't had it so easy, either because they were divorced, married to the wrong man, or just couldn't seem to find happiness temperamentally. For some reason my mother was an easy mark for women with troubles. I suppose part of it had to do with her tremendous capacity to connect with other people's pain. If she saw a person bump into a parking meter across Madison Avenue, she would let out a loud, sudden cry, as if she had felt the blow herself. She often startled me that way when we were walking down the street together.

Once my mother welcomed one of these troubled women into our lives, she would be generous with words, with sympathy, even with money, perhaps helping one of them redo her bedroom or buy a new couch. My father's tolerance for this state of affairs was on the low side. He felt that some of these women were taking advantage. On occasion he turned out to be right. My mother would have a huge falling-out with one of them and vow never to speak to her again. Sometimes we were left with things as a result. I never knew exactly what happened, but the sparkly chandelier in the guest bathroom had a negative charge around it simply because it had once belonged to a woman named Doris.

Through all my mother's friendships, my sister and I watched and learned. There was the tiny divorcée who moped around in slinky leopard pants; the highly independent woman who had two lives, each of which came complete with an unknowing boyfriend; the woman who, after years of being unhappily married, was at last reunited with her childhood sweetheart. My mother was a big believer in the sway of one's emotions. When she was a young girl in Belgium, learning to play the violin, she didn't understand that when the music called for vibrato, there was actually a technique to achieve the required sound. She thought such expressiveness had to do with the violinist's soul, that it was an outpouring of feeling, and felt she would only truly be able to play with vibrato once she had experienced more of the world. Perhaps wanting us to have a leg up on her youthful naïveté, my mother talked to us about her friends' emotional struggles. We didn't always understand what everything meant, but she thought it was important for us to know about life.

My mother filled my head with women's hidden secrets, their touching vanities, their sorry and glorious stories of love and loss.

She was a good storyteller, with a passionate sense of right and wrong, but her morality was supple, interwoven with sympathetic strands, and it cloaked whomever she was talking about in a forgiving sheen. Being younger, and more judgmental, there were times when I could see through a set of facts in a way that my mother couldn't—she was too close to her subject. So when a friend of hers, a wife and mother who maintained both a large city apartment and an equally sizable country house, avowed that she could just as easily live in a shack, I was a bit skeptical, seeing that it was very easy to make such a statement when there wasn't the least threat of it being borne out. My mother took it more at face value, admiring the woman for her sentiments, feeling with a twinge of guilt her own strong attachment to things, to a certain lifestyle. I was nine, ten, eleven, twelve, but having these conversations with my mother made me feel mature, like I was a part of the world at large. I got used to the fact that she would stop midsentence if my father came into the room. He wanted us to learn too, of course—to improve our vocabularies, every night he pretended he had brought home in his briefcase a new word, which Stephanie and I tried excitedly to guess the meaning of—but he didn't think we needed to know yet about divorce and sadness and human folly.

My mother was a collector, and as a result, every corner of our apartment was filled with objects, ranging from the purely decorative, like the multicolored tassels hanging from each doorknob, to the artifacts of her existence, which she could never find it in her heart to throw away. She had hundreds of books, spanning several languages, from the different phases of her life. They took up half a wall of shelves in our library: thick, shiny biographies of Proust and Mary Queen of Scots, worn paperback classics of French and Spanish literature, feminist manifestos from the likes of Steinem and Friedan, books about Yiddish culture, a slender pile of Japanese novels from a course she took with Donald Keene, all of them secretly marked on a particular page with her initials, GNS. My father's books, mostly by heavy-hitting American and Jewish writers, Elmore Leonard, James Michener, Philip Roth, Bernard Malamud, Norman Mailer, lined the shelves on the other half of the wall. Separated by a couch, the two sides had little to do with each other intellectually, but together they gave a cohesive coziness to the room.

In silver bowls and Lucite boxes, my mother also kept every single key that ever passed through her hands, including a few dozen from hotel rooms and many whose uses she no longer remembered. She held on to all the letters she received, every photograph we ever took, and the fancy invitations—besparkled productions in and of themselves—to each party that my parents attended. In the early days of her marriage she made albums for these stockpiles. Later, as their numbers grew unwieldy, she just crammed them in boxes and drawers. My mother couldn't even bring herself to throw out her yearly planners—thick red books, the year embossed in gold across their lower spines, whose pages would fill up in her handwriting over the course of the months with our family's appointments and activities.

My mother's desire to retain things seemed like an effort to document her life, but her energies in this respect weren't directed only at her own *pupik*—one of her favorite Yiddish words, meaning belly button. She catalogued our lives as well, keeping the letters we sent her, our childhood drawings, each notebook we brought home from school. As far as my mother was concerned, she wasn't merely guarding the past, she was also preparing for the future. Once my sister or I had grown out of a piece of clothing, she would ask if we liked it enough to save it. If we said yes, she would take the too-small sailor suit or velvet party dress and store it in a back closet for "the children," by which she meant the ones my sister and I would one day have. Another closet was kept stocked with presents that she bought in advance, silver frames and pens, fabric-covered photo albums, suitable for any occasion, which meant that she never arrived anywhere empty-handed.

My mother drew her inspiration for living from a wide variety of sources, which always involved her amassing more things. One of her most frequently used belongings was a silver Tiffany paper cutter she kept by her bed; its thin metal pincer curved up within a square frame of black plastic, catching the paper in between like teeth. Whenever she saw an ad for a dress that she thought would suit me, or an article she thought I might enjoy, she would cut it out and leave it on my desk, marked with a V. She did this for each of us, according to our interests. If she liked the look of someone's home in a magazine spread, she might tear it out, circling with a black felt pen the fantastic drapery. My mother had an obsession with window treatments, and eventually every room in the apartment had its windows furnished to her satisfaction in a different style. For the living room she put up pale blue silk valances, their dainty short skirts cinched by fabric rosettes; for the library she chose heavy red damask, trimmed in two kinds of ribbon and held in place with antique brass tiebacks. The more stunning the final result, the more unused components my mother had garnered in the process. She was tireless in her quest for the right embellishment, going to old-fashioned trimmings shops and coming home with envelopes full of intricately threaded borders. Thanks to her continuous foraging, she had brown accordion folders teeming with fabric swatches and loose pages, organized under headings like "Design," "Cooking," "Fashion," "Travel."

My father, sister, and I took my mother's caches for granted. In addition to enhancing our day-to-day reality with her projects and plans, she was teaching us that it gave life meaning to have a record of it. That was why each summer that we went away to camp, she encouraged us to write letters to her instead of just calling. We were never surprised by her insistence on the importance of writing—there was no question in our minds or hers that my mother was a writer. She had boxes filled with notebooks, short stories, and essays, and had even taken creative writing classes at Hunter College. In 1975 she penned a first-person account of her childhood, of being hidden during the war, as an introduction to an epistolary work she put together, made up of letters in French between her and her brother after she moved to New York from Belgium at the age of nineteen. She had even gone so far as to send it out to publishers, unfortunately without success. It was clear to us that all this stuff she had around her was material, that at some point my mother would sit down and produce something truly spectacular. In the meantime, she gathered to her the accoutrements of the trade, tapering silver letter openers, graceful Japanese scissors, marble-papered journals. She had a set of Victorian lap desks inlaid with mother-of-pearl and filled with all kinds of hidden compartments that she said gave her a "great elegant feeling" when she used one of them to write in bed.

My mother had a mania for tchotchkes, which manifested itself in numerous ways: a love of crystal goblets, a weakness for velvet-lined boxes with cameos of nameless noblemen on their lids. From time to time I liked to go around and open all of these; you never knew what you might find—a blue-eyed marble, a shred of paper, mysterious for being old. She especially prized curios that had more than one function: an antique photo album that concealed a music box, a wood-paneled table that pivoted around to become a stepladder or a bookcase. My father did too, but then he was an engineer by training and liked contraptions in general, fascinated by their inner workings. My mother, on the other hand, couldn't have cared less about the mechanics of these pieces; she was drawn to them in appreciation of their transformative quality. For that matter, she also liked objects whose appearance disguised their use, like the bendable iridescent-scaled fish whose firm open mouth was a bottle opener. On our kitchen table lay a pair of bladed silver tongs in the form of a stork, which my mother had brought back from Belgium and used to cut sugar cubes into smaller pieces. She was in the habit of placing a half cube in her mouth, right behind her front teeth, before taking a sip of coffee, liking the intensity of the sweetness, the quick dissolve of the granules across her tongue. My *tantes* drank their coffee the same way, a familial proclivity that had no visible ill effect on anyone's teeth.

As a result of all this collecting, almost every surface in the apartment displayed an assortment of bibelots. A given shelf might bring together an Italian blown-glass paperweight, a standing leopard-shaped lighter with beaded eyes, and an antique silver shoe brush. My mother had a knack for choosing each *objet* so that it worked in relation to the others, producing pleasing tensions of form and function. In the otherwise French-style living room, she set a collection of Buddha statues from India and Nepal across the mantelpiece, which gave the entire room a sense of calm. In marrying my father, my mother had found a fellow collector.

Although she was in charge of decorating the apartment, she was very proud of the way he artfully suspended a selection of his flutes from all over the world above the piano in the library, or that on the wall leading to the kitchen he had hung in tidy rows his collection of sleek, somber-colored homburg hats, mostly from Gélot in Paris. (He never left the house without one.)

From both sides, then, my sister and I inherited this love of keeping things, either those that came to one naturally in the course of one's life, such as books, letters, and photographs, or those one went after and brought home, almost for sport. I went through the obligatory stuffed-animal phase—night after night of carefully laying my hodgepodge of friends around me before I went to sleep, only to find them scattered across the floor in the morning—followed by a stickers frenzy, and a passion for souvenir-shop dolls in flashy dresses. Once we got a little older, my mother thought we should collect more seriously. Stephanie had a liking for elephants, which my mother indulged with porcelain and glass figurines. Having no such predilection, I got stuck with thimbles. I think my mother must have seen them around a lot as she made her way through the tables of various antique fairs, and figured they would be easy for a young girl to accumulate. At first I thought it was a very boring thing to have to collect. Eventually, though, thanks to my mother's enthusiasm, I warmed to them. They were interesting things, thimbles, tiny cupfuls of air meant to protect domestic fingers. Over the years artisans had strayed far afield, using the idea of a thimble as a basic starting point from which to embroider all kinds of fanciful creations. The best one in my collection was in the shape of a miniature woman. She had a body made of red Bakelite and an ivory thimble for a head, which was removable, revealing a narrow hollowed-out space along the length of her where you could store your pins. I liked to hold her in my hand and shake her a little, to hear the needles jostling around inside.

At the constant center of all this collecting were the four of us: my mother, my father, my sister, myself. Four pairs of legs, two-headed rulership (although my sister and I knew who was really in charge), eight eyes. We each had our own room. It was understood that my mother had full command of the master bedroom, even though my parents both slept there. We all, even my father, called it Mommy's Room. As for him, he had his den, which was right next door to it, the place where he got dressed every morning in suit and tie. Then came my bedroom, flower-dotted peach walls, matching peach curtains, a shaggy brown rug, and lastly, my sister's, smaller than mine because she was younger, and covered in blue-elephant wallpaper. Since every room had three doors, one to the main hallway and one to the rooms on either side, our apartment was ideal for playing hide-and-seek, blindman's bluff, tag, all games that could go on for hours when we had friends over. The setting was like our family itself, everything interconnected with everything else.

It wasn't only physically that the rooms were linked. A system of intercoms had been set up by the previous tenants, so we could buzz one another from any other room in the house. My mother had a certain way of using the buzzer, a strong, impatient, repeating drone, that immediately announced itself. Even before picking it up, on an extension labeled "local," you knew it was she, calling to tell you to practice the piano, clean your room, put on your slippers (she hated when we ran around barefoot, susceptible to splinters and dirty soles). Often you could hear the buzzer growing louder and louder as it went from room to room, trying to find you. Unless my parents were going out for the evening, we all ate together, and my mother often buzzed us to tell us it was time for dinner. Sometimes the buzzer interrupted the night, catching me middream, but I would roll over, knowing it was just my mother using it to draw my father to bed from the library, where he would have fallen half asleep watching television. That was the only time she ever used it softly.

I usually spent the night in my own bed, unless I had had a nightmare, in which case I went running down the hall to my parents' room and snuck in on my mother's side of the bed. Every once in a while, when my father's snoring got the best of her, the reverse happened, and my mother crawled into bed with me. I liked it when she did this, but she was a light sleeper, and I knew from experience that any extraneous movement got on her nerves. I would have to hold my body tightly, feeling suddenly like I had ten arms and ten legs, all of them dying to flail the covers right off the bed. My mother was cold at night, warm in the morning, my father the opposite. At night she relied on him; in the morning he depended on her. They had a good arrangement that way.

Between the multiple doors and the network of buzzers, inside the apartment it felt as though we were connected to our mother at all times. Upon entering we yelled, "Mommy, I'm home!" or, if she was out when we got in from school, we still felt her presence because she left us little notes, in the kitchen, on the table in the foyer, on our beds, saying where she was, when she would be home, how much she loved us. If she was home, she always knew where we were in the house, and vice versa. The timbre and pace of her footsteps alone coming down the hall could tell us not only her position in relation to us but what frame of mind she was in.

Whether you wanted to or not, you knew right away how my mother was feeling. My father, a born optimist, liked to put a positive spin on everything, but my mother could no sooner lie or pretend about her mood than she could do her own hair. She almost always started out in good spirits, coming to hug and kiss us in the morning to wake us up. We had a tradition of tangoing through the foyer on our way to the kitchen for breakfast. My sister and I took turns. My mother would lean down so we could be cheek to cheek, and then, one set of arms clasped about each other, the other set extended out in front of us, we would begin, our opposing legs moving in sync to the same rhythm. She kept the tune for us, humming it in deep, haphazard dees and dums—her usual way of singing because she never knew the words—and propelled us right through the foyer, until we had made it to the pantry or been dipped, whichever came first.

Through the course of the day, however, my mother would generally get vexed about something. It was a common occurrence to hear her voice rising in dismay. Any number of things could annoy her. She might get frustrated if she was calling me and I didn't hear her immediately, or if she felt that the table hadn't been set properly (the minute we finished cleaning up the current meal, she had us set the table for the next), or if something else hadn't been done the right way. She herself was so quick that slowness of any kind regularly got on her nerves. For this reason she often got impatient with cabdrivers. (One of them gunned the accelerator on her once, but she saved herself by shouting repeatedly out the window, *Help, I'm being kidnapped!* until he gave up after a few blocks and let her out.) She also inspired strong passions in waiters— they either loved her or hated her.

Sometimes a burst of irritation came straight out of worry. At the age of five I fell asleep one afternoon in the oversize cardboard dollhouse they had set up in my room. It was white on the outside, with a moss-green roof, and had pretty pink painted flowers climbing up its sides. My mother stuck her head in, saw me there, and yanked me awake. She had been so anxious when she couldn't find me anywhere that she slapped me. I started crying, feeling very wronged. My mother had no compunction about hitting us when required. She had been raised that way herself. Her spanks, on our arms, or whatever other part of us she could reach, were fast and sharp and stung a little, but they were never premeditated. They sprang forth uncontrollably from the exasperation of the moment.

Of course my mother's anger went both ways. It could just as well be roused on our behalf if she felt we were in danger of being maltreated. Against my will she called up the mother of a boy in my fifth-grade class to demand that her son stop teasing me, which only made things worse. Another time my sister borrowed a favorite jacket of mine, without asking, for an overnight class trip. As luck would have it, it rained a lot, and at the end of the day she put the jacket near the furnace, where it accidentally caught fire. She brought it home with large charcoal rings that you could stick your head through. When my mother saw how tearful my sister was, she came into my room, told me what had happened, and absolutely forbade me to say anything about it. *Your sister is already upset enough!* she declared emphatically, and even though I was furious, I knew I didn't stand a chance against my mother's protectiveness.

Whenever it was directed at you, my mother's temper felt like a fierce current against which you had no recourse. It could take your bearings away, her anger. Normally I knew how much she loved me, felt it in a hundred little ways every day. If she was mad at me, though, a cloud passed over everything, barring me from the light of her admiration and love. My father rarely got riled up, but if he did, it was always clear why, and so I didn't take it personally. It was like the cryptograms he used to devise for me and Stephanie, an echo of his days as a member of the team that broke the first Japanese code after Pearl Harbor. Using the established guidelines—A equals 1, B is 2, and so on—we could figure out exactly what he meant. My mother's line of argument was harder to follow, often ending with an irrefutable "Because I said so!" She thought she was being very logical, so if she told Stephanie and me to stop playing so roughly because someone was going to get hurt, she didn't understand why we were compelled to keep going until one of us was crying. She didn't accept that this was just something children did—our tears were a betrayal every time, and then her disapproving words felt sharper than any physical pain we had incurred.

The worst, though, was when she felt we were being spoiled, which of course deeply implicated her and aroused a strong sense of guilt in all of us. We asked for too much, weren't grateful enough, were too lazy to clean our rooms. *What kind of daughters have I raised?* she would cry in despair, her voice running from low and guttural to high-pitched and plaintive. I knew we were spoiled, in the sense that she gave us so much, but we had good heads on our shoulders, didn't whine or expect the world at our fingertips. We weren't spoiled as in ruined. This was an important distinction, which in her calmer moments she appreciated.

Thankfully, my mother's temper was surprisingly swift-changing. She had a good sense of humor about herself, which could alter the current, like the time she was so mad she un-characteristically cursed at us—*I'm not going to take this chit!* she yelled—and her mispronunciation made us all collapse in giggles. Other times her anger would just dissipate by itself. One minute she would be mad as a hornet that you hadn't done something she had asked you to do (you might not have even left her room yet), and then half an hour later, if you were still sulking about it, she would ask genuinely, *What's wrong?* This often occurred when we were getting ready for a trip, which was typically quite a production. My sister and I knew the drill: shoes went into protective bags, clothes were layered between gossamer sheets of white tissue paper, toiletries were securely fastened in zipper-topped plastic bags. She had us packing for ourselves early on. She still called to us frequently, however, regulating what we should take. If she needed us to find something for her, we would have to leave off whatever we were doing and come help. Dashing from room to room, remembering everything we might need down to the last tube of Bain de Soleil sunscreen, my mother managed to get into quite a state. Just when it seemed like we would never get out of there, we would suddenly be ready, the black suitcases neatly marked with my father's initials lined up in the foyer in their various sizes, my father himself groaning, looking at all of them. The minute we were in the cab, on our way to the airport, my mother would turn to us in contentment, excited about our trip. It took the rest of us longer to recover. She won us over with a ritual we had. Each time we left Manhattan she made us all shake hands with one another. It was a promise to ourselves that we would enjoy the coming adventure, that whatever our vacation turned out to be, it had begun, and we were all in it together.

My mother's flash floods weren't directed only at us. Sometimes I heard her arguing in the bedroom with my father. Her last-stop line was always the same: *You can stand on your head until you turn blue in the face, I'm still not going to . . .* One time a friend of mine was over, and we overheard my mother get so agitated about something that she swore she would divorce him. I was embarrassed. I was used to my mother's impassioned words, knew she didn't mean her threat, that she was just mad in the moment but would come around. I knew how much my parents loved each other, I had proof of it every day. The minute my father rang the doorbell, home from work, my mother dropped whatever she was doing, the phone, a book, and went to the foyer, where they embraced, ignoring for a few minutes everything else pressing in around them—the roast beef in the oven, their quibbling daughters.

Outside the apartment, give or take a little, my mother's territory covered a five-block radius, from 67th Street, where the beauty parlor was, to 62nd Street, where Stephanie and I went to elementary school, a collection of blocks that provided us with everything we needed. There was the tailor where my mother might have a skirt adjusted or an evening gown made, the temple where she sent us to Sunday school, the dry cleaner who returned our father's shirts like new, with origami-like strips of cardboard folded into them.

Within that domain, my sister and I couldn't go into a single store without the shopkeepers knowing who we were. This was true of Gristede's, whose cramped aisles provided everything from mint jelly to roast chickens; Cambridge Chemists, which kept us stocked in Mason Pearson hairbrushes and dark-purple cough syrup; and J. G. Lemmon's, the cluttered hardware store run by old Jewish men and women who joked and kidded with my mother (often in Yiddish) whenever she went inside. My mother was a great favorite in the neighborhood, chatting in her distinctive accent with each teller in the sky-blue building that housed our bank, the nice man who sold antique silver frames down the street, the maître d' of the local French bistro, site of her frequent ladies' lunches.

Because she deemed the vicinity safe, once I gained permission to cross the street by myself my mother sent me on minor errands, to the lingerie shop, where the lady knew exactly what kind of stockings she liked, or the hardware store, for lightbulbs and batteries. It made me feel very grown up to be entrusted with these missions, until invariably the phone would ring in the store, and I would know it was for me, my mother calling to remind me of something. No matter where I went, or how long I was gone, she always seemed to have me within her reach.

Although it wasn't far—only four blocks—and we felt we were old enough, my mother held out as long as she could on letting us walk to school alone. We were probably nine and six by then, and this was unfair—we knew plenty of other children who were allowed. Finally, after our begging enough, she relented. That was usually how it happened in our house. My mother tried to be strict, but she had a soft spot for her children as big as Central Park, and unless we were asking for something outrageous or downright harmful, it was clear that she found it hard to say no. I didn't know it at the time, but for months she followed us from about a block behind, never letting us out of her view. At least we had the illusion of independence. I held on to Stephanie's hand and, feeling free to do whatever I liked, had conversations with the wind. I thought of it as my friend, each gust it offered was a thoughtful response to a question I posed. *Hello there,* I whispered under my breath as soon as I was outside, and the wind would brush my face lightly in greeting. I never told anyone of my relationship, the way the wind ballooned me to school and back, allowing me to float along on its benevolence. Once when I was very small, before I knew the wind so intimately, a blast of it lifted my feet right off the ground while I was holding my mother's hand. I always wondered what would have happened if I hadn't been.

A few years later, we switched to a school that was farther away, and my mother started setting out a bowl of quarters for us on the windowsill in the foyer, from which we were meant to take our bus money. Instead, ages fourteen and eleven, we got in the habit of grabbing fistfuls of change, going downstairs to Madison Avenue, and hailing a cab. Pretty soon we had it down to a rhythm. To ride up Madison Avenue from 66th Street to the corner of 91st cost $2.10 and took about four and a half minutes. In due time my mother caught on to us and tried to put an end to it. She told us she would be watching from her bedroom window, so she could make sure we didn't take a taxi. This hardly stopped us. We just walked up a block and half, hugging the side of our building as we passed underneath her nose, until we were safely untangled from her sight and could do as we pleased.

✦   ✦   ✦

My mother didn't keep such tight reins on my father, probably because she considered him to be a man of the world. From time to time she would sit me on her bed just to tell me how wonderful he was, how kind, how generous, how smart. Her friends teased her that his name must be "My Jerry," since she often began sentences that way. Even his signature moustache was a source of pride to her, and more than once I saw her get worried when he started talking about shaving it off. She delighted in the fact that he was an amateur musician—equally good on alto sax, flute, guitar, and piano—and every so often arranged jazz parties for his pleasure, inviting only those of my parents' friends who played an instrument to join them for the evening. My father also practiced the art of legerdemain, or close-up magic, which depended on what he called "digital dexterity." From our perspective, this meant he could pull quarters out of our ears or unfailingly divine which card we had picked out of the deck. My mother rarely tired of his tricks, and at parties would act as his unofficial helper.

Each morning that my father left for the office—he was a mortgage banker, expert at finding solutions to the complex financing needs of large real-estate developments—my mother was full of admiration, and at night would listen closely as he discussed with her the ins and outs of his latest deals. She didn't have a business degree from Harvard, as he did, but what she lacked in schooling she made up for in common sense.

Once she had us, my mother never had a full-time job, but she was, as she herself liked to say, a doer. Even at night, lying next to my father in their sleighlike bed, she often didn't sleep but lay awake strategizing about the next day and beyond, the feats she wanted to accomplish, the activities she planned for us to do, the trips she hoped we would take. She was always absorbed in a few projects outside the house, working as an assistant producer on several theatrical productions, getting involved with our schools, serving as an active member of numerous charitable organizations. Because there was a constant stream of things running through her head, she had the habit of starting up a conversation, switching subjects, and then, out of nowhere, going back to the original topic an hour later. My family followed these interrupted lines of thought without blinking. Only later, when I noticed how often my college friends would stop me to ask what I was talking about, did I appreciate how much it assumes a common footing to move around like that, leaving such gaping seams between thoughts.

In all her doings, my mother preferred to stick to her own methods. Gifted with an innate sense of the best way to go about a given task, she didn't have much patience for being told how— unless it had to do with something mechanical like a stereo or a video camera, in which case she threw up her hands and let my father handle it. With everything else, she acted by instinct, which almost never led her astray. There was the case of the Aubusson carpet, for instance. Its faded threads of cerulean blue, rose pink, and dulled gold wove baskets of flowers all over the floor of our living room. She must have known the second she saw it that it would be lovely there, even though it was far too big for the space. When she explained her dilemma to the people at the auction house, they told her to fold the carpet under at the edges to preserve its integrity. Instead, much to their chagrin, she had the rug cut to fit the room and then used the ends to upholster things—my parents' bed, a Norwegian settee. Friends and family alike were outraged. But for us it showed that the carpet was my mother's, to do with as she wished, and that she intended to be in that apartment for a long while. Where was the sense in hiding something beautiful away? Useless bits and pieces of the rug—its margins—had now taken on an authority and presence of their own, as vital to the general scheme of things as the center of the carpet itself.

Nor was her wedding dress sacrosanct—a high-necked, long-sleeved, white brocade creation that she wore on December 26, 1966, to marry my father. Some women carefully preserve their wedding dresses, perhaps hoping that their daughters will wear them down the aisle. Not my mother. The following year, she lopped off the sleeves and added white ostrich-feather trim to the neck and hem, transforming it into a sexy black-tie evening gown in the wink of an eye. Of course there were some things that my mother did in her own fashion that didn't work out so well. She never could figure out the right way to open a milk carton. I don't know if it was because she was too impatient to read the brief instructions, or because she thought she could make the carton conform to her will, but upon opening the refrigerator door, we could easily tell which one she had attacked. There would be a single mutilated carton, its top ripped open in several directions, standing out conspicuously among its more demure, neatly folded cousins.

Other mothers might go away on a trip and bring their daughters back clothes. My mother fretted that the clothes wouldn't fit right unless she first measured us within an inch of our lives. One of us would sit on the bed, taking notes, while the other stood with her arms out. Droopy dark-blue tape measure in hand, my mother charted the distance between wrist and elbow, elbow and shoulder, ankle and knee, even drawing the band around our heads to determine their circumference. The eagerly awaited presents she brought back for us didn't always fit that well, so I don't have the faintest idea whether she actually used these measurements once she arrived at her destination. Nevertheless, it made us feel like she was doing a thorough job of things. It also made us feel like she was taking us with her, just as she always traveled with a small, oval-framed portrait of her own mother, the first thing out of her suitcase when she arrived in a new hotel room.

I often felt that my mother was taking my measure. It seemed like she knew every inch of me. She noticed each changing mark on my body—if I had fresh scars on my knees, if I had grown another freckle on my nose—and took it upon herself to monitor these new and sometimes undesirable developments. It was her duty as a mother to make sure we grew up as intact as possible. Whatever the season, she had strict ideas about how we should protect ourselves from the elements. From the first shivery day of autumn, she had us wearing thin leather gloves, like she did, but despite this mandate our hands never felt as soft as hers. In winter, she kept humidifiers going in all the rooms, so that our skin wouldn't become too dry, and forbade us to leave the house with wet hair. In summer, long before it was the custom, she was obsessed with the damaging effects of the sun. She herself got deliciously brown just sitting in the shade, but she was always after us to put on sunscreen, often interrupting our watery games to make us come out of the pool and reapply cream or put on white T-shirts. We had such fair skin that this didn't stop us from getting frequent bouts of sun poisoning.

The year my sister and I got chicken pox, my mother stayed up with us each night until it was over, making us wear little white cotton gloves on our hands while we slept, vigilantly catching our arms midflight and putting them back at our sides if we tried to scratch one of the burning itches during the night.

It was my mother's job to watch over us. She was in charge of all our doctors' appointments, keeping track of whose turn it was to go to the dentist, the ophthalmologist, the pediatrician. She made it her business to know everything about our health, itemizing every one of our symptoms. With me it was always the same: I had a nervous stomach and a tendency toward headaches. Whenever any of us, including my father, had an appointment, my mother came and brought a list of questions for the doctor, holding long discussions with him about our problems and their solutions. The one childhood malady that continually stumped her was growing pains. Our pediatrician had told her they definitely existed, but that there was no real remedy—it was just a part of growing up. She didn't quite trust him on this one matter. I frequently felt the telltale aches shooting along my legs, a kind of pain that was almost sweet. My mother, not quite believing they were real, decided the solution was to have me lie in a dark room and drink ginger ale until they went away, which usually worked.

If my mother registered everything about me physically, it often seemed that she knew what I was thinking, too, especially while she was cleaning my ears. For a long time she wouldn't let me do it alone. It was too tricky an operation, she said, and I could hurt myself. I didn't mind. I liked having her do it. After a bath, I would go into her room with two Q-tips, one wet and one dry. Sitting next to her on the bed, I'd lay my head on her lap. She'd begin by running the wet Q-tip under and over the ridges of my ears, leaving a pleasingly clean cold trail. Then she'd use the dry end, going over the same labyrinthine paths, finishing up with a final spin in the center pocket. Even if I wasn't saying anything, she'd ask me a question, maybe about something we'd talked about the day before. It was often the exact thing that had been on my mind. Whenever she did this, it made me wonder if she knew everything that was inside my head. It was as if she had used my ear canal as a passageway to enter a warm, slightly sticky area that, until that moment, I had foolishly imagined as beyond her reach.

During my junior year in college, I spent a lot of time trying to figure out how life worked. I was twenty years old, and after mulling it over for a while, I developed a theory that there was a web. Anytime something uncanny occurred, I would say the word out loud. Web. It was a kind of shorthand for my growing belief that all events and signs were somehow connected, that it was just up to us to figure out how. When I pictured the web manifesting itself physically, it was as a giant shimmering net, its lattice stretching unevenly across the night sky.

For some reason my life had always been filled with coincidence. A friend once remarked that she didn't know whether I actually experienced a greater number of coincidences than anyone else or whether it was simply that I paid more attention to them than most people do. I didn't know the answer, but something about my life certainly seemed to invite chance correspondences. The only reason I got my big break at the college's weekly newspaper was because the regular film reviewer became ill one night right before a deadline and the film being screened was *The Unbearable Lightness of Being*, based on the novel by Milan Kundera. I was hanging around trying to get on staff, and it just so happened that thanks to my mother, who loved the Czech author, I had read every single book Kundera ever wrote. I begged to be given the chance to write the review, and at the last minute, with no other option in sight, the editors relented. I loved the film, wrote a fervent piece, and thereby became a regular arts reviewer.

Gradually I decided that it wasn't merely by chance that fortuitous events came to pass. Having things come together in that way was a part of who you were, a result of the energy you sent out into the world. And so I came up with the idea of the web, a model that could connect one part of your life with another, your past to your future, your self with the cosmos. The one thing I didn't know was whether this web of connections was something that you fabricated solely in your imagination, as a way of making sense of the world, or whether there was something greater than you, on the other side of it, guiding the links and associations, revealing the pattern of your life to you in darting, silvery glimpses.

A few years later I went to see a Louise Bourgeois exhibit at the Brooklyn Museum. It was the summer of 1994, over five years since I had lost my mother. (I never say my mother died, even to myself. I always say I lost her.) I wasn't familiar with the artist's work, but it immediately spoke to me. I didn't know if this was because she was French, a woman, or simply because I could tell she was strong-minded and had eclectic taste. In one marble-floored hallway she presented a series of cell-like installations, structures the size of small, square rooms, each of which functioned as a world unto itself. I walked among them slowly. Stuffed with curious bits of lost furniture—old doors, misshapen chairs, antique faucets—as well as disturbing biomorphic forms and luminous white orbs that the artist had sculpted herself, the cells were like cages or poems, each one mournful and ·distinct. The bringing together of such disparate articles resonated with me, with my childhood spent surrounded by objects. As I thought of my mother's collecting, I noticed with pleasure the artist's inclusion in places of blue-stoppered flacons of Shalimar, my grandmother's perfume. They appeared in all different sizes, from tiny to gigantesque, as if they had dropped in from the pages of *Alice in Wonderland*.

Downstairs, in another set of rooms, the artist presented a series of works entitled *Ode to My Mother*. There were two parts, the first being a series of works on paper. As I looked at each one in turn, I saw that they were all drawings of spiders, large and small, in watercolor, ink, and charcoal, every creature precisely articulated and of an inexorable elegance. In the accompanying wall text, the artist had written that she had been drawn to the spider as a metaphor because, in addition to her parents being tapestry restorers, her mother was "as delicate, discreet, clever, patient, soothing, reasonable, dainty, neat, and useful as a spider, simply indispensable." *Yes,* I thought to myself. With the exception of "patient," I understood exactly what she meant. I had to laugh a little, though, because I knew my mother never would have wanted to be compared to an insect.

Walking past the drawings, I went into the last room, where I found myself caught, as it were, under the final work, a giant sculpture of a spider that the artist had cast in bronze. As I turned around, I saw there was no escape. Spindly and dark, the spider's legs loomed over the entire circumference of the room, casting odd shadows on the walls and ceiling. Standing there, I felt flooding through me the force, the dangerous safety, of being held in something larger than oneself. From the time I was born, my mother had spun a world for me. She had given everything meaning, made living itself beautiful and comprehensible. She was the absolute center, from which all other parts of life sprung. I didn't realize quite how strong she was, just how much she had made me feel sheltered and loved, until I lost her. It was only as it fell about my feet in dust-weighted strands that I realized the extent of the web she had woven, a frame through which I had always understood and experienced the world.

Orange Butterflies

For many years my mother kept large bunches of orange lilies—midcentury lilies, they were called—in our apartment, even though my father didn't like them. The smell was too intense for him, he said. I myself hated orange anything else, but all through my adolescence I loved those lilies. There was something vibrant and unrestrained about them—they weren't cold or classical, like roses. They seemed more fiery than that, their gorgeous petals lush against the dark green of the library, as if they had alighted there from some faraway, exotic place.

The lilies also reminded me of the time that Lucy lived with us, as our au pair, or mother's helper. My mother had hired her for the summer to take care of me and my sister, ages seven and four, at a house we had rented on Long Island. Lucy was tall, tan, blond, athletic—everything that we two pale, dark-haired little girls were not, and so of course we adored her. From the moment we saw her, in all her seventeen-year-old glory, she fascinated us. There was her room, tantalizingly next to ours, which she made clear was off-limits. Whenever we were lucky enough to be invited in, we would be dazzled by her dressing table, laden with perfume bottles of every shape and size, which we could look at silently but were not allowed to touch. If she had casually left her closet door open, we might catch a glimpse of towering piles of sweaters— "Cashmere in summer!" I heard my mother exclaim to a friend— a frosted rainbow of pistachio green, lemon yellow, and strawberry pink, shimmering on the dark shelves.

Sometimes Lucy was slightly cruel to us. She would tell us she liked other little girls better, or taunt us, without affection, for not knowing something. By the strange logic of childhood, this made us love her more. One day, toward the beginning of the summer, she told me that flowers could talk. Perhaps I had been fussy that morning at breakfast, and she had wanted to get rid of me for a bit. It worked. From that day on, I would regularly go out to the front lawn, to the overgrown row of tiger lilies that bordered the white gravel driveway. For long minutes I would stare into their faces— orange skin, dark freckles, thin yellow stamens—talking quietly to them about I know not what. Even when they didn't respond, I was patient and loving, and attributed their silence to their feeling shy, as I often did.

At some point during that summer, my mother lost her watch. She was disconcerted for a while, but then thought no more of it. It was easy to lose track of things in the bustle of driving to the beach, playing tennis, running in and out of the house. A few mornings later, she said to the three of us that she was going out but would be calling later to get a phone number from her address book. She didn't want to take it with her, so she would be relying on us to be there. When she called, Lucy pushed the book toward me on the kitchen table and said, "Why don't you take care of it?" I was very excited. I put the phone to my ear and carefully opened the book. Lying along its seam was the watch. "I found it!" I yelled happily. My mother's voice over the phone was rich with surprise.

The summer drifted on. My mother had sewn a number of outfits for us to wear, a seemingly endless supply of brightly colored skirts and tops with large ruffled edges. On a given day, my sister would be in turquoise checks; I would be in red and white stripes, like a candy cane. We had matching kerchiefs, which we liked to wrap around our heads as if we were babushkas. Wearing gilded Chinese slippers, we would walk to the candy store with two friends, also sisters. We spent a long time there, in the musty old store, with its jars of treasures and comic-book racks, its floor covered in sawdust. The smell was a combination of rust and Bazooka gum. My sister loved the mini-Coca-Cola gummies. I loved the bottle caps, which came in a bright green package and tasted like soda flavors: orange, grape, cola, root beer.

In the midst of our routine—eating early dinners at the local pizza parlor, locking our parents out of the car until they promised to take us to Dairy Queen, making sculptures out of driftwood and shells that we would gather at the beach—a necklace of my mother's disappeared, a gold choker with two ruby-eyed lions snarling face-to-face that she and my father had picked out in Greece. My mother was very distressed this time, and held whispered conferences with my father around the house. A week or so later, it turned up. The woman who came to clean once a week had moved the dressing table in the course of vacuuming my parents' room, and there it was, perched against the wall, as if it had landed there accidentally.

Just as my mother was calming down from this incident, her diamond ring went missing. It was a ring her mother had given to my father after he proposed, for my mother to wear as her engagement ring. They realized it was gone just at a time when Lucy had taken a few days off to go home to Connecticut. My mother began talking to Lucy's friends, other young girls who were out on Long Island for the summer. She learned that Lucy had worn the gold choker to a beach party, where everyone had complimented her on it. My mother then had a long phone conversation with Lucy's mother, who admitted that her daughter had a habit of "borrowing" things, but that she always gave them back. At the end of the conversation, my mother asked for her ring, but Lucy, speaking through her mother, insisted she didn't have it. The police came and snooped around the house for evidence, and I was so put out by their invasion that I kept claiming I heard a kitten mewing. They ignored me. Later I learned that my mother, saddened by Lucy's behavior but not wanting to ruin a young person's life, did not press charges. In talking to people about it, we found out that Lucy's obsessive femininity—the maniacally perfect collections of sweaters and perfumes, the fact that she took only jewelry—was often the dead giveaway of a female kleptomaniac. We never saw Lucy or the ring again.

This was some years before the armed heist, but in some ways it was much more frightening. For three months Lucy had lived among us, and in that time she had become a part of our family. Her turning against us was inexplicable. I would feel the same way years later when I found out that certain cells within my mother's breasts had grown malignant.

But I was only a child at the time, unable to express in words my sorrow over Lucy's betrayal. A few days after all this happened, I woke up and decided to put on a poncho of mine that had become too small for me and was now unofficially my sister's. It was from Mexico and profusely embroidered, and I determined with all my seven-year-old might to make it fit. As I pulled it over my head as hard as I could, I sprained my neck and was unable to move my head for a few hours. I remember feeling very sad as my mother and sister went out that day. I was left alone with my father, who didn't coddle me, but left me to my own devices. As I lay there, immobile, I decided it was silly to believe that flowers could talk. After that I never went out to the tiger lilies anymore. The magic had flown right off them.

If the orange lilies reminded me of that summer, they also had the same powerful effect on me as my mother did, as I stood on the edge of adolescence. For all of the seventies I had taken her European exuberance in stride, in part because I went to a coed French school that was filled with the children of all kinds of parents. Among my friends had been an Iranian exile, the daughter of a mob boss (for her birthday he took forty of us in a string of limousines to see *Hello, Dolly!* on Broadway), and lots and lots of kids of foreign mothers. When my mother came to pick me up from school the first day, I whispered to her, *Mommy, so-and-so's mother has an accent!* It would take me a few more years to realize that she herself, whose voice was normal to me, had the strongest one of all.

At the age of twelve, I switched to a more sedate, homogeneous all-girls' school, and this made me begin to see my mother in a different way. She would come to pick me up dressed from head to toe in Sonia Rykiel or Emanuel Ungaro, with matching hat, gloves, shoes, even the occasional cape. She was the most colorful mother there, with her rich French accent and her shining red nails, and I was alternately thrilled and mortified by her presence. I soon realized that the mood of our apartment was different from the somber elegance of my friends' homes, from the foyer, where my mother had had the walls covered in red-flowered fabric, to the dining room, which was Gothic, with brilliant orange-painted walls and a black wrought-iron chandelier that clung to the pale yellow ceiling like a giant insect.

When I was nineteen, we took what would be our last family vacation together. The four of us went to St. Moritz, ostensibly to ski, although there was no snow that winter. People who did try to go down the slopes would come back with holes in their skis and stories of mud and rocks and ice, so we spent our time doing other things, like playing indoor tennis and ice-skating and walking around the lake. Although I had a boyfriend at college, I was feeling bored and rebellious. I had never flirted with anyone, never enjoyed someone's attentions just for the fun of it. On the plane ride over, I announced to my family that I wanted to have a fling. No one paid me much attention.

Every night, we dressed formally for dinner. It was the eighties, so the general feeling was that the more black-tie one had to wear, the better. There was the Persian couple who sat across from each other night after night, dressed to the nines, without uttering a word, the famous Russian ballerina with her turban, husband, and child, and the Swiss family of five boys, ranging in age from ten to twenty-five. I cast my eye in their direction, and my gaze settled on the twenty-two-year-old. He wasn't my type—he was too slender and too blond—but he was gallant in spades and that was enough. Within a few days my sister and I became part of a group of young people who went out together, and every night he organized another event for our amusement. There were moonlit rides through the snowy woods in horse-drawn sleighs, and a sit-down dinner for thirty in a chalet with wood fires and candlelight. Seated next to me at dinner one night, he picked up one of my hands, my nails gleaming red like my mother's, and declared, in all seriousness: "They are perfect."

It was a pleasure to dress up in the evenings as our mother did, dipping every night into our closets for another dress. In the month leading up to our trip, our mother had come home from department stores with shopping bags full of dresses in our sizes. We had fashion shows for my father in the living room, all of us voting on which ones we liked best. At the same time that we loved the decadence of it, it also felt like make-believe. We knew that life was about other things. Our mother was in remission from breast cancer. We were grateful, trying not to take things for granted. This was a sumptuous gift my parents were giving us, but we didn't confuse it with reality. St. Moritz was a place where people went to outspend, outdress, and outski one another. There was an American man there, a known tax evader, who hosted one party after another in his chalet. I felt sad for him that he could never return to his home country, seeing him as a character out of a movie, not as a guide for how to live one's life.

At the hotel there was another family from New York, also

of two girls, a father, and a mother. Like us, the daughters and mother appeared in full regalia each night, but talking among ourselves, we agreed there was something unimaginative about them. Their shoes matched too well; there was no flair to their self-presentation, just impeccable protocol. Every time we saw the other mother, we noticed she wore a different frock and the same smile, framed by the same shade of lipstick. Like a friend of mine once said about the sunny climate in Los Angeles, her smile no longer corresponded to a mood. It became meaningless, an empty signifier. It wasn't like my mother's smile, which came from within, her spirit bubbling up inside her. (A man watching her at lunch one day came up to her and said, "You are the source," quoting the Perrier ad.) They were all outer, no inner, and when we tried to talk to them—my sister and I with the blank-faced girls, our mother with their mother—we realized we had nothing to share beyond the banalities of weather and fashion. It was as if that other family wasn't understanding the spirit of all these rituals, the fun. They took the whole thing too seriously.

Like her laugh, my mother's style came easily. Sometimes it was a form of expedience, the result of throwing something together at the last minute. When my parents went to Carnevale, my mother got a terrible bee sting on her arm that swelled into a large red welt. It was hot in Rio, she had nothing with her but sleeveless dresses and halter tops, so she had my father tie a silk scarf high up on her arm before they went out into the streets, to dance, to drink, to enjoy the night. The next evening my parents were surprised to see that a handful of women had done the same thing. By the third night, the trend had caught fire. Every other woman at Carnevale had a bright band of silk tied around her arm.

In St. Moritz that New Year's Eve, I wore a strapless black

gown. It had a gigantic black bow in the front, which cinched my waist and spread out on either side of me like wings. After dinner with our parents, my sister and I went to the local nightclub with a large group. Mr. Gallant was there, trailing me as I flitted about trying to mingle with other people. I felt jittery, regretful about what I had started. Twelve o'clock was approaching, and the last thing I wanted was to be alone with him. Sure enough, as the clock blazed midnight, he pinned me to a wall and kissed me. Much later, on the walk home through the deserted streets of the village, he stopped and said: "I guess I love you." I cringed, thinking how little he knew me. He was a fool, responding to a mere show of womanliness, a wan, delicate imitation of something vivid and fierce. I was so embarrassed that I avoided him the next day. By the time I reemerged, he had found another girl to court, and I was free. My family was very amused, and I left chastened, knowing that the whole thing had been a fiasco. I had been passive and false, my outer hadn't remotely corresponded to my inner. I had somehow mistaken the flares of womanhood for the real thing.

When I lost my mother, in the spring of the following year, I lost the color in my life. My father, sister, and I went away that summer, the three of us alone for the first time, and we brought only black-and-white film with us, as if we all intuited that it would be impossible to live in color without her. It was the beginning of a cocoon stage, when the three of us entered a kind of stasis and, for a time, were unable to come into our own and break free.

A year later, I found myself driving through Connecticut to a friend's graduation party. My own graduation was two weeks away. I had rented a car for the trip, and was driving along in the right lane. I was daydreaming, thinking about what lay ahead. I didn't have plans yet, didn't know where I was going to go, who I was going to be. In the left lane ahead of me was an eighteen-wheel tractor-trailer. It had been there for a while, and wasn't signaling that it was going anywhere, so, unaware that it was illegal to do so, I decided to pass it on the right. As I came neck and neck with the cab of the truck, I looked up and saw it veering in my direction. I honked my horn madly, but it kept coming toward me, so I swerved farther to the right to get out of the way. Within seconds, we made contact, and the force of the impact sent my car spinning in front of the truck counterclockwise. I let go of the wheel, which had locked into place, and I sat there braced against my seat, watching the landscape speed through the front window in slow motion, a green blur. Heading down the left lane of the highway backward, I prayed for my life not to end. When the spinning finally stopped, I saw that we—the car and I—had been flung onto the grassy embankment, and that it was only the thick net of bushes that had stopped us from going into the opposite lanes. I opened the door and shakily stepped out onto the grass. Still trembling, I looked down at the nose of the car, and there, stuck to the front of the grille, was the broken body of a Monarch butterfly, the burnt-orange panes of its wings framed dramatically in black, like a rare fragment of stained glass. The sight of it flew straight to my heart, where I understood two things at once. Everything was different, a way of life I had known had ended, but in this new life without my mother, all that she represented— her extraordinary spirit—would save me.

House of the Mouse

The first time I ever saw one, I was four, hiding behind my mother in the narrow hallway off my parents' bedroom. My father was seated on the bed, and my mother, standing in front of her closet, was asking his advice about what she should wear that night. She pulled out her brown dress. It was the one I loved best, with its tumble of pink and yellow flowers, the delicate tea-stained lace at the neck and sleeves. She held it out in front of her for him to see, and then brought it closer to her body. The hem dragged on the floor uneventfully. Then, as if appearing in one of my father's magic tricks, a small, round bump took shape, and, as my mother continued to pull the dress toward her, a mouse materialized, seeming to have come from nowhere, and now stranded in a sea of burgundy carpet. My mother screamed, and, holding the dress in one hand and me in the other, ran from the room. At bedtime that night, she comforted me—the mouse was never coming back, my father would take care of us—and I felt safe.

Perhaps as a result, I never particularly liked mice. My sister had a thing for them, though. When we were children, she collected stuffed-animal ones. The first was small and white, and wore a green skirt with white polka dots. When my mother, sister, and I crossed the English Channel on a large boat, my sister and I devised a game wherein she would toss Mousie up over the rail and catch her, water threatening below, while I pretended to protest. In the excitement of her chant—*Look, Mommy!*—the plaything slipped through her hands and we watched, horrified, as Mousie plunged alongside the massive wall of the ship and disappeared at once in the dark, churning waves. To placate us, my mother invented a dreamlike existence for Mousie under the sea, her visits with mermaids, her necklaces of shells.

Although this was the end of Mousie, it was the beginning of mousies. My sister had a miniature horde—ballerina mousies, cowboy mousies, clown mousies—the whole gamut you could buy at the Paper House party store two blocks from our apartment. Whenever Stephanie was frightened by a nightmare and couldn't sleep, my mother would soothe her with the image of a group of mousies having a birthday party. As they danced and sang and ate cake, my sister would nod off to sleep.

But that was my sister's thing. For my part, my feelings of antipathy for them were heightened when I was riding on the train one night from New York to Washington, D.C., where I had moved after graduating from college. It was late on a Sunday night, because I hadn't wanted to leave New York. I smoked at the time, so me and my magazine and my cigarettes were installed in a smoking car. I was completely enfolded in a large navy wool wrap I had, with a ruffle at the end. After about two cigarettes and half the magazine, I felt nauseated, so I decided to move to a non-smoking car. I stood up, and there, wedged in the crack of the seat, was a tiny, almost embryonic mouse, its eyes shut, its paws frozen in position. I realized it must have tried to come up for air and been stifled by my navy wrap. I almost threw up from the shock of it, but managed to collect my things and move, all the while chewing an entire pack of gum to stave off the salty taste at the back of my mouth.

In Washington, I lived alone in a bland one-bedroom in Dupont Circle. It had been a year and a half since I lost my mother. As long as I was still in college, I had known what to do, how to keep going as she would have wanted me to. This felt different. It was my first year out in the world, the first time that she didn't know where I was, what I was doing. Washington was a city my mother had no connection to, and yet going there reminded me of her anyway, and the way she had randomly moved to Los Angeles at one point in her twenties, simply because it wasn't Antwerp, where she had just broken up with her first love, or New York, where she had already lived and he had recently moved. My mother had been heartbroken at the time. I don't think she much cared where she lived. I felt the same way. My new apartment came furnished, which was perfect for me. I didn't want to make any lasting decisions, had no desire to clutter up my life with things like beds and desks when I didn't know where I was going to end up. My boyfriend, T., someone I had turned to six weeks after I lost her, worked on the Hill. We had decided to move there together after I graduated. He pressured me to move in with him, but I wanted my own space, the possibility for retreat. It was an experiment, not yet real life. I wasn't going to live in Washington forever, and by not going to New York I didn't have to face the apartment empty of her day after day. Part of me could even pretend she was still there, playing backgammon every night with my father in their marriage-long tournament.

So there I was in Washington. I liked it, the way the whole city seemed to panic at the merest sign of snow, followed by the spring rush of cherry blossoms. I worked for an art gallery in Georgetown, just as my mother had worked at one in L.A. Not being in politics in D.C. seemed a bit like ordering fish at a steak house. I enjoyed my work, though, and had friends there, and kept busy, writing for various publications, doing a freelance project for Time-Life on the personal effects of Tutankhamen. But I slept all the time, too. The cold of the winter couldn't penetrate my lethargy. At night I wore my boyfriend's red pajamas, and was lost in them. He would get mad because he'd go to brush his teeth, and by the time he got back I'd be asleep. In the morning, we would argue about it. I would leave his apartment crying, and cry all the way home on the bus, and when I got home the phone would be ringing, and it was him, calling to apologize. But I still couldn't get out of bed in the morning. I took cabs to work and was always late. I was frozen and gray on the surface, like the Potomac River in January, and I didn't let myself think of the emotions streaming wildly underneath. That spring in D.C. a local boy was killed during soccer practice. The tree his team stood under to stay out of the rain was struck by lightning and he died. I wept for him, for his family, for the unbelievably bad luck of it.

And then, just as easily as I fell into the rhythm of the city,

I fell out. (My mother left L.A. abruptly too.) As summer approached, I decided to move to Paris for a year. It would be a way to get in touch with a part of myself, with my mother, who had spent a year there as a young woman. I went on a ten-day jaunt and had job interviews. On my last day there, I was hired, by a woman I knew vaguely through a connection of my mother's. I was happy. T. didn't want me to go. He couldn't join me because of his job, his career. He didn't understand how important it was to me and kept talking about how hard it would be to be separated. I thought he was looking at things in a small way. I had lost my mother. That was a real separation. If he and I were both alive and loved each other, then how could mere geographical distance matter? We had long talks about what our expectations were. I told him that if his feelings ever changed, he would have to tell me right away, because I wouldn't want to walk around thinking we were really together when we weren't. It was very hard to leave him, because I realized it meant I might lose him, but I felt I had to go. I called my father from the airport, crying. He said, "A thousand girls would change places with you in a second." I replied, choking on my tears, "But a thousand girls don't go out with *him*."

I arrived listless. At first, things were difficult: I couldn't find an apartment, I quit my first job and had to find another. But gradually Paris won me over. I stayed. I settled into a job I loved at a museum, found a band of friends. I took the bus to work in the morning from my fifth-floor studio apartment on the rue St. Sulpice. I sat drinking my *café crème* at the Café de la Mairie until the last possible minute, then threw my change on the table, and hurled myself onto the bus. It traveled along the Seine, the sun hitting the water, the monuments cool and white in the morning light, the river still as if unmoving. We went past the Place de la Concorde, and crossed the water at the Pont Alma. And then I was at my museum, where I worked as an intern with a group of spirited Frenchwomen, who cooed over me like protective hens.

I became friends with an older woman named Julia. She had been a good friend of my mother's, and I remembered going as a little girl with the two of them to lunch at Maxim's, and wanting to order a hamburger. I called her when I first arrived, and she welcomed me into her home and her life. She herself had come to Paris from Hong Kong when she was a wispy, sheltered eighteen-year-old. When she arrived at the girl's dormitory of the Sorbonne, she immediately went out to explore the city, and was surprised upon her return to see that her suitcases hadn't been unpacked. After a week of this, the dorm mistress called her into her study and explained that she had better unpack her bags herself, since no one was going to do it for her. That was her introduction to Parisian life, and within a year she was swept up in the fever of 1968, handing out birth control pills in St. Germain and organizing bus trips to England, where abortion was legal. She studied fairy tales with Roland Barthes, and then went into finance. She became the right-hand woman of a powerful financier, overseeing his expansion into Asia. In the seventies, she married a jovial and titled Frenchman with whom she eventually had a little girl. Despite the fact that she was so clearly the director of her own destiny, Julia always attributed her decision to have a child to my mother, who encouraged her, saying it would bring her greater joy than anything else in life.

For me Julia went from being a slightly imposing figure of my childhood to a warm friend, strict about the right way to do things, but infinitely generous and loving. She would take me to intimate bistros for dinner, or to the market on the rue Mouffetard, where we'd stand at the bar of the café on the corner for a breakfast of steaming cups of coffee with milk and buttered baguettes still warm from the oven. When, after arguing with her husband over something, she would relay the spat to the butcher, he would smile and laugh, because her husband had already told him his side of the story. I did my laundry at her house. Whenever they went away, I walked their dog, a handsome black-and-white spaniel named Polka. I remember those early morning walks as unearthly—the feeling of waking up hungover, a faint trace of lipstick from the night before marking my lips, my hair disheveled, my body dry from too much wine.

And so my life assumed a rhythm. I was alone a lot of the time, and I loved it. I felt more beautiful in Paris than anywhere else, as if, walking the boulevards, I were a woman of mystery. I had my boyfriend at home, so I did not think of love. I concentrated all my feelings into idealizing him and what we had. I wrote passionate letters. And I rebuffed anyone who tried to disturb my long-distance attachment.

When the anniversary of my mother's death came around, I was determined to spend it alone. I walked everywhere, admiring the architecture, the children playing in the park of the Palais-Royal. I discovered a bistro nearby, with long wooden tables and smoky air, where I ordered cheese and bread and red wine. I got a little drunk and went outside, dazed by the sun shining, the wind whipping my hair. I walked home, lonely and triumphant.

When I got upstairs, I called my sister, to tell her I was thinking of her, of the day, of our loss. As we spoke with each other, and I told her I planned to stay home that night, I saw its head peek out from behind the refrigerator. Suddenly it scurried toward me. I started yelling, and it retreated slightly. Then, gathering its nerve, it came toward me again. I started throwing things at it—books, a shoe. I hung up with my sister and called my landlady. She told me there was nothing she could do—she was, after all, in her seventies—but if I wanted to buy some poison, she would reimburse me for it. She even offered to come up and remove the body once I found it. I was getting slightly hysterical. I called friends of mine, a couple who lived nearby. Richard answered the phone. I explained the situation. He said, *"J'arrive."* I ran out of my apartment and into my neighbor and her boyfriend. They were coming to see what the noise was about. By the time I had told them, Richard had arrived, and the four of us started chasing the mouse around my little apartment like a dog after its own tail. We were lifting up my bed, shouting at one another, pointing too late at the sudden streak across the floor. Finally, we gave up. Richard and I left the apartment and went out to dinner.

I called Julia from the restaurant, and she told me to come over. When I arrived, and explained tearfully what had happened, she sent her husband out for cigarettes and opened a bottle of Chivas Regal. We drank and smoked and talked about my mother until three o'clock in the morning, when I fell exhausted into the bed she set up for me in her daughter's room. I ended up staying there three weeks. Richard, who had shown he understood the situation when he said, *"Soit c'est la souris qui meurt, soit c'est Valérie"* (Either the mouse is done for, or Valerie is), diligently put out poison and checked on my apartment every few days. Only when he told me he had spotted no new droppings in a week did I move back into that apartment that wasn't big enough for the both of us.

Julia joked that my mother had sent the mouse in order to get me out of the house, that my mother knew (after my living alone for a year and half) a mere bug wouldn't be enough to get me to go anywhere, and, wanting to protect me that night from being alone, sent me to Julia so I could unleash my sadness in a safe place. My friend Brooke, another American girl who was living in Paris for the year, cut out an article in a French decor magazine about a furniture maker who carved figures of mice into his wood pieces. So I pasted up the title of the piece on my armoire, a paper sign that said, "The House of the Mouse." I liked having it there to remind me of my initial fear, which had not been of the mouse per se, but of what it represented. The creature hadn't roared exactly, but its streak across the floor had been a disturbing flash, a little shiver of life itself disrupting my carefully ordered existence. It was like an unexpected thought that crosses your mind and, having done so, jars the hull of your being, leading you to adjust yourself to a different course.

The Origins
of Loving Birds

My mother loved birds as a child, or so she told me. I had some trouble imagining this, as she had such a horror of any animal that crossed her path. (It didn't even have to cross her path. She thought when people called their children "kids" it sounded too goatlike.) Each time my sister and I were about to give our attention to a pretty dog being walked along the street, or a velvety cat lying on the couch pillows at a friend's home, she forbade us to touch it before we could make a move. "You don't know where it's been. You could catch something," she would whisper. And so our hands stayed at our sides, itching to stroke fur, maybe receive a little lick. To this day I have trouble petting a strange dog, having involuntarily internalized her phobia.

Our family did have birds of a sort, though my mother definitely didn't love them. From the time we moved into the apartment on 66th Street, in 1973, and through all the years we lived there, a clan of pigeons nested on the narrow ledge that ran along one side of the windowed alcove off our dining room, abutting the gray brick wall of the building next door. The alcove itself wasn't used for anything. It was lined on two sides with a series of ornate, lead-framed windows with diamond-shaped panes. At first my mother had visions of making the area into a breakfast niche, but since none of us had any intention of eating breakfast anywhere but in the kitchen, the four of us seated at our customary places around the rectangular wooden table, she abandoned the idea. Eventually she put a screen in front of the space, and we stored odd things there—the miniature pool table my sister received as a birthday present one year, boxes of old toys, schoolbooks, athletic trophies. Every once in a while my mother insisted we clean it out, usually because she was planning a dinner party. Then she would place the flamboyant Art Nouveau lamp-vase she and my father had found at a flea market on top of the trompe l'oeil gold-and-marble ram's-head pedestal she had bought at auction. These created quite a dramatic, if slightly over-the-top, effect in the center of the alcove, the lamp's rose-colored bulbs refracted and glittering in the multitude of glass surfaces.

My sister's and my primary interest in the alcove, however, was the pigeons. We often went to spy on them in their nook. Peering quietly, we'd see a couple of birds nestling, and hear their cooing, little rolls of sound, almost like my mother's *R*s, coming at us from just the other side of the fragmented panes. Sometimes for fun we rapped on the glass to make the pair scatter, but next time we looked they'd have returned. The nest, an intricate cross-hatch of mostly indeterminable materials, grew more tattered and dirty with every passing year. Mixed in with the inevitable branches were elements of city detritus, brought back by successive generations after scouring missions and carefully layered into the creation, which, as my mother was fond of saying about our apartment, remained ever a work in progress.

Each spring the mama pigeon hatched a brood. Sometimes we realized come fall that we had missed it all, but usually we remembered at some point after it started getting warm to go peek. Straining to see the eggs, eerily similar to the ones we ate cracked and sunny-side up, we could catch only fluttery glimpses as the mother adjusted herself over them. Soon after there would be a tangle of pinkish gray, messy little things, undulating gently in the center of the nest. My sister and I were happy to watch them through the glass. It was nature at a remove. Dutiful daughters that we were, we had no desire to touch any of them, no urge to bring a single one inside.

One year my mother decided to oust the pigeons. She didn't come out and say it that way, but we immediately recognized what it meant when she decided to install an air conditioner in the dining room. Despite our loud protests that we didn't need one there, the room never got hot anyway, it was decided that the unit was to be inserted into those windows. I didn't understand what she had against the birds. It wasn't like they got in her way. Like her, they were simply raising a family in the city, acting by instinct to create a haven for their offspring.

As ordained, the air-conditioner people came, opened up the narrow windows, creaky with age, and cruelly brushed the nest right off the ledge. The birds were nowhere to be seen. My sister and I were inconsolable, but not for long. It turned out that the pigeons had one on my mother. The very first time my father, anxious to try out his new gadget, turned it on to cool the room before dinner, a dirty slew of gray and white feathers spat into the room, filling it with the most awful smell. My parents tried everything, changing the filter, calling the men back to clean off the ledge again, but to no avail. Unless my mother wanted the dining room to stink, the unit had to go. So it did, and after about six months or so, my sister and I were relieved to note, the pigeons returned, proof that certain things were beyond my mother's control.

The fact that for years you practically couldn't even look at that corner of the dining room without making my mother tense up a little made me more than wonder about her supposed love of birds. When I was four or five, she did teach me how to draw them, however. It was the only lesson she ever gave me where drawing was concerned. We were sitting at the kitchen table, and I watched as with a quick, sure hand she drew a flattened-out upside-down W, which, the moment her pen lifted, became more than itself, gaily taking flight across the whiteness of the page. I was entranced by how easily I could do it myself.

From then on I naturally assumed that my mother knew how to draw. I learned this wasn't the case only much later, the summer she signed me and Stephanie up for drawing lessons on Long Island and at the last minute decided to join us. It was funny to think of her taking a lesson, like a schoolchild. She was my mother—she was supposed to know everything already.

I was thirteen that summer, Stephanie ten, and my mother somewhere in her late forties, but I quickly realized she was just as much of a novice as we were. Gone was the confident élan of her bird drawings. She still had commendable instincts about how things should be on the page, but now her tendency to draw rapidly meant that the elements didn't always come together properly. I was more careful, trying to get every detail right. If the finished drawing in my case was more exact, it was invariably missing the vitality that appeared in any one of my mother's sketches.

Our teacher was nice, a young hippie-ish woman with long hair and lots of patience. Sometimes she came to our house, and we went out into the garden and drew pictures of the flowers and trees. Other times we went to her place, which was a little off-putting, because her area was suffering from an infestation of gypsy moths. Even before we had finished pulling up to the house, they started coming in through the car windows, and as we ran inside we had to cover our heads to protect our eyes and ears and mouths from their frenzied palpitations.

Every once in a while the four of us would go on an excursion, to a picturesque white church, or to the beach to draw the bathers, which we all particularly enjoyed. Once we'd set ourselves up on the sand, the young woman would put on a timer, giving us two minutes to capture the scene. It was amazing what you could get down in two minutes: the succession of reclining forms lying under umbrellas, the heads bobbing in the water, the shape of the waves. My mother was especially good at it, and when we asked her why, she admitted she had always had a thing for beach paint-

ings. This I believed. With their sense of air and light, they celebrated a kind of openness and carefree pleasure she hadn't known
as a child.

When my mother was twenty-three years old, she moved to
Paris for a year. She had already lived in New York for a while by
then, and felt ready for a change, but had no desire to return to
small-town Antwerp. It was 1955, a time when ladies still wore
gloves, gentlemen wore hats, and Edith Piaf—known as the little
sparrow—held sway over all of Paris. For fifteen months or so,
my mother stayed with her distant cousin M. and his wife, R., in
the Sixteenth Arrondissement, in their large, rambling, antique-
filled apartment whose prize possession was a birdcage that had
once belonged to Marie Antoinette.

My mother's cousin was a soft-spoken man who tended to
wear an expression of dashed expectation on his heavy, moon-
shaped face. When they were teenagers, in Belgium, he had been
in love with my mother and had wanted to marry her (they were
so distantly related that the idea gave no one pause). Everyone
knew that my mother didn't return his feelings. He never developed any ill will about it. On the contrary, throughout his life he
treated her with the utmost delicacy and respect.

Despite the fact that M. made her feel welcome, my mother
must have felt a bit awkward staying there. She made an effort to
befriend his wife, gossiping and comparing notes about womanly
things. When R. was younger she had been a real beauty (a photograph of her as Miss Israel, in a bathing suit and sash, decorated
one of the living room tables). With age she had taken to dyeing
her hair a brassy blond, which better suited her voluble person-

ality. R. grew very fond of my mother, who, if a little on the shy side back then, clearly had good taste, and took to squiring her young charge about town. My mother enjoyed these forays but couldn't help feeling uncomfortable when they were all three together, mostly because of the way R. walked all over her husband, and he, meek and gentle, never stood up to her.

It wasn't an especially happy period for my mother. She was living in the lap of luxury, but it wasn't her lap, and she didn't feel fully like herself. Unlike in New York, she didn't have a group to run around with, nor did she have anyone in her life romantically. Paris is a good place to be young and melancholy, she used to tell me. After she got started talking about those days—this usually involved her playing some of her Piaf records, and telling me how truly those songs about love and loss had moved her—she ended by asking me to swear I'd be married by the time I was twenty-five. I was sixteen, seventeen, eighteen, and I refused every time, unwilling to take her request seriously. Twenty-five was terribly far from where I was on the one hand, and on the other, maybe I wasn't going to be ready yet. I got mad at her for trying to boss me around about something so important, something over which she theoretically shouldn't have any say. Besides, she hadn't gotten married so young. Reminding me that she didn't want me to go through the difficulties she had experienced, the loneliness and doubt that tormented her until she finally married my father at the age of thirty-four, long after her family had given her up as a lost cause, she finished with one of her favorite child-rearing maxims: "Do as I say, Valerie, not as I do."

The fact is, I didn't believe my mother when she said it had been hard to be alone. There was a photograph of her standing in front of the Paris Opéra from that time. Wearing a plaid suit, a pair

We had gone to Paris for a specific purpose that time: to see the Pont Neuf, which had temporarily been given a new look by the artist Christo. As was his wont, he had covered the entire structure in fabric, using a heavy peach drape for the occasion, and the thought of it—a frivolity undertaken with such seriousness—amused and delighted my mother and me to no end. As a vital part of completing the operation at the base of the bridge, the artist had hired dozens of swimmers (frogmen, the French called them, with perhaps a whiff of irony) and had outfitted them with oxygen masks and black rubber suits that made them look like stylish aliens. In addition to making sure the material reached down to water level, Christo had also wrapped everything on top, the curved alcoves, the stone benches, even the lanterns dotting the bridge. From farther along the quay where my mother and I stood taking pictures, the whole thing was like an impossibly large and impeccably elegant piece of furniture.

We took many photographs of each other, leaning against the parapet with that peach bridge in the background. When we got back to the hotel, we realized to our dismay that there was no film in my mother's camera. This was not such a surprise; she had never been very mechanically minded. So the next day we bought film, I carefully loaded it, and we went back. The Pont Neuf was still there, still crazily cloaked in its sumptuous material, and we stood in the same place we had twenty-four hours earlier. It was a cloudy, perfectly Paris kind of day. For some reason, all the images came out blurred, as if the echo of our first visit had made itself visible. In one of them, I am leaning against the balustrade, looking to the bridge in profile, my hair pulled back in a black bow. It didn't occur to me at the time what an unbelievable gift it was to return together and find the moment again, and how different it would feel to go back to places alone, to revisit the past without her. And so when I look at that photograph of myself by the bridge, I feel an ache for the girl I was then, and even more for the sensation, lost forever now, of standing and dreaming and being me before my mother's eyes.

On our way back to the hotel that day, we walked along the Seine through the bird market. It was both marvelous and sad to see them in their cages: the couture-colored parrots, the luxuriously white cockatoos, the funny little canaries. We didn't linger. As with the pigeons of my childhood, I had no desire to touch them, only to look, and my mother, despite saying over her shoulder again how she had loved birds as a child, hurried us past them, on to our next destination, whatever it was.

I think now that what my mother must have meant when she said she loved birds was not that she appreciated them on a visceral level, with their odd-smelling dander, lizardlike claws, and beaks the same veined yellow as old teeth, but from a distance—as a collection of fine lines and beautiful colors. It's much the same way that I romanticized her life as a single woman. From the safety of the nest she built for our family, her earlier flights looked to me bold, dramatic, fascinating. I didn't appreciate the pain of her loneliness, her beating anxiety about the future, her general social malaise. It didn't occur to me that she felt trapped that year in Paris. I just admired the idea of her being young and free, a glorious image whose fluid, soaring outlines contributed to the grand impression I always had of her life before my father.

The Lizard's Tail

At the age of eight, as Germany made its presence known across Europe, my mother had to pin a yellow star to her coat, to mark her on the streets of Antwerp as a Jewish girl. Knowing this, I never wanted to be identified as Jewish while I was growing up. From my mother's side, I inherited my grandmother's coloring, my *tante* Bella's nose, the shape of my mother's eyes, and all of their slender hands, but I always wanted to "pass," and was happy every time someone asked if I was English, French, Italian— anything but what I actually was. Strangers sometimes came up to us at department stores and asked if I was an Irish girl, on account of my dark hair, light eyes, white skin. My mother would laugh and say, "No, she's my daughter, and we're not Irish."

There was no mistaking my mother for an Irishwoman, with her trilling accent, olive skin, and strong nose. My mother joked that one day her nose just fell, and wasn't as delicate on her face anymore. People used to tell her she should get it fixed, especially before she got married, but she never wanted to. It was a part of her, and she didn't want to change such a distinctive feature. Several times I heard her say that even though she might not have chosen to be Jewish because it made life more difficult (and for her it had made life itself almost impossible), in the end she was glad she was.

She hadn't always felt that way. She often told me that when she was a young woman she went through a period of not wanting to be so Jewish, of being embarrassed by it. Every time she went out to dinner and my grandmother started speaking to her in Yiddish, my mother would stop her, whispering, *"Parlons français, Maman."* Later she was ashamed of herself for having behaved so badly, and as if to compensate went headlong in the other direction, becoming increasingly active in a number of Jewish organizations and speaking Yiddish whenever she could. I think it also helped that she could be truly herself with my father, who from the beginning found her equal parts exotic (in having a French accent and a general European flair) and familiar (she could make as good a matzoh ball soup as his mother). Because he had had such a different upbringing—he was the son of Russian-Jewish immigrants and had grown up in the Bronx—my father never ceased to be fascinated by my mother's Belgian-Jewish background. They often joked that they had a mixed marriage, which of course they didn't, but sometimes, especially when it came to hankering for certain foods, it almost seemed that way.

By the time Stephanie and I came along, my mother had developed a strong sense of pride in her heritage. Whenever she found out that a writer or actor we admired was Jewish, she would tell us right away, offering proof that we came from a distinguished and intelligent people. I remember her tears of relief when President Carter negotiated the peace treaty, the many marches she took us to in New York, for Soviet Jewry, for Holocaust survivors. In 1981, when I was thirteen years old, the National Women's Division of the American Jewish Congress gave my mother an award "in recognition of outstanding commitment to a world at peace and to the security and dignity of the Jewish people." I was very proud to be her daughter at the lunch held in her honor. Clearly, being Jewish was who she was, an integral part of her being.

I still had some conflicted feelings, however, about my own Jewish identity. There was the way I presented myself in public, camouflaged by a strong desire to fit in, and the way I was with my family. Part of my ambivalence had to do with knowing that the Germans would have wanted to kill me no matter how non-Jewish I looked. The memory of the war, and my mother's experience in it, haunted me. For me, being Jewish was a double-edged sword— something that offered the possibility of immediate acceptance within a community, something that had once carried the threat of death.

Through a friend of my mother's, who was a booking agent at Ford Models, Inc., I modeled as a child, for department-store print ads, catalogs, the occasional magazine. At first, it was a novelty. I got to dress up and meet interesting people. I was naturally quiet, so the long hours of staring into the camera were easy, a chance to reflect almost without interruption. As I grew a bit older—nine, ten, eleven—I appreciated modeling on another level: it was the chance to feel like an all-American girl. I felt as if I were fooling everyone, that if people knew who I really was, they wouldn't want me to wear their Wonder Woman bathing suit or their Girl Scout uniform. At around twelve or thirteen, I decided to stop, more and more uncomfortable with the falseness of not presenting the whole story of myself to the world. I told my mother, "I don't want people to think they know me from looking at my face."

And yet I wasn't ready to embrace my Jewishness either. I viewed it as a drawback, something I had never asked for, like the birthmark on my right arm, a brown, hairy spot that looked like a dirty thumbprint. My mother called it a beauty mark, but that was wishful thinking. It wasn't pretty to look at, just another thing that prevented me from being perfect. When I went to a dermatologist to have it examined at the age of thirteen—the same year I had my bas mitzvah—he took one look and said, "Cancer." I felt like he was telling me something I already suspected, that if I wasn't careful, the ugliness could grow and destroy me. My mother and I came home that day, got into my bed, and pulled the covers over our heads, sick with worry. After going to several other, more reassuring doctors, we learned that it wasn't that I had cancer, but that the mark had the potential to grow into something malignant in later years. Although they all agreed I could wait and see what happened, I decided I wanted it off right away, and so I had the operation. It left a long scar on my arm, which grew as my arm grew, and became much more unsightly than the original discoloration.

I found out that I was one of those people who scar easily, which is why there is a series of marks riding along either side of the scar itself, a raised white spot for each time needle went into skin, and I regretted not having waited until I was older.

Of course there were many things about being Jewish, and about our home life, that I treasured. My mother made sure we celebrated Shabbat together. Even if we had plans to go out separately afterward (which happened more frequently as we grew older), we usually gathered for a few moments on Friday evenings. In the warm glow of the dining room, she would light the candles, her hands circling the flames and then stopping to cover her face. We could hear her speaking softly, in Yiddish. Her voice hidden in her palms, she began every prayer the same way, *Liebe Gott bitteh* . . . , and then we couldn't make out the rest of the words, but we knew she was asking for God's blessing over our family. My father, whose approach to Judaism had always been more ethnic than religious, nevertheless seemed to relish his role at the head of the table during these moments. With great gusto he sang the blessings in Hebrew over the wine and the challah, and then two at a time we hugged, my parents last of all.

Before holiday dinners, it was I who polished the silver candlesticks. As a young girl, my mother had polished the very same ones for her mother, and I cherished the continuity of it, the weight and gleam of the silver, the tarnish disappearing before my eyes. I also liked going to temple, not so much to Sunday school, which I found tedious, but dressed up for the high holidays, the four of us walking one block together into the imposing syna-gogue. Like many of the women, my mother often wore a new hat for the occasion. My sister and I took turns holding hands with her during the services, enjoying her occasional absentminded caress. I liked being part of the congregation, the way that, after standing up and wishing one another a happy New Year, we all filed out solemnly into the brisk fall air. My parents leisurely saying hello to friends, my sister and I impatient to get home for dinner, to the eating of apples and honey to guarantee a sweet year. After we lost my mother, my father, sister, and I made an effort to continue those traditions—to polish the candlesticks, to go to services together, to cook the holiday meals. We would have done anything to re-create the spirit that she had surrounded us with. Sometimes it felt like we succeeded, the three of us gathered in the orange dining room with a guest or two, briefly kindling a sort of painful happiness.

Throughout my childhood, whenever we traveled, wherever we went, my parents would seek out synagogues where we could go to services. We went to synagogues in Prague, Cairo, Budapest, Athens. I never wanted to go, didn't feel the solidarity that my mother and father felt. I resented being dragged somewhere for a makeshift Passover dinner with people I didn't know, and would much rather have gone to a restaurant, just us. As I grew older and traveled more on my own, I began to feel differently. On a trip to India I found myself at a sparsely populated service in Delhi, stunned when I was told that week after week the handful of people in attendance prayed to have the required ten men arrive, a minyan, enough to finally open the Torah.

The year I lived in Paris, the high holidays came around and, partly regretting the services I was missing at home, partly out of some strange sense of nostalgia for those adventures with my parents, I went with a friend to the synagogue on the rue Copernic. So many people showed up that they had to put the overflow in a high school stadium. As I looked around, I noticed there was something familiar yet different about the well-heeled crowd, and I realized with astonishment what it was: everyone was Jewish and yet also irrefutably French. Toward the end of the service, the family next to us gestured for us to stand with them under their shawl. Throughout the room everyone was similarly covered, all of us protected for the final benediction. Afterward, the family invited us to join them at their home for the breaking of the fast. This was France, where one is never invited anywhere without exceedingly proper introductions and long, drawn-out periods of getting to know one another. Regrettably, we couldn't go because we had arranged to go to another friend's house, but I was deeply moved to be so warmly welcomed, grateful for the feeling of being strangers linked by a common bond.

The summer after my freshman year of college, my mother took my sister and me on a trip to Germany. This was before the Wall came down, and she wanted us to see it, not just as the country of our enemy but as a place to which her mother regularly used to go to spas, and where Jewish families once lived their lives on the most elegant streets. My mother admitted she was half scared, half exhilarated to walk through Berlin with us, and kept saying she couldn't believe that there was a time when she wouldn't have been able to walk with her two daughters freely. We all responded to the museums, to the war memorials, to the spooky feeling of waiting at Checkpoint Charlie while guards with mirrors attached to long poles looked under every inch of our bus for a stowaway. My sister and I spent a lot of time in West Berlin with the daughter and son of family friends, German Jews whose families had made their way back. They took us to the hangout of the moment, the New York Café, and we felt right at home there, amid the Duran Duran music and black leather jackets. One night we went to an open-air amphitheater to see a screening of *The Blues Brothers,* with German subtitles. I couldn't help thinking it was like a rally: the stone seats were filled with good-looking young Germans ranging in age from about thirteen to eighteen, and all eyes were trained on the center. I remember feeling chilled by that enormous crowd singing and shouting in unison, frightened by their thorough knowledge of the film, the way they had memorized the English words, as if rote were more important than meaning.

After Berlin, we spent a couple of days in Heidelberg and then continued down to Baden-Baden. We were supposed to spend a few days there, and then meet my father in Italy, on Lake Como. Our first night in the spa hotel, my sister kept me awake, complaining of a stomachache. I confess I wasn't sympathetic, but in the morning she told my mother, who decided we should consult with the hotel doctor; it all felt very nineteenth century. The doctor examined Stephanie and told my mother we needed to take her right away to the local hospital, the *stadtklinik.* We ordered a taxi and went, very nervous. This was not how a vacation was supposed to be. When we got to the hospital, several doctors came out to greet us, and took my sister to be examined in another room. After a few minutes, one of them came out and explained that she had appendicitis, and that her appendix had to come out immediately. My mother was speaking German, but I understood her every word. She said that she would book us on the next flight home. The doctor shook his head no, there wasn't time. A little hysterical by this point, my mother made a quick succession of phone calls, to my father, to our pediatrician at home. They agreed that my father would be on the next flight to Germany, and my sister was prepped for the operation. We stayed with her, holding her hands and trying not to cry, until they wheeled her away. My mother cried hard then, in fear and worry. Perhaps it seemed unbelievable to her that she was entrusting her daughter's life to a group of German doctors.

My sister came back in a few hours, groggy but all right. The operation had been a success. We never made it to Italy, but spent the next week in Baden-Baden, visiting Stephanie every day, having early dinners every night. It became a family joke that my sister was leaving a part of herself in Baden-Baden, like the song about leaving one's heart in San Francisco. (Aware that at one time Germany would have wanted no part of any Jew, my parents, under the joke, must have felt a grimmer irony.) During one of those days we took an afternoon drive through the Black Forest. It was the stuff of fairy tales, the woods thick and impenetrable, with pale, golden slivers of sun splintering through the trees. Its beauty derived in part from its darkness, the enchanted existing alongside and perhaps because of the dangerous.

In third grade, I brought a little chameleon home from school. Without pausing to consider what my mother would say, I was the first to raise my hand when the teacher asked for a volunteer caretaker. It had been our class pet for a while, and I was amazed by its ability to change color: sooty brown-gray and it blended into the soil; bright green and it was indistinguishable from the leaf it rested on. We hadn't ever had a pet. As natural as she was in some ways, my mother couldn't relate to the idea of having an animal in one's home. Why anyone would want something around that could ruin furniture, track in dirt, make things smell, was beyond her.

When I got home with the lizard, my mother, her voice sounding a little pained, washed her hands of the whole thing, and said that if I wanted to I could keep it in my room, but she didn't want to have anything to do with it. I was confident she wouldn't interfere because it was a school project and, on some level, she would never stop us from being regular kids. She didn't want us to have her fears; she had a vision that her daughters could be more sporty and American than she ever was. While she had never learned to swim, wouldn't put her head underwater, she made sure from an early age that we swam easily, flipping and diving in without trepidation. *I was the promise. You are the fulfillment,* she was fond of saying.

I enjoyed having the terrarium in my room, an object filled with dirt that was allowed in the house. It was better than television to watch the lizard change its coat, from gray to green and back again. Each day that passed, I felt a little less nervous, less worried that I might make a mistake. I began to feel that the lizard and I were getting along, so to speak, with flying colors, that my mother had been wrong in thinking it was a bad idea.

One day, about a week after I had brought the lizard home, I was holding it, admiring its almost unnatural green hue, when it leaped from my hands and into its glass-walled home, leaving its tail behind in my palm. I was disgusted, and quickly dropped the appendage into the cage. I looked at the newly shortened creature. The teacher had told me that if the lizard dropped its tail, it was out of fear, a kind of survival instinct—that cutting off part of itself allowed the chameleon to fool its enemies and make a quick escape. She had also promised the tail would miraculously grow back. I remembered this, but I was worried, because the lizard wasn't moving at all. Staring straight ahead, it was freeze-framed in a belligerent pose, legs at the ready for its next leap. I tried everything to get it to move. For hours, I waited for some sign, trying to tempt it with food, a caress. Finally I had to accept the fact that its complete stillness meant that it was dead. La Fontaine in his best fable could not have made me understand something so powerfully: I had seen for myself what happens when a living thing is frightened to death.

Las Cucarachas

One summer our parents went somewhere on a trip and Stephanie and I, ages seven and ten, respectively, were deposited at the summer home of our blond doppelgängers, two sisters whose ages almost exactly corresponded to our own. This happened periodically. We would be dropped off at the big house in Westhampton and left there, seemingly for days at a time. Fortunately, Stephanie and I loved staying with Isabelle and Nathalie, who were a little wilder than we were, which meant guaranteed fun. The two girls were also our oldest friends. Our mothers had known each other vaguely in Mexico City in the early sixties, when they were both young and single and looking for love, before any of us were even on the horizon.

Ten years later the two women met up again, by coincidence, in the lobby of the large apartment building on Central Park West where we lived until I was five. Their mother, coming in with her husband, saw and stopped my mother, who was going out with hers, and said, "Gisèle, is that you?" My mother, dressed up and on my father's arm, was apparently a little embarrassed to encounter someone from her early days in the presence of my father. "What are you doing here?" she asked. Jackie replied, "I live here." "So do I!" my mother said, warming up a little, and added, "This is my husband." "This is mine," Jackie countered, and the two men were introduced. My mother then confided, "I have a six-month-old daughter sleeping upstairs." "I do too!" Jackie declared, and in their shared laughter an altogether new friendship was born.

As it happened, the two women had followed almost identical courses—moving back to New York, meeting and marrying husbands, having children. Open to experience and intellectually curious, Jackie and Gisèle had a natural affinity, each admiring the other's ability to be a woman on the go, to throw great parties, to dress with panache, to keep a beautiful home. They read Gloria Steinem together, compared notes on raising active, capable girls, and shopped in tandem for everything from titanic dining room tables to sleek little packages of glinting powdered eye shadow. They often attended the theater or an evening of ballet together, leaving their husbands contentedly at home.

It wasn't just the mothers—there were other similarities between the two households: businessmen fathers, daughters with names that sounded right in both French and English. Each family also had the travel habit, both sets of parents being adventurers, theirs even more than ours. They went rafting, scuba diving, camping in the Sahara. We went sightseeing. On a shared vacation in Acapulco, the other sisters went waterskiing in shark-infested waters, while we weren't even allowed to set foot on the beach. Isabelle and Nathalie laughed when we asked about their day—like their mother, they were fearless.

I was crazy about their country house: the soda machine their father had installed off the kitchen as a lark, the trampoline out back, the elliptical swimming pool. Then there were the girls' bedrooms, where it was as if the fantasies we read about in children's books had been allowed to explode across the walls. Isabelle's room was painted with an elaborate jungle scene, showing monkeys hanging off treetops and glimpses of tigers hiding in the reeds. On Nathalie's walls was a blue-tailed mermaid, a perfect woman-child riding at the helm of a pearl-lined, fish-drawn chariot. With an admiring octopus and a gentle sea turtle in attendance, she rested on her half-open shell ever so gracefully. Everything about her was intoxicating: the green coronet she wore, the waviness of her blond tresses, her lighthearted smile. Around the room the watery scene was interrupted by several windows, but each time the billowing midnight-blue reins just picked up where they left off, confirmation that the outside world was of little consequence to the realm of enchantment.

The most alluring spot in the house, however, was the White Room. Reserved for guests of Isabelle and Nathalie's parents and off limits to us kids, the room was devoid of such childish embellishments as could be found a few doors away. The walls of the White Room were immaculate, the color of unused chalk. White curtains, a white-brick fireplace, and white lamp shades provided the blanched setting for furniture that was mostly dark wood: an imposing bureau, a set of night tables with a tempting array of women's magazines and chunky ashtrays, a headboard against which a white chenille bedspread lapped like milk. A freestanding oval mirror, framed in ebony, was set into a corner, reflecting the room's snow-white contents back in perfect inversion, and creating an almost untenable measure of brightness. Standing in the doorway of the White Room for a moment on my way down the hall, I would dream of entering the forbidden sanctum. I longed to throw myself on the lush pile of the white throw rug, which lay in front of the bed like a guard dog, the sleeping sentry of a pristine palace.

Every so often a lucky young woman came to stay in the White Room—a friend of the family in her twenties or thirties who would be invited for a summer weekend. That was what the White Room was meant for, when it truly came alive. The dresser drawers would be left half open, dripping with pieces of yellow bikini and peacock-print shifts. Emanating from the room was the smell of summer, a siren scent of cocoa butter and the citrusy undernotes of Jean Naté body splash.

Despite the studied blankness of the White Room's decor (so unlike the style of our house), my imagination took root there. I idolized and envied its anonymous young visitors, all of whom seemed to be in sole charge of their weekends, their wardrobes, their lives. I envisioned each guest arriving at the house with her bag, her delight at being shown her accommodations, the pleasure of lying across that white bed alone and leafing through a fashion magazine or lighting up a solitary cigarette. In the evening I pictured how she would dress, offhand, in a chiffony halter-top dress, its Kool-Aid hues exquisite against her newly tanned skin. Ready at last, Indian-inspired earrings dangling softly from her pierced lobes (all the more intriguing because my mother didn't have them), she would spin for herself one final time before the oval mirror. Only late, late at night, long after we girls were asleep, would she come home, headlights lancing the hydrangea bushes that crowded the driveway. There might be laughter as she waved goodbye to her ride, and then she would take off her gold sandals and hold them in one hand, so as not to wake us as she tiptoed to her room. At breakfast the next morning, Isabelle and Nathalie's parents would tease their pretty guest about her evening. She would smile instead of answering, eyes hidden behind large sunglasses.

I loved these young women, their utter freedom. I loved them because they were so different from the women I had around me most of the time. Not wives, not mothers, more mysterious even than the teenagers who took care of us each summer, they weren't attached to anything outside of themselves. And then too they were gorgeous, as impossibly beautiful as mermaids. I was just hitting the awkward stage—I was no longer a cute little girl but not yet much of anything else either—and was prone to sunburns and freckles, with an unwavering middle part and eyes that couldn't see much past my nose unless I had my glasses on or went underwater, where my normally flawed vision became crystalline, the fleeting beneficiary of some inexplicable aquatic sorcery. What strange trajectory separated me from those young women, I wondered. How many sea chariots would I have to ride, what harrowing journey would I have to make, before I arrived, finally, at the heady province of adult femininity?

As usual when Stephanie and I went to stay at Isabelle and Nathalie's, the four of us were mostly left to our own devices.

Whereas at our house, our mother managed to watch over almost every move of ours, scheduling time in sequences of tennis, riding, Spanish, and drawing lessons, at their place, there never seemed to be anyone supervising us, let alone orchestrating our activities. This didn't bother us, as we knew how to keep ourselves busy, creating our own scenarios, running up and down the stairs, wherever whim took us. In Isabelle's jungle setting, we painted our toenails hot pink, having pilfered an old, half-dried-out bottle from their mother's mirrored dressing room. In Nathalie's room, we taught ourselves the words to *"La Cucaracha,"* swinging our shorts-clad hips and snapping our fingers as hard as we could until we fell in giggles on the red shag carpeting. When the mood struck we built fortresses of pink and orange cardboard bricks, taking turns at being the princess. Drawn outside by the simple dazzle of green grass and bright sun, we did flips on the trampoline until we felt like throwing up, swam in the pool for so long our eyes stung and our hands pruned, or wandered to the back of the lawn, to the row of twenty-foot-high bushes where ivory-colored honeysuckle, as finely fluted as champagne glasses, grew in abundant whorls. Plucking one blossom at a time, we would delicately pinch off their bottoms, which were tinged bright green. You had to do it carefully, without breaking the pistil, or the whole thing was ruined. Pulling out the long spindly wand, bubbly with nectar, you'd feel the stigma make one final pop before coming free of the base of silky petals. Then we sucked the flowery elixir, far more fragrant and ethereal-tasting than mere candy could ever be. We did this for hours, never feeling sated, until the grass in front of the bushes was littered with crumpled white corpses and the only blossoms left intact were at the topmost regions, where our straining hands couldn't reach.

It amazed us that such subtle indulgences were passed over by adults, and so we hunted for other treasures beneath their notice. What attracted us most was the rotten, the near-spoiled, the bad-for-us. We unearthed whatever we could find that was illicit or unhealthy, comic books to numb our brains, sugary stuff to erode our teeth. Any whisper of sex or drugs or curse words sent us into a frenzy. It was the summer of *Grease,* and the movie quickly became our obsession, especially Sandy's transformation from good girl to sex goddess. Strangely, none of us were that interested in Danny, the male lead, played by John Travolta. Instead we desperately loved his lanky sidekick Kenickie, with his dimpled face and suggestive swagger. Our love for him was excruciating—a shared vice, like our sneak attacks into the pantry for handfuls of sugar cereal. I don't remember how we came up with it, but whenever it was rainy and we couldn't play outside, we went downstairs and, one by one, removed the long creamy-white rectangular bolsters from the living room couches. Isabelle would put a record on the stereo, and as the music played, we would stand our bolsters on end and pretend we had Kenickie in our arms, clasping him tight, four flatbodied little girls slow-dancing with couch pillows. Towering over us, the bolsters were stiff and unwieldy, ready to squash us if held the wrong way. I wondered if this was what sex actually felt like, bodies pressed suffocatingly close, one's sense of balance teetering on the edge, the pleasure of it mingled with a fear of being caught.

I was the oldest by a week—Isabelle came next, then our sisters, forever trailing behind us—but I wasn't the leader. That role was reserved for Isabelle, she of the green, all-seeing eyes and the shaggy golden hair that lit up in the sun, crowning her absolute ruler of all our exploits. Like her sister, she never got burned, never bothered with sunscreen the way we had to every minute. The two of them simply got brown all over, even in hard-to-reach places like the soles of their feet, as if at the start of the summer they had been dipped in honey.

Isabelle was the one who discovered the pungent stash of marijuana (in a small enameled Chinese box in the living room) that we were too young to know what to do with; Isabelle who finagled the keys to her father's brand-new moped from the gardener, giving us turns sitting behind her on the big, smooth, black leather seat, hot from the sun, as she rode us roughshod over the gnarly roots of the oak trees that framed the front of the house, our screams increasing with each near-collision jounce. We placed ourselves in her hands blindly, never realizing the many miracles we were using up in not getting killed or maimed.

Frequently during those blistering days of summer, Isabelle would get in a mood and go off somewhere by herself—and not to read a book, either, the way I sometimes did. She was the only kid I knew who just wanted to be alone every once in a while. We could see her, sitting in the gazebo or at the edge of the diving board with her feet hanging in the water, but none of us dared approach. Even if it seemed as though she had chosen to do something sociable, like watch television in the den—where, after being outside all day, the sudden dark made you see stars—she could frost you in seconds with her icy stare, making you want to be just about anywhere else. At times like these, she was not even afraid (using a thin, cold, unyielding voice) to talk back to her mother, something it hadn't occurred to me you could do. It's not that I didn't have arguments with my mother. Of course I did. But I never spoke to her in a condescending way. I wouldn't have known how. If I put up a fight about practicing the piano or being allowed to stay over at a friend's house on a weeknight, it was in vain protest, in the knowledge that on some level my arguments were futile because my mother was so utterly in charge. Isabelle, on the other hand, though only ten, was in adolescent mode, battling for her independence, already traversing a vastly different terrain from the one I was still content to occupy.

In our household it was Stephanie who put up a fight about everything, Stephanie who couldn't be told what to do, who was always trying to will things her way. Once my mother wanted her to do something and she said, "You can't tell me to do that. You're not my boss." "Yes she is," I piped up, the firstborn daughter. "No," my sister insisted. "She might be the boss of you, but she's not the boss of me." I was used to my sister's hair-raising obstinacy. Isabelle, as if recognizing in Stephanie a kindred spirit, reserved a special respect for her, in spite of the difference in their ages. The two of them often acted in concert; Nathalie and I hovered a bit in the background, more docile participants in whatever we did next.

That summer was the first time we were allowed to eat out alone, which meant that one night we got dropped off by Isabelle and Nathalie's parents at Baby Moon, a local pizza parlor that to our minds represented the acme of fine dining. There wasn't much to the place—a wall of windows, an old-fashioned jukebox, a pay phone by the entrance to the more fancy, sit-down Italian restaurant in back. Up front, at the hub of it all, was the counter, behind which men in white hats spun their elastic wheels of dough, draping them in slivers of mozzarella, splashing them in bright red sauce, like fake blood, and throwing them into the hot coal-burning oven, from which they emerged glistening with oil, completely transformed. It made the four of us feel very grown up to walk in, seat ourselves at one of the orange Formica tables, and order a feast.

We savored every part of the meal: the darkly sweet soda in ice-filled waxy cups, each hot triangular slice, sure to burn your tongue if you took the first bite too quickly. Stuffing ourselves contentedly, we surveyed the scene. The rest of the crowd consisted of families with kids, most of them littler than we were, and a few tables of teenagers, guys and girls sitting separately. We were the only ones our age who didn't have grown-ups with them. The teenage girls, with streaked hair falling in Farrah-like formations, spent a lot of time sashaying past the boys' tables in their tight-fitting jeans, to the rumbling jukebox that even then seemed kind of quaint.

When our meal was over, there was nothing left for us to do but scavenge the remains, pick the crumbs off paper plates glued with grease to the table surface, loudly slurp the last of our sodas, sucking little more than air up the blue-and-white-striped straws. We were sure someone was coming to pick us up—Isabelle and Nathalie's parents, their grandparents, a housekeeper, anyone. But by now most of the people we had eaten with were gone. New customers were coming in, eyeing the debris strewn across our tabletop. The place was filling up, locals mostly, tougher-seeming than the earlier, more family-oriented crowd. We heard the roar of motorcycles outside, saw tattoos and beards and long hair on men with handlebar moustaches. A woman with frizzy hair and short shorts came over and asked if we were done. The four of us looked at one another, as it dawned on us that we couldn't hang on to the table forever. Reluctantly, we relinquished our turf and went outside, where it was getting darker, and cold.

There was no one in the parking lot, just cars. We leaned against a blue one and waited. After what seemed like hours, Isabelle came up with a plan: we would call the house. Lining us up in size order (I was second), she marched us back in to use the pay phone, whispering, "Right . . . right . . . right . . . right," to keep our feet stepping in unison. Arms swinging to the beat of imagined drums, we felt smart and brave—none of us had ever used a pay phone before—yet the only effect our show of independence had was to make everyone in the restaurant snicker. Somewhat disheartened, we crowded around Isabelle as she pushed the dime in and dialed the number. We could hear the phone ring and ring. We had no choice but to march back out, trying to hold our heads high after the failure of our mission.

This time there was a dog in the parking lot, one we couldn't see. It was barking incessantly, like a wolf at the moon, and I could tell even Isabelle was frightened. We ran around the lot for a few minutes, hiding behind cars, trying to distance ourselves from the dog's cries, until we realized we had to go back inside. We paraded in again, this time the ritual of it not enough to keep us from the embarrassed sense that we were making a spectacle of ourselves. I don't think any of us were surprised when, again, no one answered. A waitress came over and asked if we needed help. Isabelle muttered, "No, thanks," and we stumbled outside, forgetting our lockstep altogether.

We walked home on the side of the road, on the border where gravel meets grass, the flashing headlights of oncoming cars making it hard to see. We were cold in our sandals and T-shirts—no one had told us to bring sweaters—and the night breezes kept sweeping over us, chilling. Cars on the same side whooshed past so close we could almost feel them, and we would freeze in place, waiting for them to pass. We didn't speak, all of us aware that we could be flattened on the asphalt at any moment, like the dozens of defenseless ants who regularly met their fates under our racing sneakers on the flagstone terrace. The moon, a perfect circle of white, hid behind the darkly swaying treetops, only showing itself every so often, whenever I had forgotten it was there. Even after all that pizza, I felt a sickening emptiness in the pit of my stomach. No one had come to pick us up. I couldn't believe we were so alone, completely vulnerable to the world, without the barest shield of authority to protect us. Even Isabelle's tough-girl act had disappeared, leaving her as subdued as the rest of us. I kept thinking, Stephanie is seven, too little to be out at night. I didn't understand it. Children weren't supposed to be forgotten about, ever.

Just when it seemed we had been walking our whole lives, Isabelle, murmuring to herself, began pointing out landmarks—a stable where they had once kept a horse, a road she recognized as leading to the beach. And then, miraculously, the dusky street we were on became recognizable. I could see the stony white tongue of their driveway spilling out onto the road, and past it the familiar dead man's curve sweeping out of sight. Pushing past the hydrangeas, whose cloudlike blossoms dissolved under my fists in silvery droplets, we walked wearily to the front door. It was unlocked. We trudged upstairs to put on our pajamas and get ready for bed. It felt strange to do all the humdrum things, to brush our teeth, to pull back the covers and slide into our sandy-footed beds, as if this were any other night. I was so happy to be safe I felt like weeping.

The next morning at breakfast their mother laughed when we told her what had happened. She had had no idea. Every adult in the house had thought someone else was picking us up, and by the time their parents got home from their party and peeked into our rooms, we were fast asleep in our beds. It never would have happened at our house, I thought to myself. My mother guarded us too closely. I had to admit, though, that in the light of day it no longer seemed so dangerous—more like a funny story, really—that the four of us had walked three miles home alone from Baby Moon. But for a long time that fierce, lonely feeling, of not being ready for something but having to do it anyway, lingered in me—my first, wary intimation of what growing up would be about.

At fourteen I was still my mother's daughter. At sixteen I was back again, loving her. But the year I turned fifteen something happened, as I left the comfort of her affection for other things. Suddenly I was distant and critical, the lure of my friends, of nightclubs and cigarettes, infinitely stronger than the familiar pull of her embrace. Almost overnight, my relationship with her became fraught. Though I knew she was only asking out of love, I couldn't stand it when she greeted me with an innocuous question, such as, "How was your day?" I could hardly bear to answer, all at once filled with a dire need to have my life be my own, no longer hers in any way. "Fine," I'd mumble as I sped to my room, where I could shut the door behind me, pick up my glossy black phone (a birthday present from my parents), and call one of my own kind, a friend my age.

This compulsion to forge an identity on my own took many forms. My mother had always played a huge part in my self-presentation, helping me find clothes that I liked, encouraging me to feel and look the best that I could. Now I let a friend cut off my hair to a ragged bob, enjoying my mother's shocked intake of breath when she met me at the door. I quickly abandoned the candied palette of young girlhood for a new look, which entailed dressing exclusively in black. The sweet little pink sweaters and striped-ribbon headbands my mother had tenderly helped me pick out were shoved to the back of my closet, replaced by black turtlenecks, black V-necks, and tight black stretchy skirts and pants. My new favorite item was a pair of black, punky, silver-buckled shoes, imported from London, so pointy my mother joked uneasily that they reminded her of weapons.

However loathed by my mother, my new wardrobe suited my dark mood, which manifested itself most eloquently in desolate poems. "My mind screams / and echoes its despair / in flashes which drip / from a faucet of hate," I wrote, finding no relief from the crushing bleakness of things except in the company of my friends. As far as I was concerned, my mother couldn't fathom what I was going through, even though my affliction—adolescence— was quite common to girls of my age. And in truth, to my mother my behavior *was* incomprehensible. The lovely, loving daughter she had raised so carefully was becoming an ungrateful scourge. Worst of all were weekday mornings, when I would sleep past my alarm and she and the rest of my family would make fruitless attempts to wake me up for school. *"LEAVE . . . ME . . . ALONE!"* I would roar from my bed, my voice hoarse with rage at their intrusions. Unlike Gregor Samsa, who physically turned into a giant bug in Kafka's story "The Metamorphosis," I looked the same but acted grotesque. I was a monster, drenched in hormones and resentment. And so I alienated myself emotionally from my mother, creating an environment in which it soon became impossible for us to have any kind of conversation at all.

On the rare occasions that we did speak, I was highly critical. Suddenly everything she did drove me up the wall, from the way she kept a store of crumpled tissues under her pillow at night to the fact that if she couldn't find me in an overrun department-store restroom she began yelling my name indiscriminately, making me cringe inside my stall. With sullen expressions and curt responses, I let her know how much she irritated me.

I didn't stop there. My mother and I had always been very affectionate with each other. It was a part of our relationship that we took for granted, the way we often found ourselves spontaneously hugging in the hallway, or showering bursts of kisses on each other's foreheads and cheeks—"but not on the lips," she warned me once (and never had to again). Countless times she'd sit on my bed and lightly trace her fingers across my T-shirted back as I drifted off to sleep, and whenever we walked down the street, we held hands, the back of hers facing the world, mine safely tucked behind. Out of the blue I announced that I no longer wanted my parents to touch me anymore, as if to put up an inviolable shell around myself. It was the first time I had dared make a rule, and I was surprised by how easy it was. My father's feelings were hurt— he liked it when Stephanie and I came to the door to give him a hug when he got home from work—but my mother felt it like a blow, and soon developed the anxious look of someone housing a stranger in her home.

Perhaps most insulting of all, however, was that I willfully renounced all our familiar pleasures—going out to lunch together, schlumping down Madison Avenue, spending an afternoon at the Museum of Modern Art with a quick stop afterward at Godiva for our favorite oyster-shell pralines. By saying no every time my mother suggested an outing, and never offering to accompany her anywhere, I made it clear that I vastly preferred being with my peers. It wasn't as if I did anything particularly exciting with them. After school we either went to each other's houses to listen to music or haunted local coffee shops where we could sit in back, away from the sun and the city streets, and smoke to our hearts' content. (The fact that my mother hated cigarettes only added to my enjoyment of taking up the habit, and I soon grew adept at scrubbing my hands and face and dabbing perfume on my hair and clothes the minute I came home.)

This was just when MTV was taking off, and my friends and I were obsessed with music videos. I remember watching one in my mother's bedroom, and feeling her come into the room. After briefly glancing at the screen, she spent the rest of the song watching me be entranced by the British punk rocker, and I, sensing how little she understood the words or the appeal of the scrappy singer, strangely enjoyed the experience both a little more and a little less.

How could my mother understand anything, I thought. She had grown up in Belgium. I, on the other hand, was an American teenager—not precisely what she had in mind when she said, "I was the promise, you are the fulfillment." We were on new ground. I began imagining ways of escape, asking my mother whether I could go to boarding school, an Anglo-Saxon ritual she didn't relate to at all. I cried for a week when, after much discussion with my father, she said no, that she wouldn't be ready to lend me to the World at Large until I was eighteen and ready to go to college.

I should say in my defense that I wasn't completely bad. Certain habits were so ingrained in me that I don't think I could have shaken them if I tried. (I didn't try.) You could even say that on paper, everything about me remained the same. I was the oldest daughter, got good grades, set the table when I was told, and regularly (if indifferently) practiced the piano at my mother's bidding, counting the exact number of minutes until I could leap off the bench and scurry back to my room. When I think of all the things I could have done, like skip classes, or plunge into drugs, or go too far with the wrong boy (or any boy, for that matter), it's hard to imagine what all the fuss was about. Who knows, perhaps my mother would have been relieved to find me committing such typical juvenile offenses. At least then the problem would have been external, easily identifiable, something she could have rallied to solve and conquer.

When we were very little, my mother used to keep us in line with the specter of a girl from her childhood, also named Gisèle, who had the effrontery to go by "Gigi," something my mother never did. Gigi had been a bad girl. She never listened to her mother, ran around with boys, did poorly in school, talked back. For a long time my mother's merely saying "Gigi" in a certain tone of voice would be enough to get Stephanie or me to behave. Now I was beyond Gigi, as evidenced by the fact that my mother didn't even have the heart to bring her up. My crimes, being corrosive to the haven my mother had built for us, were much more insidious than those of her ancient nemesis. It was the warmth of our relationship I destroyed, thereby upsetting the balance of all relations within the family. My mother, endlessly conferring with my father and sister on how best to handle me, took my behavior very much to heart. I knew it pained her terribly, but I couldn't—for my life, didn't want to—stop.

Around this time my mother wrote me a letter, mourning the

trying to marry my mother off. Boy after boy was presented as a potential life partner. Deals were struck, then by necessity broken, since my mother exhibited no interest in anyone presented to her, displayed no desire to settle down and become a good Jewish wife before she had seen anything of the world. After the initial euphoria of the war ending, of being free, her life in Antwerp was becoming more and more untenable. She began begging my grandmother to be allowed to leave, always using the same argument. "If you loved me, you'd let me go," she'd say, day in, day out, until finally my grandmother gave in. My mother told me that as soon as she was on the boat, about to sail for America as she had always dreamed, she started crying. "She doesn't love me, she's letting me go!" she sobbed on the deck as she leaned over the balustrade waving goodbye to my grandmother (now a little speck on the shore), her entire future lying unknown before her like the great Atlantic itself.

Perhaps in response to her own experiences, my mother never gave us much of a hard time about the little things. She was often bossy about how and when we should fulfill our various obligations, but it was always clear that she wanted us to enjoy ourselves, to make the most of life. She never begrudged us a pleasure, whether it was going to the movies, staying at a friend's house, or taking up an extracurricular activity, as long as it wouldn't interfere with schoolwork and the getting of a good night's sleep. It made her so sad that after all the efforts she made to be different from her own mother, to have a smoother relationship with me, I felt the need to "escape" from her grasp. What she didn't understand was that I refused to become a mere repository of all the dreams she had for me.

It was during this period that I began living a double life. There was the Valerie my mother knew, who went to school and did homework and hung out with friends, and another whose existence I believe she didn't even remotely suspect. That winter I started going secretly to nightclubs. I never asked if I could go. But I had heard enough of her discussions with other mothers to be aware of her feelings about it, to know in my bones that such a thing would be strictly forbidden. So I just didn't tell her. I felt a little guilty about it, but her finding out would put an end to the whole thing, and with it my whole social life, meager as it was.

I started running around with a different set of girls—they were a grade younger than me, and faster than my usual crowd—and every weekend we did the same thing. On Friday nights we went to Studio 54, and on Saturday nights to Xenon. It was way past the heyday of disco (Bianca and Liza and Halston had long since moved on), but we went anyway. The clubs were filled with prep-school kids like us, equal parts worldly and idiotic.

Half the fun was in getting ready. We would all arrange to stay over at the house of whoever's parents weren't home. Each of us would bring a bag of clothing and accessories, pooling our resources to come up with the best ensemble. Telling her I was going to a party (or some other lie) and wanted to look my best, I invaded my mother's closet for sophisticated pieces, which she gladly lent me, happy that I wanted anything at all from her. Sometimes things got lost. I remember bringing a hat of hers that everyone loved to a friend's house, a little black number meant to be worn pitched forward, like a stewardess's cap, with a big bow

sprouting from one side, and not being able to find it in the morning, though I'd seen it in the house the night before. My mother
didn't notice—or if she did, she didn't mention it for fear of creating more strife.

It was the era of big. Big hair, big shoulders, big accessories. We were not so much dressed as rigged, with fat clip-on
earrings, huge square clutches, sharply creased pants, and stiff
hairstyles, hundreds of minuscule antennae poufed up high and
sprayed motionless. We spent hours on our hair, not to mention
our makeup, vainly applying layer after layer of pressed powder to
soak up the oil that naturally kept collecting in the pockets of our
teenage faces. We all, without exception, wore shoulder pads,
which jutted squarely from our necks as if we were football players, practically overshadowing our disproportionately small, oval-
shaped heads. Perhaps the pads functioned as a kind of defense
against the night—not that we thought we needed any. It never occurred to us that we weren't completely safe.

We usually didn't have a problem getting in. Either we knew
someone at the door, or our names were on a list, or we tried looking as alluring as possible to get the bouncer's attention. (Despite
the fact that we were a bunch of overdressed fifteen-year-olds, this
actually worked.) Once inside, we were immediately accosted by
the lights, the music. It was unnatural, that environment. Our bodies were pummeled by the bass coming from the speakers, the
strobe lights that made it hard to see. And there were still other
boundaries to cross. At Studio 54, the VIP section was straight
back, an island of velvet couches adjacent to the dance floor. At
Xenon, it was to the left as you walked in, but it was also considered O.K. to go up to the balcony and watch the dance floor from
above.

Whenever my friends and I danced—and there were certain songs we went crazy for, screaming at one another in excitement before we raced out onto the floor—we piled our bags one on top of the other and moved around them in a circle, as if we were part of a pagan ritual, paying homage to a strange unlit fire. It was hot on the dance floor, damp and smoky with the exhaust of a thousand cigarettes. And for that time, it felt like I had never been anywhere else, there was just me and the music and the enigmatic stare of strangers and a sense of giddy connection with my friends, who were as alive and sweaty and crazy as I was, as we danced to "Creatures of the Night," or some other awful anthem with a driving beat.

When we weren't dancing, we were going up to the bar to get ourselves another cocktail. I liked gin and tonics, screwdrivers, White Russians—I wasn't picky about my poison. Every time I drank, it felt like one side of my head was tilting over, and I was walking around off center. It seemed weird to me that no one could tell. It was as if I could feel my brain cells diving into oblivion with every sip. To steady myself, I smoked cigarettes, pretty much nonstop. We all did. It was the only thing to do as we stood there trying to see who was there, which wasn't easy in that lighting. No matter who was there, there was the sense that the most important people, whoever they were, hadn't come.

It was always the same crowd. We would see girls we knew from other city schools, boys from Collegiate or home from boarding school. And then there were the guys who seemed kind of ageless already. They had been kicked out of boarding school at least once, done a stint at a rehab center or two, and now the clubs were their life. They usually had their names on the invitations that came regularly in the mail. One night, to be different, I wore a mock tuxedo: black pants with satin stripes down the sides, a black fitted tuxedo jacket with a shiny black collar, a white shirt with the collar turned up, and a black bow tie I had lifted from my father's drawer. As I was standing in the VIP section, one of those guys looked at me and asked me to turn around, he had to see this. So I did, moving slowly under his gaze like a doll on top of a music box, waiting to see the approval on his face when I finished turning. By the time I did, he had moved on and was talking to someone else. I felt like a fool, momentarily thinking I mattered.

Sometimes it came as a relief to pile into a cab at the end of the night and go home. (I had a 2 A.M. curfew, which I had wrangled out of my mother after pointing out that it was safer to leave when my friends were leaving than to be out on the street alone trying to get a cab.) If my parents were on Long Island, we would go to my house. If someone else's parents were away, we would go there. Wherever we were, we would change into our pajamas and go into the kitchen, invading cabinets, ransacking the refrigerator, designing an elaborate spread. After all that dancing and drinking, we were ravenous.

This was just at the time when construction work was being done on our building—the entire façade was covered in scaffolding—and we had an infestation of cockroaches in our apartment. My mother was on an urgent campaign to get rid of them. She brought in roach motels, all kinds of exterminating experts. We had dozens of Combat traps placed strategically around the kitchen. Nothing helped. The roaches stayed and proliferated, as if on a mission to drive my mother crazy. Sure enough, it wasn't long before she became a fanatic. She had us empty the garbage every night, refused to allow a single dirty dish to be left in the sink. At her insistence, we left the lights on in the kitchen all the time (the roaches preferred to come out and play in the dark), but you still had to stamp your foot before going in, to announce your arrival and make them scuttle back to their hiding places behind the sink and under the counters. It was horrible, but at least my friends all lived in apartments too, and understood that roaches were just part of city life.

Until then I had never done anything my mother wouldn't have approved of. She trusted me. That was the very crack in her protectiveness through which I slipped out, into contraband places of which she never dreamed, away from her watchful, worrying eyes. Stronger than any fear of retaliation was my conviction that I should be able to go anywhere in the city, do anything. I thought myself terribly urbane. And I was desperate to meet boys. I had been kissed only once, and if I hadn't adored the sensation, I was at least willing to give it another try. I didn't know what I was risking in going into that kind of environment. I didn't know how often girls got lost along the way, crushed by the unrelenting pressure of their peers to do more, drink more, have more sex, take more drugs, until they were permanently trapped on the downside of glamour. I only wanted to fit in with my friends, to be part of the pack, anything rather than stick out as an individual. Renouncing my unique role as my mother's oldest daughter, I hoped to become like every other adolescent girl I knew. It was an act of rebellion by way of utter conformity.

One Saturday night I found myself at Xenon. I was wearing my favorite red sweater, worn backward—backs were "in" then, so I used to take my plain V-necks and wear them the wrong way, imagining this to be sexy. My friends and I had gone into the VIP section, but we got bored, so we went up to the balcony to survey the scene. I saw him right away. He was wearing a burgundy sharkskin jacket and cowboy boots. His blond hair fell perfectly over one eye. As I stood with my friends, I felt nervous and shy, as if I were at a fifties prom, waiting for the boy to come to our side of the room and ask for a dance.

Suddenly I heard a voice in my ear.

"Would you like to do some lines with me?" it said.

I turned to look at him. I didn't understand. "I'm sorry, what?"

"Lines, you know, like cocaine. Would you like to do some cocaine with me?" he repeated.

"Oh. No, thanks," I said, disappointed.

"Well, in that case, would you like to dance?"

"Sure," I said, and as if it were the most natural thing in the world, he took my hand and led me downstairs and onto the dance floor. I was in heaven, my only distraction being that I knew my friends were watching and laughing it up above us.

Afterward, we went back up to the balcony and made out. He was a good kisser, so accomplished I was able to tune out the obnoxious guys sitting beyond us who were shouting and egging him on. Whenever we weren't kissing, he told me about his horoscope that day, how it had told him that something amazing was going to happen that night. He was so handsome, I was so drunk with the thought that he was mine for the evening, that I believed everything he said.

For the first time, I let my friends leave without me for their common destination. It was late, I would tell my mother my friend hadn't been feeling well, and so I thought it better to come home. I had gotten good at lying. After the first few times it was easy, especially given how much my mother wanted to believe me. In the cab up Park Avenue, he kept begging me to let him come upstairs, I could sneak him into my room, he would be very quiet. I wasn't that drunk. "No, it's impossible," I said, and we made plans to speak to each other the next day.

I was supposed to go to a friend's house that Sunday to study for a history test. I called her up to confer. She had a laid-back mom, which meant that boys were allowed in the house, so we decided to invite my new guy over with his friends to hang out and watch TV. I took a lot of time with what I was wearing, and then went to tell my mother goodbye. "Have a nice time studying," she said, looking at me with love as I stood there with my bookbag on my shoulder, itching to run out of the house.

Within a half hour of the boys' coming over, I was in my friend's room with the guy, fooling around. He kept asking me to take off my sweater. My breasts were small and relatively new. I wasn't used to them, couldn't believe he wanted to touch them. I kept saying no, and finally he just pulled it up anyway, his skin against mine like sun-warmed velvet. It felt so good I almost didn't care that everyone out there knew what we were doing.

The next day, my mother spoke to my friend's mother. "That's nice that they had the boys over, isn't it?" my friend's mother said. My mother played along, and then hung up the phone, livid. When I got home, she yelled at me. It was the first time I had ever been caught in a lie. She said she didn't know what to do—not only did we not have a relationship anymore, but now she couldn't even trust me. I had no defense. I had deliberately told her I was going to study, knowing full well I wasn't. (She didn't know that I had fooled around with a boy. That would have been a whole other level of betrayal.) The fact that I had lost her trust—that it would take me months to get it back—didn't upset me half as much as the fact that I never heard from him again.

Eventually things settled down. I got over my crush (who I heard later got kicked out of school, went through rehab, and ended up writing television jingles). I stopped going to nightclubs, stopped badgering my mother to let me go to boarding school, and gradually became affectionate with her again. It was different this time. My body was my own, I wasn't her baby anymore. We began relaxing in each other's presence, and I wasn't so critical of everything she did. She asked my opinion about things, we talked. We discovered that irrespective of our mother-daughter relationship, we liked each other, enjoyed spending time in each other's company. She appreciated that I had my own point of view, no longer took it as a matter of course that she could boss me around morning, noon, and night. If I went to make a phone call and closed my door, it didn't hurt her feelings as much. She understood that I needed my own space. On my side, I no longer viewed her as perfect, as the absolute authority of everything to do with my life. I loved her, adored her even, but I also saw her faults—her impatience, the illogic of some of her convictions. I forgave her for them, as she eventually forgave me for having emotionally gone away.

Within that year I renounced wearing all black and writing depressing poems, and found a steady boyfriend, with whom I was well matched in intellect and humor. Sometimes I even talked to my mother about him, asking advice or sharing a little story. By senior year of high school, I was much happier. I had joined a singing group, become editor of the high school paper, put on a

Dorothy Parker play with a couple of friends (my mother's closet providing the costumes for the entire female cast). Before I left for college I even thanked my mother for not letting me go to boarding school. And I became all the more grateful later, when I realized how short our time together actually was.

At the height of my hideous adolescence, neither one of us really believed it was just a stage. It was like our apartment building, which had undergone renovation to have its stone façade, turned dark brown over the years by the filth of the city, restored to its original color, a beautiful light-brown-sugar shade. There was nothing to be done about it: for the transformation of the building to take place, there had to be construction, and with construction came the bugs. For months they wouldn't go away, surviving all my mother's attempts to do them in. Then, just when we got resigned to the pests, got used to seeing their terrible brown bodies shimmy across the countertops whenever we walked in, they grew tired of being there, and left, en masse. We couldn't believe it. It happened so quickly and arbitrarily that it really seemed as if their departure had been their own decision, as if they only went away when they were good and ready to go.

Years later, long after I had lost my mother, I was invited back to Isabelle and Nathalie's house. We were still friends, and we saw each other regularly in New York, but clearly the need to stay for long periods at their country house was gone. One summer weekend, though, I decided at the last minute to take Isabelle up on her offer and go to Westhampton. I was twenty-eight years old, single, with one disastrous love affair behind me and a new story that was still playing itself out. To my disbelief, when I arrived with my weekend bag, their mother took me upstairs and walked me past the mermaid and her retinue, past the monkeys, right to the door of the White Room. It was mine for the weekend. At long last it would be my bikinis that would spill out of the dresser drawers, my high-heeled sandals casually strewn across the white throw rug, my reflection greeting me in the oval mirror as I got ready for the evening. I remembered the little girl I had been, the sense of yearning that had filled me with each glimpse of those young women, their carefree splendor. It took me aback to realize that so many heartaches later, seemingly despite myself, I was on the other side. I had become one of them.

The Flying
Duck Theory

The summer that I was thirteen and my sister was ten, my parents rented a house for us on David's Lane, in Easthampton. From the front, the house looked like a third of it had been sliced off the left side, which gave it a kind of lopsided charm. By far the best thing about it, though, was its proximity to the local duck pond. My sister and I would bike down the street in our sneakers and faded T-shirts, our faces sun-freckled, our hands sticky on the handlebars from homemade popsicles, which we would make in ice trays out of orange juice and toothpicks. Once there, we would jump off our bikes and pull hunks of bread out of our pockets. Tearing the bread into uneven pieces and tossing them into the dark green water, we would breathlessly wait for our friends to arrive. Honking loudly, they came as if pulled by magnets—bills out, eyes shining, a wake softly dividing the water behind them. As they darted their heads toward the soggy crumbs, we tried to aim for the less aggressive ones, instinctively wanting to help them. Then the little ones would start to appear, shivering in bunches, sometimes bumping into one another, their feathers like tufts of cotton stuck to their bodies. When we ran out of bread, we took walks in the shadowed trails winding through the nature preserve. Even if the great white beach had been scorching, the sand burning the soles of our feet, it was always cool on the paths. Crossing rickety wooden planks, we spotted turtles hiding in the shady water, or shrieked when a water rat came skimming into view.

By the following summer, my parents had bought a house for us in Easthampton. It was farther away, which meant we hardly ever went to visit the ducks anymore. But years later, when I was living in Paris for the year, I thought of those ducks before accepting an invitation from my mother's friend Julia and her husband to go hunting. We would be going to Touraine, and our weekend would be dedicated to ducks. I was a little nervous, never having gone hunting before, but I reasoned that since I was very fond of eating duck, I could not raise any moral objections. We left Paris early on a Saturday morning, and arrived in time to begin hectic lunch preparations. Every weekend, a different family was assigned the responsibility of organizing the meals, and it was our turn. We would be about thirty people for lunch, including the gamekeeper and the head of the hunt, the various husbands and wives and their assorted children. I was the only American there. We went into the kitchen and started preparing the meal: unwrapping cheeses and washing fruits and vegetables. There were some local women helping us; they wore heavy white aprons and, chattering among themselves, frequently broke into laughter. At one point, amid the slicing and washing and chopping and boiling, I noticed a large salad bowl filled with slivered endives. Without giving it a thought, I reached out my hand and popped one of the vinaigrette-coated leaves in my mouth. Suddenly I froze. I heard a nightmarish voice in my ears, berating me for taking a piece of salad. *How unsanitary! The salad was for everyone—what had I been thinking?*

I turned around, but I was alone in the kitchen. It was only an echo from the job I had left the week before. My boss had been a woman in her fifties, someone my mother had known socially. When I started looking for a job in Paris, I sent her my résumé and arranged for an interview. She was curt on the phone, but quite engaging in person. She looked at me intently with her clear blue eyes, and I saw warmth and interest. She asked me about my mother, and when I told her she had died, she stood up and kissed me the French way, on both cheeks. I told her I would work very hard for her. She said, "We'll try each other out for one month. If you're happy and I'm happy, we'll take it from there." I knew that she was in P.R., that she represented the best chefs and restaurants and hotels in France, and that she was friends with the likes of Polanski and Paloma and Isabelle. Her office was in her apartment, and there were photographs everywhere of her hanging out with celebrities.

Back in New York, I was impatient to start. I had two months to wait before leaving and it seemed endless. I had emerged from my Washington apathy. Overnight, I went from barely moving to overly excited, filled with bravado. I was going to Paris, just as my mother had. I was completely thrilled with the prospect of my new job. My boss seemed plugged in to every interesting cultural event and personality in the city. It would be glamorous and exciting, everything I secretly wanted for my year in Paris. I was flying high, barely able to downplay my excitement to friends who asked what I would be doing.

When I arrived for work at the beginning of September, she was away, so I met the two other girls with whom I would be working. One had been there for six months and knew the ropes, but wisely kept calm in the face of our ignorant enthusiasm. The other girl and I spent a lot of that first week smoking (even though we had been told it was absolutely forbidden) and discussing our near, bright future, what happenings we would be attending, whom we would meet there. At one point, while we were standing on the little balcony blowing our smoke into the air, the ashtray we were using fell from our hands. It went crashing down into the middle of the courtyard, the thirty stubs or so in it splaying over the stones. We giggled nervously and vowed to each other not to say anything to our boss.

Walking through the place on the first day she was back, I noticed the atmosphere was charged, electric. For one thing, the apartment was full. She had brought back her eighty-two-year-old mother, an ill, complaining woman whose one solace in life—aside from her daughter's great success—was her parrot, Coco, whom she had had for forty years. As I walked in, I saw my boss on the phone. Her eyes flashed at me. She was wearing three watches and a dozen chain necklaces around her neck, and I immediately knew that the nature of the job—along with my dreams of it—had changed.

Gone was the charm of our interview. With her staccato commands and short hair, she was a drill sergeant and schoolmistress rolled into one. At her request, she addressed us informally as *"tu,"* and we responded formally, with *"vous."* I had never known the word *"minable"* before, but I learned it quickly. It means "of a pitiable mediocrity." She used it anytime we asked a question, or if she caught us using anything but her signature brown ink. There was brown ink in the copy machine, the fax machine, the printer. We even took phone messages with brown pens. I went home in a stupor.

The next morning it was without much joy that I pressed the downstairs buzzer—marked, ironically, by a giant red heart—that rang up to the apartment. As I got off the ornate iron elevator and stepped onto the sixth floor, I saw the concierge walking away from the front door. When she saw me, she stopped, and, begging my pardon, asked whether I smoked. I looked at her for about three seconds, and decided to trust her. I knew my father would never forgive me for getting fired from a job for smoking, and I also knew that my boss would have us for lunch if she found out about the courtyard incident. I moved toward her and, clasping my hands together in a form of supplication, I stumbled out an apology, which ended with my begging her not to tell Madame. She listened intently, and then broke into a smile. "It's O.K.," she said. "I just wanted to solve the mystery. I won't tell, don't worry, Mademoiselle."

I entered the apartment in a cold sweat, only to hear my boss telling the other two assistants how the concierge had had the nerve to come up and ask her if any of us had been smoking, and how she had told her to go hire Scotland Yard, damn it, if she wanted to find the culprit, but how dare she come snooping around here.

Every day brought new horrors. I heard her say, after hanging up on the best florist in Paris because she couldn't get her way with him, "I will destroy that man." I would go into her bedroom in the morning to tell her she had a call, and she would look up at me with fifty needles in her face from the acupuncturist. I lost weight. I woke up in the middle of one night in a panic, realizing I had forgotten to take out the mail. It didn't matter that I had left after dark, long past the last pickup. The next morning I was castigated for my stupidity by the maid, the mother, and finally by the boss herself. I tried to comfort myself by thinking of one of my mother's sayings for not letting things get to you—"Let it glide over the back of your indifference"—but it didn't work. It got to the point where I talked of nothing else with my friends, as if nothing existed but her and her insane behavior. It finally made sense to me that she had had sixty assistants in less than six months. If old assistants called, to try to ask for moneys owed them, she would say, "Only if you come in person," which usually settled the matter. One assistant did come back, and even brought a man with her for protection. I had stayed late, and got to experience the tumult from another room. I overheard my boss screaming that she would ruin the girl's chances in all of Paris. Luckily, as far as I know, none of these threats were actually carried out.

Although I wasn't happy about the idea of leaving before my month was up—I thought of myself as a good girl, after all, someone who didn't quit—after about two weeks I had had it. This was not at all how I had envisioned my year in Paris. I went into work in the morning and asked if I could speak with her. "When I have a minute," she replied. It was eight o'clock at night before she turned to me and asked what I wanted. In the meantime, I had gone out to lunch and had a steak and a glass of red wine to fortify myself.

I planned to tell her I would be leaving. I looked her in the eyes and began to speak. I said, in a very calm voice, that I was not stupid, and that I was willing to work very hard for her, but that I thought the way she treated us sometimes was just not acceptable. She replied, zinging my words back at me, that she thought the things we *did* sometimes were not acceptable, and not only that, she thought my mother would think she was right, and I was wrong, and that she would be ashamed of me. I felt as though I had just been hit by a truck. I managed to stammer, "Maybe I should just leave." She replied, "No, no maybes. Do you want to *stay*, or do you want to *go*? Because if you *don't* want to stay, I would rather just close the office for the next couple of days and have *no one* here." She was leaving on a trip to Texas the following morning, so that her mother could visit a heart specialist recommended by Jerry Lewis. Before I even knew what I was doing, I stood up and said, "I'll stay." We shook hands across the desk.

What followed was utterly bizarre, like a scene out of an army movie. She led me around the office calling things out to me, and waiting for my reply. She stood next to the bulletin board and yelled, "Now, what happens when a journalist calls for the such-and-such hotel?" I yelled back the correct procedure. We did this for a while, until we ended up in the copy room at extremely close quarters. She started waving her hands around, pointing to the many files stacked up on the wire shelves. "I did all of this, this is all me. I came from nothing. If you do things the way I say to do them, you will be doing them right. I had no fancy education, I had no parents spoiling me. Everything I have I built myself." We were so close I could see her facial muscles straining. I felt a new regard for her. I felt that I could handle the challenge she was offering me, that maybe she wasn't so bad after all, just some kind of crazy perfectionist. If I could only follow her system to the letter, I would be O.K. When I left that night, it was as if we had reached a new understanding. *"Je comte sur toi"*—I count on you—she said, as we shook hands again by the door.

At home later, I felt elated, as if I had managed to tack a happy ending onto a nightmare. My father was so proud when we spoke on the phone. He had never really understood the extent of her terror tactics, so he was relieved that I had reached some kind of détente with her, that I had handled things in a calm, rational way.

I lasted two more weeks, and although things improved, and I felt she treated me with a kind of gruff respect, ultimately it wasn't where I wanted to be. The purported glamour wasn't worth the price. A few days before my month was up, I told her my plans would be changing. She said, without flinching, "You won't have it as easy anywhere else. It's not everyone in Paris who will give you your Jewish holiday." (I had taken the day off for Yom Kippur.) I pretended not to hear her. I left that apartment for the last time on a rainy night. I'd had an appointment in the Saint Germain area, but by the time she let me go I had missed it. The soft rain coated my face, soaked through my clothes. I was shivering a bit when I got to the friend's house where I was staying. She gave me a glass of brandy, the way you do with someone who has just experienced a shock. I had made it out alive, but my confidence in myself and the world, my sense that things would always work out, had been badly wounded.

Over the next few weeks, I didn't know what I was going to do. T. was pressuring me to go back to the States, but my instincts told me that if I left Paris, it would always feel like a failure. I wanted to leave on a happy note, having had a good experience, not a traumatic one, which is why I was very glad to be on a trip to the country with family friends. It was a chance to get out of the city, to get some perspective and enjoy myself again.

That Saturday in Touraine, after lunch and a walk in the woods to pick *cèpes*—fat wild mushrooms that we sautéed later in garlic—the families all disbanded to different houses. I remember feeling incredibly sleepy, lulled by the fire and the adult conversation and a glass of heavy red wine. We ate a decadent dinner, after which I was ready for bed. I was sharing a room with Julia's twelve-year-old daughter. Both of us were feeling a bit fluish, so Julia took out a miniature glass bottle filled with an emerald-green oil and rubbed it under our noses, at the back of our necks, and on the sides of our foreheads. It was mentholated, and made it easier to breathe. The spots she had touched felt cool, as she tucked us in and turned off the light.

The next morning we woke up and dressed while the room was still dark. We got in the car and drove back to the lodge. There were about twenty of us. Some of the women—in olive green from head to toe—were extraordinarily well dressed, with bright feathers in their small, jaunty hats. From the lodge, we walked on a muddy path to a nearby lake. The head of the hunt, a white-haired man with a great red nose and a shining brass hunter's horn attached to his suspenders, broke us up into groups of four.

Each group went to a point around the lake, where there were docks made of old, pale gray wood. I followed my group as we walked low, almost crouching, to the end of our dock. I could see the other groups scattered along the border and the white, cloudy sky reflected in the water between us. The ducks, hundreds of them, were in the center of the lake, quietly nosing each other and diving for food. All at once I heard the silvery notes of the horn, announcing our presence in the unfettered light. There was a great flapping and squawking as the ducks lifted themselves into the sky. They rose in a swarm, like a reverse whirlpool, and flew out in all directions. As the two men in my group shot again and again, my ears rang and my mouth filled with a metallic dust. Then there was quiet. Before I knew what was happening, the dogs we had brought with us plunged into the water. They swam in a straight line for the dead, and one by one brought them back and laid them at our feet. The ducks were long and plump, their capes of dark feathers molded wetly to their bodies. Amid the barking of the dogs and the cries of congratulations and bonhomie, I felt a secret joy for the ones that had escaped.

I realized it was the ducks that had flown straight up in the air that had gotten shot, whereas the ones that had stayed low, parallel to the water, had made it into the woods. It was a flight pattern to live by. With this job, this year in Paris, I had been too eager, too confident that I had found the answer. I cringed when I thought about how high my hopes had been. Life had humbled me by putting me through this experience. The ducks had been like a drove of young girls, like me and my friends as we set out in life. From now on, I would try to lie low, not get swept up in undue excitement. I called it the flying duck theory, a reminder not to let myself get carried away.

In the afternoon, the bounty was placed in a circle on the ground. The hunters lifted each darling by its feet and bagged it. I was handed a bag with two ducks in it. It was the first time I understood the expression "deadweight." I gave them to Julia, and once we got back to Paris, they were put in the freezer. Months later, we ate them, roasted to a tender crisp. I am sad to say that, like the bruised dreams of the young, they were delicious.

Snakes in the Grass

I am Eurydice, dying in the grass. I have been chased to this field, felled by a poisonous snake, and am lying motionless on a bed of fake grass whose every stalk has been covered in glitter.

A friend of my sister's had told us she was producing a short silent movie (an artist's first filmic effort) and thought I might be right for the lead. I dressed up for the audition, which seemed as though it could work either for or against me. I was my mother, my grandmother, in a dove-gray, fur-collared coat and ankle-strap shoes, with pearls at my throat. My hair was up. I was the opposite of my rival, a thin girl in a T-shirt, who had a kind of nonchalant, downtown cool. The minute I saw the artist's storyboard, I fell in love with the project. It was the myth of Orpheus and Eurydice, his vision of it dark, romantic. He would be using only techniques that existed in the twenties—an old windup camera, a rented smoke machine. He had wanted to film the story for a long time, and was finally doing it. I was impressed. He was making a dream happen, which is what life at its best is supposed to be about.

I got the part. I liked the idea of being the star of a silent film. It was so outside the realm of my usual life as a twenty-eight-year-old editorial assistant at a magazine, and at the same time it returned me to a part of myself I had lost sight of. Acting was something I had enjoyed since childhood, right up to the classes at Lee Strasberg's I had taken a few years before in honor of my mother, who had studied with him in the early sixties. When I arrived for the first day of shooting, the makeup artist was in conference with the director. They were looking at pictures of models in Armani ads, made up with blue-shadowed faces and purple-bruised torsos, as if the young girls had been beaten up. "Aren't they incredible?" they kept saying to each other. I was a little scared of what they might turn me into. Then they started talking about a gorgeous woman, how everything looked good on her, every outfit fell exactly right, while she maintained a look of utter disdain and incomparable charm. Who was this enigmatic creature, I wondered, and then realized they were talking about a new mannequin at Bergdorf Goodman, where the makeup artist worked as a window dresser.

I was curious to see how he would handle my face and hair, hoping that under his expert hand I might become more beautiful, that a side of myself I hadn't known might be revealed. I soon realized that this wasn't his intention. He made me up heavily, with layered stains of brown and rust, and so many fake eyelashes that it felt like caterpillars had been stuck to my lids. After he was through with my face, he added a large mass of hair to my own, with trailing braids and ribbons wrapped Grecian-style across my forehead. I felt ugly and strange, which they seemed to feel contrasted interestingly with my gossamer-thin peach dress.

As the director adjusts the lights—it is excruciatingly hot under them, and my arched-back position is killing me—I have a lot of time to think. It reminds me of modeling as a child, the lengthening of time before the camera, the space to be alone with my thoughts. The snake is made of rubber, cold and dry. It squeaks as they wind it around my legs again and again, chafing my skin as they try to get the best, most ominous shot. Orpheus had not been the lover that Eurydice thought he was. He let her down. He loved her so much that he had to look back, to make sure she was still there, condemning them to eternal separation.

My mind wanders. The snake passes over my legs again and again. My eyes are burning, hot in their sockets. I think back. On many Sundays, my mother takes us to the Museum of Modern Art, where I grow very familiar with the paintings, rattling off the artists as we enter each room. I am enchanted by Rousseau's painting of the sleeping gypsy in the desert, the way the full, glowing moon, fearsome lion, and costumed figure are all held together mysteriously within one frame. If it is a sunny day, we eat in the garden, where the crisscross pattern of the white wire chair uncomfortably marks my legs. There I eat a large slice of lemon meringue pie, which I also consider to be a work of art, with its solid yellow base and foaming white crests.

After, my mother gives my sister and me pennies. We pitch

them into the fountain, where they will join the hundreds of shiny disks already there, the copper souvenirs of other children's wishes. I don't remember what I wished for, standing on the side, or on one of the flat white-stone bridges, but I remember the pleasure of hearing the penny hit, and the way, despite its previous heft and speed, it seemed to drift weightlessly to the fountain floor. At some point during the afternoon, we visit the stone snake, a form lying dormant, almost hidden on its ivied terrace. Each time I worry I won't find it, and then it appears to me, smooth and gray and separate. I don't know who made it, but the menace of its closed slanted eyes and broad pointy head is not lost on me; this is a portrait of danger in repose. The stone is always slightly cold to the touch, the figure curving into itself in perfect solitude.

My mother had three stories of love. The third and best, of course, was my father. The first was a boy named Aby. He was the golden boy of her group. They spent summers in Knokke, on the seacoast in Belgium, the girls riding around in a red convertible, waiting for the boys to notice them, all of them going out at night to a dance club called De Hoeve. Aby was loved by all the girls, and he loved many of them in return. At some point, though, he let it be known that he preferred my mother. She was not strictly beautiful. She did not have classic features, but she had something else, what her favorite aunt—rubbing her fingers together and pursing her lips—would describe as a "commme heeerrre" look. When I examine the photographs of my mother at that time, I am struck by the mindfulness she holds in her eyes. It is after the war. She has lost her father, three years of her life, her innocence of the world. She knows pain and sadness and fear, but she knows other things, too: how to get a tailor to fit a suit, what shoe will best show off her leg, even, when necessary, how to steer clear of her mother.

On the first trip to Knokke I really remember, I am eight, Stephanie five. We love the boardwalk. There are little push-pedal cars and wagons you can rent. The whole walk is taken over by children, driving their minivehicles. Adults have to move out of the way. We beg and beg to be allowed. Sometimes my mother gives in. Other times we walk alongside her while she catches up with a friend. Her voice is rich and craggy in Yiddish, as she tells stories of her life in New York. I can't speak Yiddish, but I am so familiar with her intonations and expressions that I understand the gist of what she says.

The beach is strange, unlike American beaches. There are canvas partitions set up all along the sand. People sit inside them, safe from the wind. We sit inside ours, too cold to strip down to our bathing suits. Our aunt is red-haired and sexy. We do not know what sexy is, but we are drawn to her warmth, her lazy drawn-out laugh. She is an exceptional cook. At dinner the night before, she said something about a woman's appetite being very revealing of her sex appeal. She was eating lobster, the butter sliding down her chin. My mother, who prefers to pick at her food like a bird, said nothing. Today my aunt is surrounded by sheets of colored tissue paper. She starts with a wire, wrapping green tissue expertly down its length, until she has what we recognize as a stem. She chooses a deep pink for the petals, interspersing it with a paler pink. Soon she has a flower. She hands it to me. It is so real-looking that I lean in to smell it and she laughs at me. She makes us each a bunch. This is her signature flower. We soon find it is recognizable to all, prized for its style and intricacy, as we walk in the labyrinth of the partitions, trading at makeshift sand stores for seashells and the

tissue-paper flowers of other mothers. We see lilies, daisies, a pre-
ponderance of roses in all shades. We realize that the rose doesn't
take much. It is the easiest bloom for distracted mothers to make.

My mother has an early appointment with a friend at a hotel on
a corner. I have a plan. There is a toy store down the street, toward
the boardwalk. I ask if we can go. We don't have to cross any
streets. We know where she is. She will know where we are. Even
at that age, I am persuasive. My mother is worried about letting us
out of her sight. But she is longing to speak with her friend, and
she reluctantly agrees. I take Stephanie by the hand. Instead of
walking to the toy store, I walk us in the other direction. I cross the
street. I want to circle the whole town. I can't quite tell how big it
is, but I have a need to walk. We hold hands. I keep up a conversation, to amuse her. Stephanie has no idea where we are. We
describe a rectangle. We wind our way past stores and families,
cars and trees. When I have determined that we have walked far
enough, I cross us back over. We are going to the beach. I see it in
the distance. The ocean twinkles at us, beckoning. We walk along
the boardwalk, the sun glare making us squint. It is early. There
are few people out. The canvas partitions billow angrily in the
wind. A few gulls break up the sky with their squawking and flapping. We are just two little girls, walking. I make Stephanie swear
that we will remember this moment forever. We form a secret club,
with five initials. We promise that only the two of us will ever
know what they stand for.

My sense of direction is good, and when we get to the next
corner, we take a left, onto the street of the hotel. We stop in front
of the toy store. The hotel is at the end of the block. My mother is
in there, safe, talking with her friend. It is like candy to look at that
display, filled with foreign yet familiar toys, fake fangs, the frilled

dresses of new dolls. Lulled by the international language of games being spoken to us through the glass window, we momentarily forget where we are. We are jolted back to the real by the sound of shouting and sirens. We look up. My mother is running down the street, screaming; there are policemen trailing after her. I hold Stephanie close, frightened. When my mother gets to us, she is too angry to speak. Then she pulls us in to her, shaking us and crying. She had come out a few minutes after we left to look for us. We have been gone for almost an hour. She was looking for us everywhere. The police have been summoned. She is angry, but Stephanie and I have our club. It is as if I wanted to punish her for letting us go in the first place.

We return to Knokke many times. As we get older, we learn to appreciate its café culture. We no longer trade flowers on the beach or ride the pedal cars on the boardwalk. Now we sit for hours in the main square of Albert Plage, at one of the outdoor cafés. Everyone has one they like better than the others, but they are all almost exactly the same. My mother and my uncle invariably wave to people as they walk by. Sometimes someone joins us. It is pleasant to sit outside, to watch the colorful flags beating in the wind. For lunch my sister and I order Coca-Colas (usually forbidden) and *croquettes de crevettes,* lightly breaded and fried balls filled with dozens of translucent North Sea shrimp. We have an ongoing contest over who will make her soda last longer. We watch each other struggle not to drink it all in a few gulps.

In the afternoons, we go to one of the outdoor clubs with my great-aunts. We sit under trees at tables set in the grass and play boraco, a Brazilian card game similar to canasta. My mother has taught it to us, so we are at ease playing with my aunts and their friends. They have other words for things. *Lobbe* means winning at the first turn. A *jolie* is a joker. *Morte* refers to a package, meaning a bonus hand. The women wear straw hats, which dapple their faces. The men smoke. Many of the players have blue numbers on their arms. No one speaks of it. We eat Belgian waffles, piled high with strawberries and cream.

At some point when we are old enough, my mother tells us what happened with Aby. One night, back in Antwerp, they all went to a ball. I imagine my mother looking like she does in one of the neatly labeled black-and-white photographs from the small, embroidered, rectangular albums that contain, between sheets of white waxed paper, her childhood and adolescence. (My childhood and adolescence will never be so neatly contained. We have dozens of albums, many of them falling apart, drawers full of unmarked photographs.) In one image, she stands at the bottom of an ornate staircase, wearing a lace gown. In another, she sits on the floor, her satin dress spread out around her in a circle as if she were a flower that had been dipped in water. I cannot picture how she must have been, in color, in motion. I listen to the story. It is a story of her life, and so of my life. I am aware that if this decision hadn't been made, I would not be here. She tells of a ball. There were many after the war, the fruits of a desire to forget all that had happened. Young and old would go. It was toward the end of the night. The band was getting ready to play its last number. My mother looked up and saw Aby walking toward her. She said to herself, *If he is not coming for me, then it's over.* Her heart is pounding. He is walking, walking. It seems like it will take him forever. When he gets to her he keeps going, straight past her to his mother, who is sitting on a chair on the sidelines. My mother watches him bend down handsomely, offer his arm, and ask his mother for the last dance. My mother runs out, before she has to see them together. The next day she breaks it off. Despite her vulnerability, she is tough in that regard. I am the same way, I realize. But losing her love makes her lose weight, too. She becomes very thin, practically anorexic. We have pictures of her on the beach, amid the partitions. She is so skinny in her bikini that her bones show, at her hips, her ribs. I think she looks sexy that way. Years later, she runs into Aby in New York, on the main floor of Bloomingdale's, of all places. She is eager to show off her happiness, pulling out pictures of her family—her husband, her two daughters—us. He is subdued, his hat in his hands. He has never married. The sadness of it. But we love this story, this ending. This is how it had to be.

My mother's second love is more dangerous. She falls in love with him on a visit to Mexico, a short trip becomes a year-and-a-half stay. Weeks in Mexico City, weekends in Acapulco, this is when she perfects her Spanish. He is a Mexican filmmaker, full of machismo. He orders her around, decides where they'll eat, what she should wear. It is warm all the time, there are red flowers everywhere. She lives on ceviche, a salad of raw fish marinated in lime. A photograph shows her in a sleeveless white pantsuit with tassels at the hem, a white cap slanted rakishly over her dark hair. She leans provocatively against a flower-covered stone wall, looking like a James Bond heroine. Her expression is inscrutable, or perhaps she is just squinting from the sun.

While she is there she becomes a model and an actress. She appears on television, the beautiful girl singing and dancing and pointing in variety and game shows. For one brief week she even dyes her hair blond, perhaps wanting to see if it was true that blondes have more fun. In the album we have of her Mexico days, there are modeling shots, publicity stills, a casual photograph of her formally dressed and made up, waiting to go onstage. Sitting on her chair, legs sprawled, she looks a little bored. Clipped and pasted into the book are articles from Mexican newspapers that say things like *"Gisèle Neiman está para morir."*

She tells us a story of being invited to a house with some friends. The host and hostess were delayed but left word that their guests were to relax, make themselves at home by the pool. Lazing in the sun, the group spent the afternoon dipping into a bowl of crunchy little chocolates. When at last the hosts arrived, they informed their guests that the treats they had been eating were chocolate-covered ants, a Mexican specialty. My mother tells us that the minute she heard this, she had to run out of the room and throw up.

It takes only a few weeks for her to realize she is fully in love with him, and only then, as if she were a character in one of his films, does she learn that he is married. He lets it slip, knowing it will make no difference, she is too firmly in his grasp. It takes her another year to extricate herself. He lies to her every time they are apart—she knows he is with other women—but she believes him when he tells her he has been miserable without her. They spend one night together during which he calls his wife at four o'clock in the morning to accuse her of cheating on him. He rants and raves while my mother listens. She can hear the woman crying and protesting on the other end of the line, swearing on the church that she has been faithful. Despite everything, even the man himself, my mother loves him, his brute strength, his cruelty. She almost loses herself down there, in the Mexican sun. My sister and I come close to never having existed. We are lucky—what she had thought was a great love turned out to be merely an affair.

✷ ✷ ✷

By the time my mother met my father she was tired of love. It was a hot day in July 1966, and she was sick of everything, of living in New York, of meeting men. She couldn't even see wanting to be friends with an American man, let alone falling in love with one. I know these were her exact sentiments because she was halfway through a letter describing those feelings when she went out that night. She had the flu, and wanted to stay home, but her best friend and roommate convinced her to go to this party to meet a banker, the best friend of *her* boyfriend. My mother wasn't interested in meeting my father. She thought he and his profession sounded dull. On his side, my father was curious, but he wasn't about to stake his night on someone he had never met, so he went to the party with a date, a blond woman whom he never saw again. At the party, my father took one look at my mother and didn't leave her side for the rest of the evening. (To this day, the family joke goes, there's a blond woman who walks around saying, *What ever happened to Jerry Steiker?*) Before the party was over, he cornered my mother's best friend and asked her some important questions. Was my mother seeing anyone, was she married, was she Jewish.

The next day my father called. *I have to see you,* he said. By this time, my mother felt really bad. *But I don't feel well,* she answered. My father, already proving himself to be more than just a boring banker, had a gig downtown playing the saxophone, and asked if he could meet her for a quick coffee. They went to a place near her apartment. At one point, my father reached his hand across the table and looked my mother in the eyes. *How are you?* he said. My mother, overwhelmed by the directness of the question, the kindness of this man she had just met, tremulous that this would become another story of failed love and she wouldn't be able to stand it, started crying and couldn't stop, already opening herself up to him, once again admitting to the possibility of love. *I used to think that love meant suffering,* she would later say. *Until I met your father.*

They were married four months later, my father proposing in La Grande Place, in Brussels, on his way to meet my mother's entire family at her brother's wedding. How narrowly they almost missed each other, and at the same time, how inevitable it was, that they found themselves in the same place in the same city that summer night, a turning point from which they walked away together. On the bottom of the letter she never finished and never sent, my mother wrote, in different-colored ink, "That night I met Jerry Steiker, who became my husband." And so, like the stone statue, the stories of my mother's loves wound around, ending every time the same way, happily, with my father.

Each Saturday I went back, the artist's loft had changed. One day there was a candlelit banquet in Hades, with torches, gauzy fabrics, and strands of pearls hanging from chandeliers. Not in the scene, I watched as a heavyset man, leafy wreath placed above his somber face, became Bacchus; a young, thin guy was transformed, with animal skins and small horns, into a faun; and women of all shapes and ages took on a strange, lurid aspect, in giant head-dresses covered with feathers and fake jewels.

My next shooting day occurred a week later. The glittering field, the complicated banquet scene, were gone. Instead, just a sheet of black photographer's paper, hanging from the back wall and pulled out all the way to the front of the loft. We would be filming the scene in which Persephone, after all of Hades has been soothed by Orpheus's music, summons Eurydice from the dead. I was given a white velvet gown to wear, with a five-foot train and a medieval bodice. It took the makeup artist three hours to do my hair, an ornate wrap of braids and gold coins crowned by a fake gold-and-diamond flowered diadem, which gave me a headache it was so heavy on my head. He whited out my bottom eyelashes completely, and put in fake ones lower down, creating the illusion that my eyes had expanded, my gaze become huge, monstrous. Then he made my mouth tiny, the rosebud lips of a silent film star. Finally, he put a veil over me, so that you could just barely make out my harlequin features, my elaborate coif. Barefoot, I walked down the long sheet of black paper toward the director, who double-exposed the film. In the footage, I am a ghost, floating closer and closer to the camera.

White Goose

My first memory of my grandmother is in a hotel room in Cannes. She is on one side of the double bed, I am on the other, having just wet my pants. She is staring at me, her brown eyes twinkling with determination. Suddenly she swoops up, arms flapping, straight across the bed. She is just about to catch me when my mother opens the door. I start to cry. My mother gets angry and flies to the phone. She calls my doctor in New York, who confirms that there is nothing wrong with me, that it is O.K. for a two-and-a-half year-old to wet her pants.

She was Bomama, my mother's mother, and when she wasn't trying to spank me, I loved to be near her. I would play for hours with the zipper on the back of her dress, never tiring of pulling it up and down. Once I went so far as to ask my mother why I hadn't come from *her* stomach. My mother laughed, telling me the story later. "From the moment you were born, it was like that between the two of you," she would say. "Love at first sight."

I was four when my grandmother died. When my mother told me that Bomama was gone, I remember thinking she must have run out of blood. That's how I thought it happened then. I figured the salty red liquid had to be important, because it hurt so much to lose any. This also made me cry a little harder than the pain warranted every time I got a cut. I was afraid of running out too soon.

There were certain things I knew about my grandmother— the nubby feel of her bouclé suits, the caramel scent of her perfume—but these perceptions faded over time. Almost everything else about her I had to learn from stories.

Born in 1908, Bomama was the oldest of nine children, raised in the town of Sighet, in Maramures, a remote province of northern Transylvania that went back and forth between Hungary and Romania over the years. Like many towns in those days, Sighet was known by a host of names—among them Maramarossziget, Marmarosska, and Syhot. If Sighet's national allegiances and local sobriquets were prone to fluctuate, for a long time the place itself remained remarkably the same. Like Maramures in general, the town was a hub of Jewish life. Jews had been there since the seventeenth century, and were an accepted part of the community.

For some curious reason many Jewish families in Sighet had animal surnames, perhaps to differentiate them from their non-Jewish neighbors. There were foxes, goats, mules, hens, every farm and forest creature one can imagine, as well as several more exotic varieties. (My mother's brother recently met a Sighet man by the name of Olifant.)

My great-grandfather Berko was a Gancz, or goose. The story goes that he was riding a carriage through the snowy woods one winter day when he came upon a beautiful young woman standing in the forest, taking a rest from her walk back into town. When she looked up at him, her hair dark and her skin white, he determined to marry her. Her name was Raisel Wiesel. A weasel marrying a goose. Apparently when Berko asked Raisel's father about a dowry, my great-great-grandfather replied, "You are getting something more valuable than all the riches in the world." That settled the matter, and if my great-grandfather was disappointed, he never showed it.

Berko Gancz was respected in Sighet, a member (along with one other Jew) of the town council and the owner of a successful hotel-restaurant. His new wife did not turn out to be the helpmate he expected—she was quite a handful, that Raisel—but she at least bore him many children. They produced a flock of nine, naming their eldest, my grandmother, Blanca, and two of her sisters Bella and Rosa—sylphlike Art Nouveau names that translate as White, Beautiful, and Red. There are pictures of the girls before the war putting on a play in funny costumes. Bella with her long blond tresses looks like a Pre-Raphaelite angel, and all their faces are laden with innocent smiles.

Berko worked hard and was a doting father. Raisel by all accounts was difficult and rather spoiled. She preferred to stay in bed all day and let the maids and her oldest daughter do everything. Bright and quick, my grandmother (whose nickname in the family was Bloema, Yiddish for flower) was in charge of her eight younger siblings, of the many chores involved in running the house. Bloema had a knack for getting things done, in the kitchen or out. Even so, her mother was always on her back about something. Her brothers and sisters in turn chafed a bit under Bloema's bossy ways, but she was quick to scold, to raise her voice, even to slap if she had to, to keep them in line. They loved and resented her. She loved and protected them. The boys went to shul to study the Talmud. The girls stayed home, learning how to cook in order to become good wives. Everything made sense. They were a family, a single living breathing entity.

Although it was all she knew, Bloema didn't like life in Sighet. Day in, day out, she had too much to do, added to which her mother drove her crazy. In 1928 she decided to run away. She was twenty years old. She didn't have the nerve to say goodbye to her mother, who she knew would take it badly. Her father pulled her aside and said, "Don't worry, I understand." By the time he broke the news to his wife, Bloema was gone.

My grandmother went to Belgium because one of her younger sisters, Edith, was already there, having married and moved to Antwerp a year or so earlier. Edith and her husband didn't have enough money to take Blanca in, so Blanca did what many girls in her situation did: she found work as an au pair. (Jewish families in those days always had Jewish help—they wouldn't think of hiring a non-Jewish girl.) Although Blanca had escaped her domineering mother and was living in a more cosmopolitan city, life wasn't all that much better. Her new boss, the woman of the house, was very demanding.

Two years later, Blanca met my grandfather, Avram Neiman,

through a local matchmaker. Avram was a good-looking young man from Romania, passing through the Belgian port on his way to Australia to make his fortune. Avram took one look at Blanca and his dreams of Australia (or America, depending on who's telling the story) went up in smoke. They were married right away, and decided to stay in Antwerp.

At first Avram struggled to make ends meet. He bought a bicycle and went around selling ties at cafés to make money. In October of 1932 my mother was born, and soon after this he began a more respectable career as a furrier, with my grandmother helping him in his business. In 1934, however, Blanca fell ill with tuberculosis. She was sent to a sanitarium for eight months to recuperate, and my mother, age two, was put in a nursery. While they were gone, Avram took up the diamond trade, beginning as a polisher in the Bourse, Antwerp's diamond exchange. Blanca, followed by my mother, returned. Slowly Avram worked his way up, eventually becoming a dealer in his own right. By 1936 or so things had turned around, and the family was quite well off. My grandfather became known for handling only hundred-carat parcels of diamonds at a time when the standard packet was two or three, maybe six, carats at the most.

For reasons having nothing to do with his financial success, my grandfather was considered a gem among diamond dealers. I was always told that if I asked anyone at the Bourse about him, every person I found would tell me what a good man he was. He lent money and didn't ask for it back (no wonder people loved him), he gave wise counsel whenever there was a dispute, he was gentle with his wife and children. In one of the few photographs we have of him, he stands, under a small-brimmed hat, with his wife and daughter (my mother, age six, wears a large white flower tucked behind her ear), leaning toward them slightly in a gesture of protection and proprietorship. My mother told me that once the war started, and supplies became scarce, he made every effort to continue to bring her sweets—oranges and chocolate mostly. It was proof of his love for her, that he would treat her well no matter what. When I picture him, I see him as sepia-toned, standing in that same gentle pose, the only spot of color a bright, round orange he holds firmly in one hand.

Avram and Blanca made a chic couple. They went to synagogue, to the theater, to the opera. My grandfather was religious. He would stop to say his prayers on the street. If the theater started at eight o'clock on a Friday night, and Shabbat at ten, he would go to the theater, but only if he paid for the tickets beforehand, so as not to have money pass through his hands on the day of rest. In those years my grandmother kept a kosher home. The Neiman family resided at 12 van Spangen Straat, a three-story town house on a quiet street. This is where my mother lived as a child. The house is no longer there, torn down to make way for a religious grade school.

Avram was a generous man. Blanca had furs, jewels, the latest dresses, all of which she wore quite well. She developed a liking for tchotchkes, collecting animal figurines and other small objects that she displayed in glass-fronted cabinets. At some point she indulged in a new set of china, pale pink and emblazoned with calligraphic silver markings (the design had won a prize in Brussels), dishes almost too gorgeous to use.

In 1938, ten years after forsaking the place, Blanca took a trip to Sighet. (No one went back to their native village in those days. It just wasn't done.) She arrived in a luxurious fox stole, with her delightful six-year-old daughter, wanting to show her mother how well she had done in life, what a good husband she had found for herself, especially (I imagine) after the shame of having left to be a maid. Blanca was thirty years old, happily married, and a mother in her own right. She had never gotten along with Raisel in the first place, and yet none of this seems to have diminished in any way her desire for maternal approval. (Much later my mother experienced similarly mixed feelings toward Antwerp and her own mother, the same push-pull of having to get away and needing to return.) Later Blanca must have been grateful that she had gone back, whatever the reasons. It was the last time she saw her parents and most of her siblings.

Soon after this trip, right before the outbreak of war, Blanca gave birth to a second child, a son, my uncle David. He and my mother were almost seven years apart, a world of difference. It would be more than a decade before they became friends.

Life in Antwerp grew more and more stringent for the Jewish community (which numbered some fifty thousand people), with the enforcement of curfews, the mandate to wear yellow stars, and the gradual closing down of Jewish businesses and schools. Sometime in 1941 my grandmother and her children were walking back from synagogue, all dressed up, when they passed a couple of German photographers taking pictures of an elderly religious man in full orthodox garb, part of a mission to take official portraits of Jews and document their inherent otherness (and thus their threatening potential). Seeing how frightened the older man was, Blanca, according to my mother, became furious, and planting herself in front of the camera and pointing to the yellow star sewn onto her smart jacket, yelled at the man, "Why don't you take pictures of me and my children? We're Jewish, too!" The photographers told her to leave. She wasn't what they had in mind (which of course she well knew). I know from my mother's writings that she admired Blanca's nerve, not appreciating until much later how dangerous it had been for my grandmother to make a scene.

Despite the growing rumors of Jewish fates in the hands of German occupiers, my grandfather didn't want to leave Belgium. At one point he got papers to go to Cuba, but he gave them away. He was a Romanian citizen, after all, and the king of Romania famously had a Jewish mistress (her name was *Lubishka*, Yiddish for wolf). I'm not sure how my grandfather thought this would protect him all the way in Antwerp, but it strikes me that in an increasingly senseless world, people clung to whatever logic they could. In the end, thanks to those papers another family went to Cuba, where they safely waited out the war.

I've been told Avram escaped from the Germans seven or eight times. It always began the same way, with the Germans making an announcement that if the head of the household turned himself in, his family would be spared. Each time my grandfather escaped from custody. My mother saw her father for the last time in November 1942. Responding to an order of requisition for Jewish workers, he turned himself in. This time he was deported to Auschwitz. He never returned. That year my mother, age ten, made a sampler at school, the letters, *a, b, c,* stitched in multicolored threads. In our apartment it hung, framed in black, with these words written on the matted border: "To the memory of the child who embroidered this in the Tachkemoni, the Jewish school in Antwerp, Belgium, during the war years. 1942. When my world fell apart. My mother, brother, and I went into hiding and my father died in Auschwitz. To my children and all children to come. May they never live through this experience."

As for my grandmother's and mother's experiences during the war, of course I can never know what it was really like, or precisely what happened. My mother often spoke about those days to me and Stephanie, describing being forced undercover, feeling afraid, narrowly escaping—stories that we never tired of hearing. It was tangible to us that our mother had been hidden for over two years. In that sense the war became part of our childhood, too. She also wrote that 1975 essay about her war experiences, so there is a written version of the events. Other details have been filled in for us by my uncle, or from playing cards and talking with my *tantes* over the years. Every time I hear a story, though, it differs slightly in the telling, depending on who is speaking, what their mood is, the time of day. I weigh them one at a time, sifting through feathery impressions in favor of the sharp relief of familiar endings, which guarantee that my mother and my grandmother make it safely through the war.

Undoubtedly the best source would have been the diary my mother kept during the war, chronicling her days in hiding. She somehow kept it with her as she moved pell-mell with her mother from place to place in the course of two years. It was the one irrefutable record of what they experienced, but it is missing. It was among several boxes of belongings that my mother left in L.A. when she moved unexpectedly to Mexico, boxes that were eventually thrown out by a careless roommate. My mother never forgave herself for that loss. She felt it was her fault. According to Jewish reasoning, it is your responsibility to know the character of a person you're leaving something with.

My grandfather left his children in his wife's care. Once he was taken away for the last time, my grandmother went into action. She changed her official identity, got a new passport, went from being Blanca Gancz Neiman, a married Romanian citizen, to "Victorine Van Belle," a Belgian *célibataire*. As she and Avram had decided, she put their money and diamonds and a few personal effects in safekeeping with trusted Gentile friends, the Brusselmanses (Mr. Brusselmans had worked with Avram on the Bourse as a polisher); she sent David, my mother's younger brother, to stay with a childless Christian couple who had a farm in the countryside between Knokke and Ghent (the wife, Gusta Jannsen, had worked for friends of Blanca's in town, and for a good fee, she and her husband would pretend David was their own as long as necessary); and she took my mother and went into hiding.

All growing up I hear the stories. Over the next two years, my mother and grandmother stayed in seventeen different places. They kept moving, never knowing how long a situation would stay safe. My grandmother, practical and protective, did everything to safeguard her daughter, always thinking of the next possibility, the next escape. Many times, if you'll pardon the expression, they thought their goose was cooked, but they were always saved at the last minute by some miraculous confluence of luck, intuition, and timing.

At first they lodged with a family in Brasschaet, for a huge sum of money that my grandmother arranged to have paid out to them each week. It was expensive to hide. Families who risked their lives to take in Jews sometimes demanded a lot of money in return. Blanca was fortunate to have the stash of diamonds that my grandfather had amassed before the war.

My grandmother might have been calling herself Victorine, but she wasn't fooling anyone. At Brasschaet the son was an anti-Semite. He mocked Blanca and her daughter for being Jewish, for having big noses. My mother writes in her 1975 essay that every night he conjectured, "I'm sure tonight the Gestapo will come with their dogs." Other times he mused, "I wonder if Jews have red blood," and finally my mother, age ten, pricked her finger with a needle to prove it. Blanca worked on finding them another hide-out, anything to get away from his odious behavior.

Throughout this period the Brusselmanses would organize payments on Blanca's behalf and help her figure out where she and her daughter should go next. Blanca was lucky to have the Brusselmanses to rely on. In her account my mother writes that she liked them because they were kind and had children for her to play with, which meant that she didn't have to be quiet all the time. (Many times while hiding, she notes, she and Blanca couldn't make a sound, couldn't even go to the bathroom during the day while the family was out, for fear of attracting the attention of neighbors.) She also reveals that it was the older Brusselmans daughter, age twelve, who explained to her where babies came from, and that for days my mother was disgusted at the thought, distancing herself as much as she could from Blanca in the single bed they shared at night.

The closest Blanca and her daughter came to being caught was at the end of 1943, while staying at 90 de la rue Lamorinière, in the second-floor apartment of a Belgian man, a non-Jew, of course. For eight months he hid four Jews, my mother, my grandmother, Max Ament, an erudite German Jew, and his wife. The Belgian man liked to play cards. My grandmother was a great cardplayer—she took games quite seriously and very much liked to win. During one game Max was looking over Blanca's shoulder, kibitzing, and saw she had the cards to go out, so he nudged her to lay them down. She ignored him, and within a round or two their host won the game. Later Blanca told Max, "I prefer to lose a few dollars than to lose our lives." She knew that the kindness of strangers could evaporate at the smallest provocation.

One night the Belgian man went out and got drunk. He began bragging at the bar, "You'll never believe what I have back at my apartment . . ." Perhaps, astonished at his own bravery, he felt reckless. Within the hour there was a pounding on the front door. Knowing that such knocking could mean only one thing, my mother, my grandmother, and the other couple ran to a back window. One after another they jumped, first my mother, then Blanca, landing in the courtyard below. The Germans were breaking through the apartment door at this point, there was no time. Sure that his wife was about to follow, Max jumped, too. His wife hesitated, and was left behind. He never saw her again.

Blanca and my mother ran back to the Brusselmanses', where they hid out for a while again until making their next move. It is because of this experience that my mother refused to live on high floors: if they had been up any farther, they could not have fled with their lives. Years later my mother took me to that street and showed me the second-floor window from which she jumped. I found it disturbing in its ordinariness. How could it pretend to be like any other window?

✦ ✦ ✦

In the beginning of January 1944, Blanca and her eleven-year-old daughter were still at the Brusselmanses'. One evening the family heard there were going to be raids, and decided to hide my mother and grandmother in an old cistern in the courtyard. The father lifted the heavy stone, my mother and grandmother slipped into the pit, and all was darkness. Sure enough, the Gestapo came in the middle of the night. They woke up the little boy of the family, age four, and said, "Are there Jews hidden here?" Half asleep, the boy said, "No. There's no one here," but the Gestapo kept looking.

My mother and her mother remained in that dank cistern for seven or eight hours. Though it was no longer in use, the smell was almost unbearable, and this, combined with the drumming fear, marked my mother, making her intensely claustrophobic for the rest of her life. My mother told me about this night many times. Added to the dread of listening to the shouts and clanging steps of the soldiers, the fearful barking of the dogs who might detect their presence through the stone at any moment, she said, was their knowledge that even if they weren't caught, there was no way to lift the stone from the inside. It would be years before she and her mother discussed that night, how each imagined the worst—that the good-hearted family above would be taken away or would in the end submit to temptation after all and conveniently forget she and Blanca existed in order to keep my grandmother's money.

Hours later, when the Brusselmanses finally determined it was safe, they opened the stone lid and called out "Blanca . . ." My grandmother thought it was a trick and put her hand over her daughter's mouth before she could reply. The moment she was sure it was really her friends and that they were safely lifting out her daughter, Blanca, who had steadfastly held my shivering mother in her arms through the night, collapsed on the wet stone floor.

Blanca turned out to be brilliant at the game of survival. Time and again, during those two years, she rose to the occasion and did the necessary, whatever it was, whether shushing her trembling daughter, losing at cards, or cutting her losses in other ways. Running low on funds at one point, she gave a packet of diamonds to a colleague of Avram's to peddle on the black market. (As my uncle commented to me recently, my grandmother was "eating her money," selling and selling to stay alive.) When the man returned with the cash, it was less than she expected, so she asked how many carats had been in the parcel. The man replied he wasn't sure. My grandmother knew this couldn't be true—he had been a polisher, it was his business to know. His vagueness implied he had probably skimmed some off the top. Although it went against every fiber of her being, she let it go. Never again would she display this kind of reserve.

When I look at my grandmother's actions during the war, I see a woman of impressive resourcefulness—a tough, brave lady. But in the course of their hiding together, my mother saw a different, more melancholy side of Blanca. In the night she would fold my mother, her Gisela, her little gosling, in her arms, and they would cry together. If Blanca was up to it, my mother, relying on half-remembered school lessons, tried to distract her by teaching her to read and write in Flemish. Other times my mother watched as her *maman* played long games of solitaire, softly crooning Yiddish folk songs under her breath (how different from the Blanca who brazenly stood up to the German photographers). Seeing her mother this way would make my eleven-year-old mother so depressed she felt like she was going crazy. Unwittingly they would switch roles: daughter would have to comfort mother. Years later I occasionally caught my mother playing solitaire in her room, and I liked to sit beside her and watch the silent permutations of the cards, fascinated by the fact that the same game never unfolded the same way twice.

My mother and grandmother's last hideout in occupied Belgium was at a hotel in Brussels, where the owner, a former ballerina, took a liking to stylish Blanca and her daughter. There, my mother said, she learned to roll cigarettes, at the behest of some men down the hall who were selling them on the black market—work that took her mind off the disquieting realization that her unattached mother was an attractive woman, noticed and flirted with by all the men.

In 1945, my grandmother and my mother were finally free. They walked in disbelief through the streets of Antwerp on the day of liberation, hugging and crying with other Jews. Soon after, Blanca went to retrieve her son from the Jannsens, who couldn't conceal their disappointment that she had survived the war. My uncle hadn't seen his mother in two years. Until the age of four he had been called David and spoken Yiddish. Under the Jannsens' care, he had learned the local Flemish dialect, answered to the name Monneke (a diminutive of the Christian name Dominique), and had even begun to call Mrs. Jannsen "Mother." No wonder that when my grandmother took him back and enrolled him for a year in a French school in Antwerp, he began to stutter. Unlike Blanca, my uncle wasn't old enough to be able to doff and don his identity at will, as wartime survival seemed to require. Traumatized by the separation from the only family he really remembered, not understanding why they couldn't all live together in one big house, he would take months to treat Blanca as his mother again.

For weeks my grandmother went every day to Antwerp's brand-new Jewish Center, where lists of survivors were generated, to see if her husband was by any chance still alive. Once and for all she learned that Avram had perished in Auschwitz, that she was a widow. Her sister Edith, too, had died in the camps, along with her husband and their twin children.

Back in Sighet, the Jewish community had been annihilated during the war, a way of life brutally ended. Over ten thousand Jews, more than a third of the local population, had been forced into a ghetto on the outskirts of town, from which they were eventually transported to the camps. The Gancz children disappeared one by one. The youngest son, the darling, went first, on a train, Bella and Roszi running after it, waving and crying. Berko died of a heart attack. Raisel passed away three days later, of a broken heart it was said. Bella and Roszi, who had never left the town, were deported to Auschwitz. When they arrived, and stood before the man in charge that day, they were separated, Roszi, redcheeked and hardy like Blanca, sent one way, Bella, pale, ethereallooking, sent another. One of the guards took pity on her and said, "No, he told you to go *there*," pointing to the other side, the side of the living. She looked up at him, about to protest, and then understood, running to join Roszi.

Hiding the fact that they were sisters, Bella and Roszi were able to stay together and help each other. If a guard, out of some strange form of compassion, threw one of his gloves on the ground in front of them as they worked in the fields, the sisters shared it, passing it back and forth to ward off the cold. At night they slept next to each other, holding on. For months they were forced to do the horrible task of sifting through the clothing of the newly dead.

Years later, on a trip with my parents in Hungary, my *tantes* were eating dinner at a romantic restaurant in Budapest, surrounded by candlelight and violins. From across the room, a woman walked, as if in a trance, toward Bella, and when she got to their table, she murmured, *Bella? Bella, is it you?* My *tantes* immediately started crying and embraced the woman. They had all been in the same barrack together. It was a miracle to have survived and then to find one another after all those years.

Once the Americans came and liberated the camp, Bella and Roszi were taken to a hospital in Italy to recover, Bella so frail she would never be able to have children. When they arrived there after long travels, an American soldier opened the door, welcoming them inside. Bella screamed and fainted, never having seen a black man before. Later he gave her candies, talked to her about his skin, and generally tried to reassure her that there was nothing to be afraid of. For the rest of her life she wished she knew the man's name, so she could have apologized to him.

After being released from the hospital, Bella and Roszi were transferred to a DP camp. We have pictures of them there, sitting in a group around a kitchen table with tired smiles. They spent nine months there, and then, in 1946, the two sisters, ages thirty-one and thirty-four, came to Antwerp to live with their sister, my grandmother. My mother fell in love with her *tantes* right away, forging passionate relationships with them that she would cherish for the rest of her life. Blanca was more businesslike. She decided that Bella and Roszi should find husbands immediately, that the best way to recover from the war was to move on. She took it upon herself to make it happen, forcing her sisters to pretend they had lost their Romanian papers so she could present them as being five years younger—it would be easier to catch men that way. By this time Blanca, already a respectable widow with two children, had married again, a man named Maurice Landau. (She had had an earlier offer, from a handsome American soldier who fell in love with her right after liberation, but after all they had been through, she couldn't see spending her life with someone who wasn't Jewish.)

Blanca found Roszi's husband first, in a food shop. She saw him across an aisle and said, "You, aren't you so-and-so's son?" Yes, he nodded shyly, not used to being spoken to by a woman he didn't know. "Come with me," she said, taking him by the arm. "I have someone I want you to meet." Léon (Leib) Domb married Roszi and they had a son, who later became the father of four daughters. They are my second cousins, living a different way of life in Antwerp, each one married off as she turns eighteen.

After Roszi moved out, Bella was miserable. She was sick of being in her sister's house, tired of Blanca trying to run her life. She sat down at the kitchen table one day with Blanca's friend Max Ament—the man who had lost his wife when she refused to jump from the second floor—and cried. She let all her frustrations tumble out. She was still weak from the war but she looked like Bette Davis, with waved blond hair and impossibly large blue eyes. "I'm tired of living here. I'll do anything to get out. I'll say yes to the next man who asks me, I don't care anymore. Anything to have my own kitchen, my own bed, my own life." "Bella," Max interrupted.

She looked up, her face damp with tears. "Bella, will you marry me?" My *tante* Bella reenacts this story for me, putting her head in her hands, mimicking herself forty-five years later, blushing with remembered happiness.

From the age of four I no longer have my grandmother but I have her beloved sisters: Roszi, the sensible one whose dark coloring is so much like Blanca's; Bella, the flaxen-haired beauty who has a similar élan. I love my *tantes* dearly—Roszi's deep chuckle, Bella's high, sudden laugh, their warmth and humor and loving kindness. They are always ladylike, dressed to go out in little heels, with the right jewelry and a good coat and bright lipstick, but even in their robes, preparing a Friday-night Shabbat dinner or an afternoon cup of coffee, they are lovely. Both are religious, Roszi perhaps more so than Bella, who has a twinkle in her eye, a greater openness to the ways of the world. Bella makes lace curtains, dappled with flowers and cherubim, for our living room windows in New York. My mother puts them up proudly; they are magnificent, a protective netting whose tatted squares let the sunshine pour in.

My family goes to Belgium regularly to visit the *tantes*, or else they come to New York to visit us. I love to be with them—they are ties to my grandmother, to my mother's youth, to another world. They adore my tall, hatted father, spoil him, treat me and my sister as paragons of goodness, praising us constantly and kissing our cheeks. Tears spring to their eyes the moment we walk into one of their homes, as they usher us to the table quickly to sit down and eat, the emotion in the room too much to handle. My mother relaxes in their presence, gossiping about people they know, catching up. With my father, my sister, and me they speak French, but with my mother it is Yiddish. Bella and Roszi's deftness in telling a story is striking, full of feverish gestures and rollicking inflections. Their lilting voices clamber over each other, painting the past.

Once Blanca settled her sisters' lives to her satisfaction, she turned to her own. She had no money left after the war; she had spent it all to survive, a last substantial sum right at the end, when she and my mother were arrested at the hotel in Brussels and forced to pay a fortune to the Belgian police so as not to be released to the Germans. (My mother observes in her essay that the war was almost over by then, and the Belgian S.S. was more interested in getting credit for not turning in Jews than in continuing to collaborate.) Her only option was to start over.

Before the war my grandmother had been a lady of leisure, whose duties comprised looking after her husband, her children, her toilette, and her home. After the war, with Avram's money gone, Blanca had no choice but to become a *femme d'affaires*. Her new spouse wasn't much help. Maurice fancied himself an inventor, but nothing he came up with worked. (He famously ruined a man's car one day by insisting he test out a homemade polish.) Blanca, on the other hand, turned out to be a relatively intrepid businesswoman.

Over the next fifteen years, my grandmother owned as many as ten different businesses, among them a vegetarian restaurant, a handbag store, and a lingerie shop. Many of her ventures enjoyed moderate success and then would inexplicably fail, leaving her to start from scratch. There was nothing she wouldn't try her hand at, from working in textiles and selling blouses to investing in a photocopying machine at a time when the technology was hardly in use.

In wartime, when the stakes had been at their highest, Blanca had controlled her more foolish instincts for the greater good. In life she didn't always manage to do so. Her restaurant, for example, flourished, but in a fit of pique she sabotaged the entire venture by accusing the chef of cheating her. He left in a huff, and went on to become the caterer of the entire Bourse, while she was forced to close her establishment.

Despite these setbacks, Blanca's fiscal situation steadily improved, until she was once again considered a woman of means. She became a lender in the community, financing other people's enterprises and earning interest. Fortunately she was successful enough that it didn't matter so much that she wasn't always terribly good about collecting debts.

Partly because of all she had suffered, and partly, I think, because of all the worries she carried on her back, Blanca had a lot of nervous energy after the war. She became quite high-strung—a condition that wasn't helped by the fact that she and her new husband didn't get along. They fought incessantly, usually over nothing, at such a pitch that my grandmother frequently threatened to throw herself out the window. (Little did her husband know she had already proved she could survive such a fall.) Neighbors would call the police in the middle of the night because of their yelling. They would divorce after twelve unpleasant years.

It was during this time that my mother and her mother grew apart, my mother exasperated by Blanca's anxiousness about everything. My uncle told me that my mother often said, "I don't want to become like Mother," meaning that she didn't ever want to be that difficult, and at the same time that she didn't want to have a bad relationship with her mother, as Blanca had had with Raisel. But a daughter, imprinted at an early age, can't help walking in the footsteps of her mother, like the gosling after the goose.

Throughout her travails, Blanca never lost her reputation as a coquette. Aside from her looks, there was something engaging about her, about the way she went through life. She could be funny about herself, changing her mind in a flash when the occasion warranted it. For years she kept kosher, making a point of comparing shrimp to worms, wondering aloud how anyone could eat such things. One evening, at a formal dinner in someone's home, she was presented with a plate of shrimp cocktail, and feeling like it would be rude not to eat what was in front of her, she tried it. From then on, shrimp became her favorite thing to eat, and she ordered it, if somewhat abashedly, whenever she could.

My grandmother was especially admired as a dancer. (People still tell me how her legs went "up to here.") I have a photograph of her and Bella dancing in each other's arms, at a wedding or ball of some sort after the war. They have been through so much, and yet there they are, utterly beguiling in modish black dresses that leave their ankles and arms bare. An entire row of guests watches them, transfixed, as they clasp arms. Bella's gaze is wide, uplifted, but my grandmother looks down, her mouth in a close-lipped smile, as if she knows that the image of the two of them dancing can meet only with approval.

In 1962, a few years after her second husband left, Blanca got married for a third time. Abraham Bloemenfeld was a nice man, but the marriage didn't last long. My grandmother was still too impossible. From then on she lived alone.

In her final years, Blanca changed, her apprehensiveness perhaps eased somewhat by her witnessing her children get married and become settled in their own right. She was diagnosed with cancer, and perhaps as a fatalistic response to her growing sickness she became more and more passive. No longer the easily agitated Blanca of old, my grandmother in the end seemed to have found a kind of peace.

Whatever her shortcomings, there is no question that my grandmother was a remarkable woman. During the war she saved my mother, her daughter. She saved her son by sending him away. (He remained in touch with the farm couple and invited them to his wedding, in gratitude.) Afterward she saved her sisters, making sure they got off on the right path in their new lives. My mother told me her mother could faint on command if things weren't going her way. She was a force to be reckoned with, a different woman on different occasions. When she walked into a room, a ball, a restaurant, all eyes turned to her, riveted by her presence. She was many things, with her white skin and apple cheeks, Bloema, Blanca. To me, she was Bomama. Apparently she was always offering pieces of apple to my first cousin, her other granddaughter, who until recently thought her grandmother's name was Pomme.

The Leopard Hat

In the fall of the year I lived in Paris, I stayed in a cavalcade of apartments, finally moving to the rue St. Sulpice sometime in November, just as the rainy season was ending and it was beginning to get cold. My studio, which I discovered through a friend of a friend, was small, but I found it charming, with slanted wooden eaves and recessed windows covered by brown velvet curtains. Each piece of furniture had its own sense of humor: an uneven little table, two chairs whose legs splayed at odd angles, an armoire whose door wouldn't close.

Walking around my new neighborhood one day, I noticed a beautiful leopard hat in the window of the hat store across the street. I loved hats, so without thinking about it too much, I went inside and put it on. As I looked out from under its brim, I felt as though I had my mother's view of the world—giddy and warm and defined. Although the hat was outrageously priced, I was determined to make it mine. I knew that my Paris experience wouldn't be complete without it. I had places to go, wearing that hat: the races, La Coupole, the bar at the Ritz. Besides, I had been called a leopard once, and I was ready to become one again.

The first time had been just before Christmas of my junior year in college. My mother was very ill that winter. Despite our best hopes, the dreaded cancer had come back, after a mere year and a half of her being free of it. My parents weren't letting my sister and me in on how serious things were yet, but it was hard to ignore the signs. Every time I went home, my mother seemed more worried, less her energetic self, and then she would say things to me as if trying to prepare me for what lay ahead. The summer before, she had commented, in the kitchen one morning while we were preparing breakfast, "You know, eventually your father will date again, and I want him to, it will be good for him. It's important." I put my hands to my ears and made nonsense sounds until she stopped talking about it.

I'm not exactly sure why I auditioned for a play that fall. I suppose I thought it would take my mind off things to do something light. I was trying to be normal, to go to classes, to keep up with my life. That's what my mother expected of me. She and I spoke almost every day, as usual. She had always been able to tell over the phone if something wasn't right, and would ask me right away, *Are you O.K.?* These days she wasn't asking anymore—it was too apparent what was upsetting me. It was what was upsetting my entire family. In one phone conversation, she must have wanted to respond in some way to the pain couched in my voice because I remember sitting on the bed of my college room and her saying to me, "Just keep your head up and keep cool." I wrote it down, and kept the slip of paper in the pocket of the black Filofax she had given me, taking it out and looking at it whenever I felt myself becoming something other than the stalwart daughter she knew and loved.

I had always been kind of superstitious: touching screws when driving over train tracks, avoiding walking under ladders. My friends and I had this ritual of crossing our fingers and making a wish if we saw a Ryder truck. The rule was you could uncross them only at the sight of a dog, a taxi, or a pregnant woman. We did it religiously. Although in many ways she was quite logical, my mother was superstitious, too. She had always told us that finding a piece of white thread on your clothes brought good luck, and that a white spot in your nail bed was a sign that you could expect a present. But more than looking for portents in the everyday, my mother strongly believed that when you were blessed, you were also susceptible to having bad things happen. Some innocuous person, just by saying something nice about you, could bring you to the attention of the evil eye, a roving force eager to dissipate too much luck or happiness. Anytime anyone complimented us, she would turn her head to the side and make a low spitting sound, three times in a row, to protect us from the consequences of being smart, beautiful, loved. She was constantly rapping her knuckles on wood to punctuate her sentences, or else she'd say in Yiddish, after mentioning any sort of future plans, *Mirtsishem*—God willing.

Now, on my own at Harvard, I became obsessive. Heading back to the dorm late one afternoon I saw a Ryder truck. I crossed my fingers and made my wish, for my mother to live, for the sickness to go away. I waited to spot one of the redeeming figures. It was getting dark, around dinnertime. I saw nothing that would help me. I slept that night with my fingers crossed, a withering feeling in my stomach in the morning when I saw they had unraveled during the night, as if confirming that what I wished for was impossible.

Usually it was enough to imagine the worst: that would keep it from happening. So I kept imagining the worst, hoping to stave it off. I had also developed a strange habit. Whenever I walked around Cambridge, I had to check every person I saw coming toward me on the street for all four limbs, systematically searching for wholeness, praying that something hadn't fallen away. If I couldn't see a leg at first, I would hold my breath, praying for it to be momentarily out of sight, like a paw lifted before being set down. The times there actually was a limb missing, my heart shuddered, the sight of it showing me that life could go on without all four parts, despite their all seeming so necessary, so vital to me.

Friends of mine were putting on a December production of *Blithe Spirit*, and I had always liked Noël Coward, had loved going to see *Private Lives* with my mother on Broadway with Elizabeth Taylor and Richard Burton. I auditioned, hoping for the lead. Instead I was given the part of an older, exceedingly proper Englishwoman, a prudish type. There were eight of us in the cast—including the director and the producer—and we rehearsed for weeks. I enjoyed those rehearsals, for the chance to get loose, to do things I wouldn't normally do. We'd dance around, limbering up our bodies, and do improvisational exercises, like the one in which one person left the room while the rest of us came up with an adverb. When that person returned, he or she would ask each of us to do something in the manner of that word. One time I left the room and when I came back in, I asked the guy playing the lead, who was a pretty good friend of mine, to drink his glass of water. Staring straight ahead, he lifted the glass up to his ear in one quick motion, so that the water went shooting in a spray behind him. I couldn't figure out what word he could possibly be acting out. "Spastically," I said. "Awkwardly." After ten minutes or so they told me. The adverb had been "surreally."

A week before the show opened, we used real gin in the endless martinis called for by Coward's script. Everyone got a little loopy—Mr. Condomine (the lead) did his entire part in a fast-paced Hindi accent—and it was hard to get our lines out through the laughter. At the end of the night someone came up with the idea that we should be Secret Santas to one another for the holiday season. Even though I was a little drunk, I immediately appreciated the absurdity of the proposal. I was losing my mother to cancer and I was Jewish—what could a Secret Santa possibly do for me? Nevertheless, the director wrote our names down on slips of paper, and we each picked one out of a hat. It was fine by me, as long as it wasn't going to take up too much time.

A few nights later, when I went backstage after the last dress rehearsal, I found a note and a watergun on top of my things. The note said: "Meet François Le Piu at Au Bon Pain at midnight. Better bring your gun . . . " They had to be from my Secret Santa, but I was a bit surprised. Normally people gave chocolate, balloons maybe. This was different. I was too tired to change back into my regular clothes for my rendezvous, which meant that my hair was in a chignon, and I was wearing my costume, a velvet dress of my mother's, under my coat. It was bitingly cold as I made my way over to Au Bon Pain. The wind was like a whip on my stockinged legs, and I remember thinking that there were so few people around that Harvard Square itself almost looked like a stage set. As I approached the outside tables, where in warmer weather men gathered to play chess, I saw a guy sitting alone, wearing a beret and holding what looked like a baguette. I went over and sat down across from him on the cold stone seat.

"The Basque has heard of you," he said to me, in a fake yet strong French accent, his words smoking in the chill night air. "He is quite impressed with your reputation, and wants to hire you for a very delicate operation."

I was almost frozen, and I had no idea what he was talking about.

"Of course we do not speak of payment, but the Basque asked me to give you this, as a token of his appreciation. He assumes that you accept the assignment. He will be in touch."

With that, he handed over the baguette, stood up, and disappeared.

Bewildered but amused, I walked back to Dunster House, holding on to the unwieldy baguette. It seemed rather heavy for just bread. I unrolled the bag it was in and looked more closely. The inside of the bread had been carved out and filled with Hanukkah gelt—there must have been hundreds of the gold-wrapped chocolate coins. It made me instantly smile, this hidden show of extravagance, the thoughtfulness of it. That night I comforted myself to sleep with memories of Hanukkah. I was a child again, playing dreidl in the foyer with my sister while my mother looked on.

The next day, when I got home from classes, there was a message on my answering machine. "White Leopard, this is your next assignation. You must meet Mustafa the Happy Turk at Café

Algiers, Tuesday night, at ten P.M. You will approach him and ask him for a match for your cigarette. Don't be late."

So I was White Leopard now. It was funny to be given a code name and instructed exactly on what I had to say, like being cast in another play. I had new lines to learn, a whole other set of stage directions. As I got ready for my Turkish tryst, I made up my mind to fully plunge into the part that had been assigned to me. All I needed was the right ensemble. By coincidence, I had a white leopard-print velveteen skirt. I put on knee-high black suede boots, a pair of dark sunglasses, and red lipstick. Looking in the mirror at my new persona, I realized it would be good to lose myself for a while. Costumed this way I could step out of my identity as my mother's older daughter, a role in which, for the first time in our relationship, I could do nothing. Yes, if she had trouble going down the marble steps of our lobby, I held her hand and reminded her to take deep breaths, to diffuse the pain. *Thank you,* she said. *You're always helping me.* But I couldn't make a categorical difference, I couldn't change what was happening to her, to us. Forget the Coward play, this phone message was offering me the chance to act like a true blithe spirit. I left my room and wandered down the hall, to a suite where a group of eight guys lived together. I borrowed one of their trench coats, which I belted tightly, and then begged someone to keep me company. No way did I want to venture alone into this escapade. One of them agreed to come with me, and before we left, I loaded my gun with water and put it in my pocket.

When we got to the café, my friend went to the bar while I cased the joint. My heart was pounding. I saw the producer of the show, seated by himself at one of the small, round tables, wearing a bright red velvet fez and a long, curling moustache. Mustafa. With cigarette in hand, I went up to him and asked him for a match. He looked at me, and in a thick Turkish accent (or what I imagined a Turkish accent was supposed to sound like), he said, "I have a lighter, better still." He lit my cigarette with a snappy chrome Zippo, and then handed it to me, my gift for the evening.

I sat down. He gestured to a stack of papers on the table. "This is your dossier," he said. "It has all the information you'll need." He started going through it. There was a black-and-white photograph from the twenties, with hundreds of men dressed in top hats and tails. A tiny arrow pointed to an indistinguishable figure in the back. Above the arrow was written: "The Basque, Age Ten." There were other photographs, of châteaux and estates, old maps and train stations, even a tear sheet from a fashion magazine that showed a sexy model dressed in red, and next to her, in pen, the words: "The Basque's manicurist." At first I was delighted, looking at so many pictures, amazed by how much work it had taken to put them together, but then, when the file didn't end, it struck me as more and more inane, these images that didn't correspond to anything, such care lavished on an enterprise that had no bearing on reality.

The producer was my friend, though, and I was impressed with his performance. As Mustafa, he never broke a smile, never let me in on the artifice. In a steady accented stream, he told me that the Basque's most valuable possession, a priceless bottle of wine, had been stolen. They suspected his former mistress, a woman known as Arachne the Spider Woman. It had been a torrid affair, but after a while the Basque had tired of her. When she didn't want to end things, he had gotten her hooked on cocaine to get rid of her. Now it was believed that when she ran out of money for drugs, she had stolen the one thing that truly mattered to him—his prize bottle—and would soon be demanding ransom. The plot seemed awfully convoluted, like that of an old thriller in which the pieces don't quite fit but you're hooked by the drama of it anyway.

Suddenly Mustafa stopped talking. I looked up. There was a dame in a black strapless dress, complete with long black gloves and gold serpent bracelets running up each arm. A little hat—an ostrich feather number—partly obscured her face. I couldn't imagine what was going to happen next. She was smoking, using one of those lengthy gold cigarette holders. "Mustafa," she said, prolonging the word in a pretty decent imitation of Marlene Dietrich. "Vaht are you doing in dis neck of de voods?" She drew deeply on her cigarette, and then exhaled a large cloud of smoke in Mustafa's direction. He began stuttering and coughing, and then boom, he up and fell over. There he was, sprawled in the middle of the café floor. I couldn't believe it. The waitress stood over him, holding a trayful of cappuccinos. As Arachne slinked away, I heard someone ask, "Is he O.K.?"

I was just in the process of absorbing the high theater of all this when, next thing I knew, François Le Piu was at my side. "This is turning ugly," he whispered in my ear. "We'd better get out of here while the getting's good." Outside, he held me by the shoulders, looked me straight in the eye, and said: "Father Martin, St. Trinity's Church, Thursday at noon. Go up to him and say, 'Forgive me, Father, for I have sinned.' " Then he dashed into the night. I thought to myself, if only in real life someone whisked you away when things got messy, if only someone always gave you directions on what to do next. As my friend and I walked home, we couldn't help but be enthralled by how the evening had turned out.

He told me that once François Le Piu and I left, the whole place had burst into applause.

Later, after I had put my White Leopard getup away for the night, I called home. Half laughing, I told my parents and sister what was going on, the type of awesome peril I had been in that evening. I had been flattered to be the focus of so much attention and effort, but now I felt self-conscious, recounting the details of this fake drama to my family. Maybe because I myself didn't sound convinced, my mother said she didn't like it, it made her nervous. "Tell whoever it is that they should stop," she instructed me. I tried to explain that whoever was doing this had to be a friend of mine, because otherwise they wouldn't go to so much trouble. She wasn't persuaded, and I couldn't say anything to change her mind.

Two days later, on the appointed Thursday, I went to church. Father Martin was there, looking suspiciously like François Le Piu. As I walked up to the pew, I noticed two people in the back, a man and a woman in trench coats and fedoras, holding newspapers. As I slid into the seat next to Father Martin, I dutifully asked his forgiveness. "Bless you, my child," he said, and then handed over a brown paper bag. Before I opened it, I looked back at the henchmen, who hid their faces behind their papers with loud rustles. I turned my attention back to the bag. Nestled inside was a plastic pouch filled with white powdered sugar, which I gathered was masquerading as cocaine. I slipped the whole thing into my pocket, bid Father Martin adieu, and walked swiftly up the aisle. The meeting had gone off without any big theatrics, and I felt somewhat relieved, glad to get on with the rest of my day.

I had promised a friend I would bring her lunch from the coffee shop around the corner where we spent a lot of time. I walked over there, went inside, and went up to place my order. The man at the counter was comfortingly rude. While I waited, I turned to have a look around. I had been followed. The couple from the church was in one of the booths, reading their infernal newspapers. This felt wrong—they were intruding on the normalcy of my life. I hastily paid for the sandwich, went outside, and started walking briskly down the street. I looked back, and they were walking briskly behind me. I picked up my pace. So did they. I started a light jog, which soon—as I abandoned any pretense—became a hell-bent run. This was no longer in good fun. I was being hunted, and the last thing I wanted was to get caught. I bounded into my friend's apartment building and pressed maniacally on the buzzer until she let me in. When I got upstairs, I was panting, and kept running to check the windows. To my friend's consternation, I explained that I had a bag of cocaine on me and had been followed. She tried to remind me that this was all a game, but I was genuinely upset. Feeling too vulnerable to go outside by myself, I got another friend to come and pick me up for the one-block walk home. Later, alone in my room, I pulled down the shades and hid the bag behind a bookcase, nearly convinced I was going to be the victim of a drug bust. With characters following me outside the appointed time and place, the elaborate drama had spilled over from playacting into my life, and with it I, too, was slipping over the edge. It was as if my worst anxieties about my mother had sprung out at me in disguised form, and I had lost all sense of proportion.

That night, as we performed the play in front of an audience for the first time, I resolved to find the perpetrator, certain that would allay my unreasonable fears and dispel the danger I imagined myself to be in. I watched everyone in the cast carefully.

There were only three other women besides myself. First there was the shy freshman who played the second wife. She had been receiving Shakespearean sonnets and Hershey bars every night from her Secret Santa, and judging by her delight, I concluded she didn't have the imagination to be sending me on a wild goose chase. Then there was the woman who played the medium, an exaggerated role that called for a lot of histrionics. Somehow I couldn't see her as the artful spymaster my Secret Santa had to be. Finally there was the senior who had the female lead. She played the part of Elvira, the first wife who comes back from the dead to torment her newly remarried husband. Because I had such a minor part, it was my job to cover the star in silver paint every night. I used a sponge, and watched as her white skin became metallic, unnatural. Every night, she talked about herself, completely absorbed in her transformation. Occasionally, if she sensed my restlessness, she would look my way and toss off a compliment. One night it was: "I like your dress—is it your mother's?" I said something veiled in response: "Yes, but it's too big for her now." Some thought about what I might mean seemed to cross the girl's mind, but then she shrugged and didn't go there. She looked back at herself in the mirror and said, "I think my left shoulder needs a little more, don't you?"

I decided my Secret Santa had to be a man. I eliminated the producer. Although he had played a convincing Mustafa, he knew every Shakespearean sonnet off the top of his head. I briefly considered the director, with his shy, absentminded air, but came to the conclusion that he had enough to worry about without staging a second, entirely different kind of production. That left one of two people as the culprit: the brainy, somewhat roly-poly guy who played my husband, and the brilliant Mr. Condomine, he of the many accents. They both lived in Adams House, and they shared many of the same friends, some of whom had already made appearances in my adventure. I would be more watchful from now on, as I waited to see what transpired next.

When I got home that night, there was a message telling me to bring the goods to Arachne at the Weeks Bridge at twilight the next day. Apparently she was beside herself and, as the Basque had foreseen, would be willing to trade the wine for the cocaine. The next day was Friday, and my sister was coming up for the weekend to see me in the play. She was traveling without my parents because my mother wasn't well enough for even such a short trip. Stephanie's solo arrival made me think about how lonely it felt to be in a play without my mother in the audience.

That evening, I asked my sister to join me for the meeting. Before we left, we created an overly strategic system whereby she would stand twenty paces away with the brown paper bag and would walk over only when she got a signal from me. We went to the appointment. Arachne was sitting on a bench, looking utterly strung out. I went and sat next to her. Without taking her eyes off me, she spoke in a babble of incantations clearly meant to indicate drug-deprived desperation. I found my mind wandering. I was abruptly aware that I wanted the whole thing to end soon. Wherever I went on campus, people gleefully told me they knew who my Secret Santa was, but they didn't know that my mother was dying. In some ways, that was good. I didn't want to be "the girl who lost her mother." I knew how people described people in passing, and that tragedy bandied about that way didn't mean anything—it just became another kind of gossip. I signaled to my sister, she brought the bag over, and we made the trade. It was a bottle of red wine, whose handmade label had been slightly charred. We walked back in silence to my room so I could get ready for that night's show.

There was one last message when I got home late that night. I was to go to the indoor swimming pool at Adams House at 6 P.M. on Saturday, the evening of our final performance. The pool had been built in the twenties and was supposed to be fantastic-looking, but I had never been there. I dressed up once more in my White Leopard ensemble and, holding the bottle close, set off for what I suspected would be my last encounter. On the way over I resolved, somewhat irrationally, that if anyone threatened me in any way, I would retaliate by dropping the bottle.

When I opened the door to the poolroom, I found myself in the midst of an elegant soirée. I experienced the sinking sensation that I was underdressed, especially since the party seemed to have been arranged in my honor. Waiters in white jackets and ties were passing out trays of caviar and champagne. Fifteen or twenty men and women in black tie and evening gowns stood around the pool, chatting politely.

After a few minutes, François Le Piu came forward and ushered me into the room. I looked back. A dual flight of stairs, curving and graceful, led up to a platform situated above the door I had just entered. Upon this platform, with its back to the room, was a figure swathed in white. Flanking the figure was a series of attendants, also dressed in white, who stood along the stairs at even intervals. As I took the party in, I heard a piercing, birdlike cry from the top. It was the Basque. Instead of speaking, he squeaked. The attendant on his right appeared to listen very carefully, then leaned down and whispered to the attendant below him, and so on, until the whispering reached François Le Piu, who was standing next to me at the base of the stairs.

"The Basque wishes to thank you for your expertise. He is most pleased with the results." The sharp twittering continued. François waited a beat, and then spoke on: "As an expression of his gratitude, he would like to offer you the most precious thing he owns: the bottle of wine which you are holding. And now, eat, drink, and be merry." François bowed, then walked up the stairs and took his place next to the Basque, surveying the room and occasionally leaning down to say something to him in a low voice.

I stood around for a while, holding the bottle, and then snagged a glass of champagne from a passing waiter. I recognized him. He was in my American literature class. Even though it was clear that this party was the pièce de résistance of the whole intrigue, I was uncomfortable. Everyone seemed to be talking around me, but it was like a dream, where you can't be a part of things, and you can't make yourself understood. There were people I knew there, others I recognized only vaguely, and some I had never seen before, but no one spoke to me or addressed me in any way, either in or out of character. There were no congratulations for having completed my mission, no claps on the back or champagne toasts. Until then, I had mostly enjoyed my role as the White Leopard, but all at once I felt ridiculous, wearing a trench coat that was too big for me and holding a leaky watergun and a fake old bottle of wine. It was like everyone around me was laughing, but I wasn't being let in on the joke. And at the same time, knowing it was all over, I also felt a little bit abandoned, sad that the curtain had finally come down on this charade. As I left to get ready for our last performance, it occurred to me that the party didn't need me, that perhaps things would only really get started after I was gone.

Every night, just before the last scene in *Blithe Spirit*, while the lights were completely out, a few of us would sneak onto the stage and hide. My job was to crawl under a large table covered by a tablecloth that hung to the floor. There I would wait, crouching patiently until the scene was over. Right at the end, when the audience was expecting complete quiet, we would strike from our respective places, banging and shaking the set as if the whole place had been taken over by spirits. Night after night, no one in the audience could figure out how we did it.

After the last performance, and a particularly good bout of banging and shaking, we agreed to reveal ourselves to each other. Someone suggested that we each point to the person we thought was our Secret Santa. I thought for a minute. I had two options: the guy who played my husband and the guy who played Mr. Condomine. It could have been either one, so I thought about how each one would react to my choice. I figured that if I chose Mr. Condomine and I was wrong, my husband would be hurt that I didn't guess him, whereas if I chose Mr. Condomine and I was right, Mr. Condomine would be disappointed that I hadn't been fooled. I went with my husband. If I was right, my husband would be thrilled that I got him. If I was wrong, Mr. Condomine would be thrilled that I didn't.

Sure enough it was Mr. Condomine, and he was thrilled. I thought back to the first meeting and remembered seeing him walk by, his collar turned up against the cold. I learned that he had been at every "assignation," had in fact almost fallen through the high window where he was perched outside Café Algiers because he was laughing so hard. I even learned that the two flunkies in the coffee shop had been reading *Pravda*, the Russian newspaper, to be more authentically spylike.

A few nights later I went out to dinner with my friend the

producer. He was losing his father to cancer, and we could talk to each other openly about what we were experiencing in a way that we couldn't to anyone else. I remember saying to him, "I can't lose her because I don't know everything that she is. You can't lose something that isn't perfectly defined." Suddenly I was crying into my hamburger. "She is so many things and all those things will be gone, and I won't have known them all."

When I got to New York a few days later for Christmas vacation, I was exhausted, the result of no sleep and constant paper writing. I was also nervous. It was the first time for as long as I could remember that we weren't going away somewhere for the holidays. Before I left, I tried to explain to my roommate how different it was, how it showed that everything was changing, but I could tell that she didn't fully appreciate what it meant in the context of our family.

My mother was relieved to have me home, safely out of the international spy ring. She was extremely anxious during that Christmas break, partly in response to the medications she was taking, which heightened that aspect of her personality, and partly, I think, because she wanted to make every effort to ensure that things were in place. My parents' wedding anniversary was December 26th, and she forbade us to get her a gift. *The house is full, I don't need anything. I don't want you to get anything,* she kept saying, more and more insistently. Not thinking about the implications of her wanting to freeze our inventory, Stephanie and I got them a present anyway, a slim marble backgammon set that fit perfectly on the table by the window in the library, a monument to my parents' marriage and their love of the game.

My sister's and my passports were about to expire, and my mother was after us the whole vacation to go and get new photos taken. It seemed weirdly appropriate that she focused on our passports so intently: these were the documents that guaranteed our ability to travel the world as we had always done together. Things kept coming up and we kept putting it off, but finally, on one of the last days I was home, we went to do it. I liked how the picture of me came out, but it struck me as very strange that I would have that passport for ten years. The image of myself then, a daughter fulfilling one of her mother's wishes, would remain the same, but in that time, what would change, who would I become, where would I go?

In the end, I wasn't quite sure why my mother had been so against my brief stint as White Leopard. She had always been proud of me when I got the lead in any production, and after all, hadn't this been a kind of improvised play? The theater was certainly something she had been a fan of all her life. She was passionate about going to see plays, movies, the ballet, and spoke with great fondness of the years she spent studying to be an actress before she met my father. Even her frequent hat wearing was a kind of role playing. She would take down her dove-gray cloche or her burgundy tricorne, and she would be "on," ready to face the world. She loved herself in a hat. Others did, too—sometimes when I was with her, people stopped her in the street. Since she herself often went up to people to tell them how great they looked, when she received a compliment from a stranger it almost felt like it was her own energy coming back around.

After I thought about it for a while, I remembered a story that my mother sometimes told. Once, as a girl in Belgium, she had gone to the train station to pick up my grandmother, who had been away on one of her customary visits to a spa. Standing on the tracks, my mother, young and impatient, watched as the passengers descended. After a few moments she saw a beautiful, hatted woman emerging from the stopped train. It took her a moment of longing and admiration before she realized that it was her own mother who was mesmerizing her. That was the power of the hat: it opened up the possibility—and the danger—of changing one's spots, becoming unrecognizable altogether.

This caper had swept me up into a new role at the exact moment when we both needed me to be utterly myself. And maybe the experience frightened us a little, too, because it hinted at the way in which I might really change over time, turn into someone other than the daughter my mother knew so well.

As for Paris, it was the right place and the right time for a leopard hat—my experience wouldn't have been complete without it. Every time I put it on, I did seem to become someone else. When I took it to the races, I was photographed for *Vogue* standing next to a prince. When I wore it to a nightclub, a young American movie actor started talking to me at the bar, assuming I was French. At Easter, I donned it to go out for lunch with a group of gorgeous blond girls, all friends from home. It was fun to be with them because everywhere we went, the French went wild. After lunch, we roamed around the Eighth Arrondissement—I remember laughing while holding on to my hat as we crossed the Place de la Concorde—until we descended en masse upon a rococo-style tea salon on the rue de Rivoli. Once seated, we devoured a feast of hot chocolate and pastries. An hour later we stood up to leave. I was third in line as we filed out—a parade of youth and high spirits—and I heard a woman say to her companion: *"Regarde, surtout, la troisième."* Never was coming in third such a compliment.

The Girl Who Cried Wolf

When I was very young, I decided that when the time came I would lose my virtue to a prince. I imagined that he would sweep me up in some sort of chariot, take me to his villa—located somewhere in the South of France, of course—and there, in a pristine, high-ceilinged bedroom, with large windows and billowing white curtains, he would ravish me.

I never slept with anybody while my mother was alive. I told her as much one night, sitting on her bed in her dimly lit room. She was lying still under the covers. She said, "Don't do it because the moon is just so, or because it's a beautiful night. Wait until you can't help it." I put my head down next to her, and she stroked my hair.

In her last months, I fell in love. Tall, with lustrous black hair that he brilliantined daily, T. seemed to be from another era, especially because he wore a lot of his grandfather's clothes from the forties, which gave him an odd yet dapper air. He lived in Dunster House, as I did, and we had a couple of friends in common, but we didn't really know each other. We had eaten lunch together once, in the fall, when I had come out of the cafeteria line holding my tray, looked around the room, and decided to join him because I didn't see anyone else to sit with. I don't remember what we spoke about, but I remember thinking how smart he was, how full of energy and plans. After that I noticed he was always intent on doing something, learning a new language, planning a trip, going to the screening of an old movie in Harvard Square. He kept saying he wanted to show me this monastery he knew about on the Charles River, but I demurred, knowing he wanted something from me I wasn't yet ready to give. He had an intensity I wasn't used to, but as I got to know him better I realized he wasn't serious-minded all the time. He had a good sense of humor, so deadpan that it always took me a minute to realize he was joking. As winter thawed, as my mother grew weaker and weaker, I fell more and more prey to his anachronistic allure.

By early spring I was spending most weekends at home, where I wouldn't let myself think of him, of his dark good looks and the way he eyed me when I walked past him in the courtyard. Instead, I tried to immerse myself in being her daughter. Often, when I went into her room, she asked me to tell her funny stories. I tried to make her laugh, and hated the silences when I couldn't think of anything to say. I loved my mother, I loved her. I wanted to find new ways to let her know how much. I told her that every time I looked at old photographs of Hollywood actresses—Elizabeth Taylor, Natalie Wood, Marilyn Monroe—I saw her face in their faces. I needed her to know that in my mind she had the same mythic quality—her femininity was as complete, as iconic, as knowing. But I couldn't say any of that. As if understanding what I meant anyway, she answered, "I guess you really do love me."

Every Sunday afternoon I was split between fear and relief when it came time for me to go back to school. Once, toward the end of her last hospital stay, she seemed especially anxious to hurry me off, nervous that I would miss my shuttle. My father followed me out of her room and guided me down the hall to the empty waiting room, with its bleak views of the East River. We sat down. "Valerie," he said, and then he put his head in his hands. He told me what the doctor had told him, that the cancer had attacked her bones, was feeding on her liver. "There is no hope," he said, and I realized that if my father, the man who habitually walked on the sunny side of the street, was telling me this, it had to be true. We cried together awkwardly, side by side on the stiff plastic chairs. It was the first time I understood she was going to leave us, the fact of it cold and ugly. I flew to Boston in blank solitude, listening to my Walkman and staring out the small airplane window at the clouds, which refused for once to transform into anything else. Before I knew it I was in a cab, speeding along the Charles River, and then the red tower of Dunster House appeared, a beacon telling me I had made it safely to another world.

It was spring, and I felt my pain as a kind of private melody. I was obsessed with show tunes, especially Gershwin, and would sing things like "Someone to Watch Over Me" under my breath while walking to class. I went to lectures and the library and the dining hall like everyone else, but I was in a state of mild fever, continually bruising myself by knocking into chairs or unseen corners, as if my body were attacking itself in confluence with my mother's. As I passed by the cordoned-off campus greens on my way back to my dorm, the cool air and the tender grass shoots made me tremble. I couldn't write the simplest three-page paper, and measured time by old sitcoms, watching them until I could hardly remember who I was. Seven in a row took up three and a half hours of time. I pretended to get work done, bringing all my books to the library, glad for the comforting warmth of its wood tables and low, glowing lamps, its walls of embossed-leather books and the thoughtful scattering of deep red armchairs.

T. was often there, so I could admire him when he wasn't looking up, feel him staring at me whenever I looked down. He was from Brooklyn, and teased me for being an Upper East Side girl. Soon, despite my numbness to everything else, I was always aware of his presence, noticing right away if he wasn't in the dining room, scanning the courtyard for his person. It was hard to miss him in those old-fashioned suits, and then, too, he was six foot four, big and unfamiliar, not like the gentle boys I was used to. He rowed crew, and I was fascinated by the way he drove himself, and, at mealtimes, by his rapacious appetite.

At the beginning of March, my mother's doctor let us know there was truly nothing more he could do for her in the hospital, and my father decided we should bring her home, where she would be more at ease, surrounded by the family and things and memories that she loved. She was happy to come home—we could hear it in her voice as she directed us to pack up her belongings—as if she had worried without telling us that she would never see it again.

The last week of her life I spent at home. It was spring break. My sister and I sat by her bed, talking softly, watching television. We played the sound track to *A Room with a View* over and over, all of us soothed by its ethereal quality. "That's nice," my mother said at one point from her bed. We took turns bringing her things: lunches she couldn't or wouldn't eat, highball glasses filled with 7-Up or ginger ale. She drank constantly. The disease parched her and nothing was enough to quench her thirst.

Although there was a nurse, it was we who administered her pills, careful to take note of the time and to follow the doctor's instructions. At one point, she was in so much pain she threatened to kill herself if we didn't give her another dose of medication. Frantic, we called the doctor so he could tell her we weren't doing anything wrong, and she got on the phone and accused us of all being in a conspiracy to hurt her. My mother, once so full of warmth and love and vitality, had become suspicious, paranoid. The morphine was taking her usual anxieties and feeding them until they grew to monstrous proportions. One afternoon she insisted I escort her to the library. Painted hunter green and filled with books and musical instruments, it was the best-loved room in the house. She explained to me, her voice strict with instruction, that she wanted us to make sure there were no samurai there. Without questioning her, I held her, felt her body's efforts under the peach satin robe as we walked slowly down the hallway, through the bright red foyer where she had so often entertained, and into the library. I turned on the light, and said softly, "See, Mommy? There isn't anyone here." In her quasi-dream state, she seemed satisfied, and we returned to her room. I helped her to her bed, wondering at the speed with which we had all had to surrender our grip on normalcy.

On one of those twilit days, T. called. He was in town, and asked if I wanted to spend an hour at the Museum of Modern Art. I asked my mother in French if I could go, feeling guilty and wanting to please her somehow with the sound of her mother tongue. She got impatient with me. She didn't want to speak French, didn't want me to go, it wasn't right. I went anyway, feeling I needed air, as though I had to get out of the stifling apartment, away from its sickly sweet medicinal smell. He and I went to see the Warhol show. A year later I would write my senior thesis on one of the paintings. Although he knew my mother was ill—I had mentioned it one night at school a few months back when we were talking, and he had been taken aback by my sudden, easy tears—I did not explain anything, or talk about it in any way at all as we walked through the pop-filled rooms. Afterward, we got hot dogs by the park. While we were sitting on the bench, his shirt gaped open between buttons and I saw a glimpse of his stomach, covered in black hairs. I was repelled and thought to myself: that's not for me.

A few days later, Bella came from Belgium. Bella, one of my mother's beloved *tantes,* whom she had been close to ever since she was a child. I went to pick her up at the airport with my uncle, my father's older brother, and on the way back we got caught in traffic on the Fifty-ninth Street Bridge. It seemed inconceivable to me that my mother could die without me, while I was trapped in something so mundane as a traffic jam. When we finally got home, Bella wept over my mother's weakened body, her stark skull, her unblinking, watery eyes. Later she cried to me that she hadn't seen a human being look so ravaged since Auschwitz. None of us knew what to do with ourselves, with the pain—hers and ours—that was everywhere, pervading every available space in the house. With the exception of her bedroom, which was filled with the plastic accoutrements of illness and no longer recognizable as her usual headquarters, the apartment looked as it always had. Only everything was very still. On the tables my mother had arranged so lovingly, the silver-framed photographs of past adventures and delicate porcelain bouquets and figurines sat silently waiting. The couch pillows puffed just so, the tall chairs standing at attention around the dining room table: all was in abeyance. The spirit that had animated each room, every seductive curve of furniture, every woven flowery vine, was withdrawing, its life force waning. She was being taken from us, and nothing, not even our boundless love, could stop the process; no amount of knowledge or money existed that could keep her from going away.

On the morning of the day she died, I looked in the bathroom mirror and cried for myself, for the almost unrecognizable girl before me. I didn't get dressed, staying in the same nightshirt I had slept in, which was covered in dark burgundy stripes, and which later I would put away at the back of a shelf, never to be worn again. Whenever I wasn't in my mother's room that day, I spent time cleaning mine. My belongings had gotten out of hand, so I cleaned furiously, folding the clothes that were strewn everywhere and angrily putting books and papers in order on my desk. When the time came—for what, I didn't dare to imagine—I wanted to be ready. A few hours later I got my period. I stared at the clouds of tissue, like pale pink roses, floating in the bowl and took the blood as a benison, a tribute to the children I would have in her memory.

Bella and my father and my sister and I spent that afternoon and evening in my mother's room, holding her hands and stroking her forehead, my sister and I begging her to promise she would watch over us always. In the middle of the night, not knowing what else to do with ourselves, we sat down to play boraco, the family card game, perhaps trying to evoke the Renoir-like afternoons we had spent in Belgian tea gardens together. Just as the cards were laid out, as if she were annoyed by our choosing to play at such a time, the steady rasp of my mother's breathing became jagged, uneven. We flew from the card table and gathered around her bed. It was a sound like something being torn. Ourselves choking, we stroked her face and arms until the last catch in her throat. The life had not flowed out of her; it had been seized.

My father and sister and I drew away from the bed and held one another tightly, a crying circle of three. On the table in her room, there was a nineteenth-century brass lamp: an angel holding up a torch of light. When I looked up from our embrace, the light from next to her bed had cast a silhouette of the angel against the white closet doors, and I remember thinking to myself that it made perfect sense, that her spirit must have been borne away by angels.

It was about three o'clock in the morning by the time we got into bed. My father slept on the pullout couch in his den—it was too upsetting for him to go into their bedroom without her. Stephanie and I decided to sleep together in my room. As we faced each other in bed, too tired and brokenhearted even to say good night to each other, I watched in amazement as my sister's features became my mother's. I was staring at the face of my mother in my bed, she was right next to me, looking at me lovingly, her eyes melting into mine. Yes, I knew that the undertaker had just come and taken her body away, carrying it on a gurney through the marble lobby where she had so often clipped in her high heels. But this was real. The next morning when I told Stephanie what I had seen as we fell asleep, she looked at me as if I were crazy and then started half laughing, half crying. She had had the exact same experience. She, too, had seen our mother's face, in mine.

For as long as I could remember, my mother had always worn a small ring on her right hand. It had been her mother's, and was pure Deco: an onyx octagon surrounded by a circle of diamonds and then another circle of onyx—black encircling brilliance encircling black. It reminded me of my sister's favorite line from the Union prayerbook we used at temple: "Our life is but a fleeting gleam between two eternities." If any object in the world had been capable of epitomizing my mother, her sparkle and elegance, it had been that ring. She lost it about a year before she died. We had ransacked the house looking for it, not wanting to believe it was gone. We decided it had been accidentally thrown out, especially since, as she got thinner, she got in the habit of taking off her rings, wrapping them in a tissue, and putting them into her purse.

The day after my mother died, our housekeeper's daughter came to help out. I went into the library and started to undo the foldout couch so that she and her two little boys could sleep there. As I pulled open the mattress, I saw something on the floor, twinkling from the darkest corner. I leaned in and screamed. From the other room, my father thought I had seen a mouse. It was the ring. It wasn't possible for it to be there: the carpet was new; the couch had been reupholstered; we had had several guests sleep there in the past few months. We all touched the ring, passing it from hand to hand, feeling it to be an unassailable sign sent by her to tell us that she was still with us, that she was all right.

The following morning, the day of the funeral, I pulled out a dress my mother had bought me when we were in Venice together. Long-sleeved and with a slightly swingy skirt, the dress was made of a glossy fabric that had a miniature houndstooth pattern on it, so that the black-and-white diamond shapes shimmered like small stars when I walked. Twirling around in the store for her, could I have imagined that I would wear it to her grave? That morning in my room, Stephanie, nervous and unsettled, saw me in the dress and wanted to take a picture of me in it. It was something normal to do, like this was any other big life event. I got angry with her, saying it wasn't appropriate. This wasn't an occasion to be photographed. We wept and hugged and forgave each other for not knowing how to act or what we were supposed to do.

We actually laughed a little bit during the services, as one of her friends described her always talking about "My Jerry," and how she would get us to practice our instruments ("That sounded so lovely, darling. Will you play it for me again?"). We cried, too, holding each other, following the coffin down the aisle. During the long ride to the cemetery, my father started talking to the rabbi, asking him what our religion had to say about eternal life. I tuned out, alone with my thoughts. When we got to the graveside, another one of my mother's friends tried to hug us to her. This was not a woman we felt particularly close to. I had met her perhaps a half-dozen times in my life. I suddenly realized that some people enjoy going to funerals, the drama of wearing black, of weeping the loudest. This woman was wearing a big hat, and as she clutched us, the only thing I could think was *Let go!* But I didn't want to be rude. I just held my body stiffly until she gave up and moved back into the crowd. Following our father in turn, Stephanie and I each took the shovel and cast dirt onto our mother's grave as Jewish custom dictates. The thud of the earth, the finality of the gesture, the thought of my mother, always so claustrophobic, trapped in there, was almost beyond bearing.

Afterward we went home. Within moments, people started arriving to pay their respects and the house was full of movement. Friends and family cried with us, tsk-tsked over us, ate the food that had been laid out for them, pulled us into their arms. We felt an outpouring of love, but some unwanted nosiness, too. *What are you going to do with the apartment, with the house, with your mother's things?* I stayed on the move from one part of the apartment to another, always at the ready to attend to something or someone else. A friend of mine flicked the ashes of his cigarette onto the carpet in my room as if the whole floor were his personal ashtray. I looked on at everything from a distance. I was in a different place, no one could reach me. The unimaginable had happened.

I started going out with T. six weeks later, weeks filled with his increasing attentions and my shameless desire to be pursued. I relished hearing things about his obsession. I found out that he broke up with his girlfriend over me, and that when the girlfriend had said, "But she doesn't know you exist," he had replied, "But I know she does." If I went down to the late-night grill to get something to eat, I would see him. I imagined him always awake at night, prowling the halls.

One night, in the middle of writing a paper, I decided to go to the 24-hour store, to pick up soda and cigarettes. Before I left, I asked my roommate if she wanted anything. It was 4:30 in the morning. I felt fearless. My mother had died and no one could hurt me. I walked at a fast pace, daring anyone to get in my way. When I got to the store, I took my time wandering through the aisles before going up to the register. It was soothing to be around other people for a moment, all of us there briefly for a random variety of reasons. Drawing my jacket more closely around me to prepare for the chilly walk home, I stepped out of the fluorescent bustle and onto the dark street. When I turned the corner, I stopped short. T. was there, standing with his hands in the pockets of his crew jacket, waiting for me. I felt a rush of relief; I hadn't known it until I saw him standing there that this was what I had been waiting for, to be saved. I said nothing as I got into the car with him, and he drove me home.

The first night I spent in his room—he had taken me to see the monastery that day—we never went to sleep. He lifted me up and we danced together around his room, my feet only skimming the ground. He told me he loved me and pressed me to say the same, but I couldn't, explaining I didn't know him well enough yet. Later, as we lay half dressed in his narrow student bed, he showed me a red light beaming in the distance farther up along the river. He said it was his Gatsby light, the light he would stare at night after night that reassured him he would be with me someday. I wanted my breath to be sweet for him, so I had brought a tin of English candies that were shaped and flavored like raspberries. We passed a single candy back and forth, the sweetness commingling in our mouths, until the candy became a thin transparent disc with a razor edge.

In the weeks that followed there were midnight walks along the river, and a motorcycle ride that without a doubt would have made my mother mad. One weekend he and I went to New York and stayed out all night with another couple, going to a gay club and dancing for hours, eating a late dinner in the meatpacking district in a diner that served French food. T. had ordered pâté, which I didn't like, and kept trying to get me to taste it. He said, "If you loved me you would try it," and finally I answered, "I do, but I'm still not going to eat any." He laughed in victory and pulled me close to him. At three o'clock in the morning the four of us ended up in the middle of Central Park, at the Belvedere Castle. The moon was out. The castle loomed against the city skyline. This was what I had always wanted, to be swept up in a love that was larger than life. With my mother's death, I was bereft of the person who had made sense of the world for me. Now I had found someone else who could lead the way. He was so much larger than I was—his thighs bigger than my waist—that being with him made me feel small and vulnerable and at the same time safe. He could lift me or place me however he wanted. He liked to take my entire hand in his and squeeze it until my knuckles cracked, or lift me up so that my back would release. Sometimes in bed my bones felt like they might splinter under his weight.

One night I told him that a part of me had died when my mother died. T. responded that she never would have wanted me to think that way. I appreciated the thoughtfulness of his answer (although it was weird to hear someone who had never met my mother describe what she would or wouldn't have wanted), but I also knew that what I had said was true. The person who had answered when my mother called my name, the daughter I was when I was with her, that Valerie no longer existed. He held me as if he could physically prevent me from thinking that way.

Part of the reason I never made love with anyone while my mother was alive was because I couldn't picture going out to lunch with her the next day. I felt as though I wouldn't be able to look her in the face, that she would find me out, realize that I was different from the young girl she had raised, and be angry or disappointed or both. I couldn't see how I could remain her daughter and yet also be a sexual being—the two roles would cancel each other out. Now that she was gone, that logic no longer held.

Nevertheless, I would be strict with myself, I decided. I would hold myself to the rules of propriety my mother had established for my conduct, like the one about boyfriends staying in separate rooms. The first weekend after school ended, I went to Easthampton with my father. T. was still in Cambridge, hanging around for graduation, but he joined us, driving his car across two ferries and arriving late that Friday night. I set up a room for him to stay in downstairs, just as I knew my mother would have wanted. When I opened the front door to greet him, I remember thinking how handsome he looked in the moonlight, with his dark hair swept back from his forehead.

The next day, we were all in the kitchen when my father picked up the phone to make reservations for us to have dinner that night at a Greek place we liked. I heard him say, "That'll be a table for four," and then fall silent. "I mean three," he said a couple of seconds later. He put the phone down, cursed quietly, and left the room. After dinner, T. and I went down to the basement and started to fool around on the couch. This time, though, things started moving too quickly. I stopped him, and, explaining into his chest, told him I had never made love with anyone. He said he had figured as much. I told him I hadn't wanted to tell him because, having seen how fiercely he pursued me, I thought that instead of the question of sex coming up naturally between us and resolving itself gradually, he would think of it as a challenge: how quickly could he get me into bed? At first he was insulted. Then he told me I was being silly, that I should trust him more. We talked about it, and it emerged that we were quite representative of our genders. He explained to me that while in his life he had gone without being in love for long periods of time, the thought of being without sex was very difficult for him. I said that for me the two were completely linked. I didn't tell him, though, how scared I was of becoming another person than the one my mother had loved.

Just as the summer began, he went to Europe. For the next few weeks, we wrote each other constantly. I put on bright red lipstick before mailing each letter, to seal the envelope with the imprint of a kiss. He wrote me almost daily, letters describing the minutiae of his days. I would skim over those parts, hungrily seeking the declarations of love, the quotes from Kundera, the words of a song.

We met up in Madrid. I had gone there with my sister; she and I were supposed to stay there for a few days, just the two of us, before meeting friends. T. was staying with friends of his outside the city. He picked us up at the airport. I was shy with him; he was a tanned stranger. That night we all went out, to a crazy restaurant that offered food, pool, dancing, and archery. In Spanish spirit, I

wore a flaming red dress. When he brought us home, my sister
went straight to our room, but he and I kissed passionately in the
hallway of the hotel, he practically removing my dress and me
struggling to prevent him, until his friend, who had to drive back
and get to work in the morning, started to ring the bell impatiently
from downstairs, and we parted, disheveled and wanting.

My sister and I were in Spain with my father's blessing, because we had arranged to go on an all-girls' trip with two other
friends, also sisters. It would be like any other summer; we would
have a wonderful adventure. We had rented a car and were supposed to drive down to Marbella, where we had taken an apartment
for a week on the beach. Not according to plan, T. came with
us, the five of us sitting cramped in a little white car with no air-
conditioning and no power steering. He drove us all the way there,
silently zigzagging through the hills, sometimes grunting with the
effort of wresting the wheel in the heat. At night we stopped in
small Spanish towns for gas and food, sheepishly grateful that we
had a man to protect us.

We finally got to the South. The apartment was in a modern
high-rise, and, with its marble floors and views of the sea, it ex-
uded a kind of tacky luxury that was too much for our mood. He
and I shared the master bedroom—the faux parents of our little
ménage. My sister was so angry with me for having invited him
that she would hardly speak to me. I felt very alone, even with
him. On one of the days he caught me lying across the bed reading one of his letters. He had written, "Do I love you with lightness or with heaviness?" He crashed down next to me on the bed
and asked, "Who do you like better, the me in the letters? Or the
me who's here?" I answered the way he wanted me to, but I wasn't
sure. I thought maybe I preferred the letters, which were calmer

and sweeter somehow. It made me sad thinking about it, about what a chasm there is between human beings and the marks they leave. My mother had written me dozens of letters and notes over the years, and I cherished them. But I hated knowing that all I had left of her could fit in a single, medium-sized box, that I could no longer put away the traces and embrace the real thing.

We didn't sleep together for almost a year, and the first time was terrible. He had been trying to convince me that we should make love for months, and his patience had worn thin. We were in his room in Brooklyn, where he was living for his first year out in the real world. I was still a senior in college. I knew him much better by then. He wasn't a tall dark stranger who could save me, just a handsome, slightly neurotic guy with strong opinions about things, good taste in music, and something of a sartorial flair. I liked his intelligence, his badgering sense of humor, his drive. Even if he wasn't a prince, he was the person I wanted it to be with. But I was scared. It was nothing like the place of my dreams. I had tried to explain my fantasy to him, but of course it sounded ridiculous the minute I began to speak. When it finally started to happen, I felt a dry rude stabbing that disturbed my whole being. He could tell I was in so much discomfort that he stopped and pulled away. I was in despair. There was blood on the sheets, not a huge amount, but enough to prove that the daughter my mother had known was gone. I prayed she would forgive me for moving on.

Wild Horses

There is a set of black-and-white photographs taken at Knokke Le Zoute, on the Belgian seacoast, in the summer of 1952, right before my mother left for New York. Although in real life she couldn't swim, she makes for a convincing bathing beauty in these images, sheathed in a strapless cream-colored swimsuit, with a tousle of short dark hair and a smile slipping across her lips. In one of the photos she is lying on a beach towel in a Marilyn-like pose, her body held by a combination of modesty and hidden corsetry in perfect restraint, her skin as luminous as a seashell. Underneath is a caption of sorts, in her handwriting, that says, "What was I dreaming of? Did I think about New York?" Another shows her seated, with prettily bent knees, looking off to the distance, and below it the words "What am I expecting? What am I looking for?"

With a navy blue felt-tip pen, my mother added these reflections many years later, in 1972 or so, when she went through a flurry of annotating photographs and organizing the albums of her life, writing little snippets documenting the moments, along with wry observations about past happinesses and sorrows. Her voice in these notes, which are written on red-lined labels tacked into the albums, or else directly on the album pages themselves, is bemused and open. She couldn't have been writing for me. I was four, five years old at the time, obsessed with such imponderable mysteries as the engraved plaque in the elevator of our Art Deco–style building, which showed a woman with cropped hair and a flowing gown—who was she? where was she going?—seated sidesaddle on a horse, arrested midgallop in all her independence and splendor. But sometimes now it feels as though my mother had in fact left all those writings for me, so that I might understand her better, be able to see the story of her life in a coherent way without having her here to narrate it to me directly.

The beach images I love because they show a young Belgian-Jewish girl testing out her sensuality, my mother before she had ever seen New York, my mother as she would shortly cease to exist. I love them because I can tell she herself was moved by them, that she easily saw through the poses of that barely dressed girlish figure, light and ephemeral as a summer afternoon, to the emotion and fear and headiness that accompany moments of great transition. Most of all I love that my mother was reflective about her life, that so many years later she could so gracefully point to herself on the cusp of change, recognizing the instant when she went from being a daughter of Antwerp, Belgium, to becoming a woman of New York.

I often wondered what had galvanized my mother to make that decisive and terrifying leap. True, she had been unhappy with her stepfather, frustrated with her mother, unwilling to marry. But what was it that had caught her fancy about New York? I got my answer one summer afternoon in Easthampton when I walked into her bedroom and caught her shedding tears while watching television. I couldn't figure it out. A musical was on, and it was right in the middle of a deliriously happy flags-flying number, with hundreds of smiling tap dancers in red-white-and-blue sequins prancing about a multilevel rotating stage set.

"Why are you crying?" I asked.

"Because," she said, pointing to the singing and tap-dancing extravaganza filling the screen. "That is why I came to this country."

Life is strange, I thought. My mother had been lured to New York by the leg-kicking optimism of the American musical. As near as I could understand, the razzmatazz of New York–centered movies like *Lullaby of Broadway* and *On the Town* had seemed to offer to her personally—as she sat, young and hopeful, in the darkened movie theaters of Antwerp—the promise of a better, brighter life.

My mother left Belgium at nineteen, much as her own mother had left Hungary as a young girl before her. I was twenty when I left my homeland, but I left it unwillingly, the moment my mother died, as I was suddenly and incomprehensibly forced to inhabit a world that didn't have her in it. I say I left my homeland, too, but I don't mean a country. The place I grew up in is not a place I can ever go back to, except for brief spells in memory or dream. Childhood is always like this, of course. But once it has ended, a mother continues to hold the key to that domain, so that no matter how old you are—in her passing remark, in her remembering to cook you a favorite dish or buy you a sweater that matches your eyes—your mother transports you back to that realm where she once ruled supreme, and where you, her child, wanted no other happiness.

Actually my mother left her childhood much earlier than I did. Or rather it left her, ripped away by the war. She was only eight years old when she lost her father and the world as she knew it was destroyed, stranding her, irrevocably, on a different shore. In that sense, her physically leaving Antwerp just over ten years later was almost an afterthought.

It was September 1952 when my mother arrived in New York, not exactly singing as her boat came to shore. Her traveling companion on the Holland-American line was a girlfriend from home who had managed to spend the entire voyage in their cabin, seasick. My mother was hardly better off: though not physically ill, she was completely overwhelmed, seesawing between terrible homesickness and panicky fear about what she had just done. Their prospects as an intrepid duo looked bleak. Upon arrival, they cheered themselves up by going to the theater by night and museums and movies by day. At the end of two weeks my mother had almost run out of money. It was time to find a job. She writes in her unpublished epistolary memoir that she was confused at first by all the ads, which required applicants to be "Good at figures." She thought that meant you had to be shapely, which offended her. A savvier friend finally explained what it meant. And so my mother went to the United Jewish Appeal, a charitable organization, and they found her an accounting job on Canal Street.

New York was full of surprises. Next thing my mother knew, she had been named Miss UJA, a transitory yet heartening title for a Jewish girl new to the city. She must have been exactly what the charity organizers were looking for, or else she had just walked into the right place at the right time. In any case, my mother was invited to Times Square for a ceremony presided over by the mayor of New York, and, very excited, she sent home newspaper clippings of the event, proof that she was making it in the big city. It had its effect. Blanca immediately thought she had become famous. It took her a long time to be convinced otherwise.

This began a long tradition of my mother sending her mother photographs of her life. Little did my mother know that my grandmother would go around Antwerp showing off the pictures of her daughter-adventurer—first as Miss UJA, later as an associate at a fashionable gallery in L.A., and then as an actress/model in Mexico City. Everyone my grandmother met would be asked, "Do you know Gisèle?" and before the person had a chance to reply, she would whip out the latest photos, bragging about her daughter's style, exaggerating the degree of Gisèle's professional and personal successes. While my grandmother openly castigated my mother for not being the domestic type (why couldn't she just settle down with a husband and children?), on some level she clearly got a kick out of her daughter's unbridled gallivanting. If only my mother had known, as she struggled for a sense of self-worth and identity, that her mother was proud of and often exhilarated by her exploits.

One could say my mother was sowing her wild oats. If she had it in the back of her mind that it would be good to marry, she certainly wasn't in any rush. Lithe and swift and clever, with a potent French accent, my mother was quite alluring by New York standards, and soon found herself going out on a lot of dates. Antwerp might not have been as big as New York, but my mother was still a city girl, one who knew how to dress and put herself together just so. It's fair to say that in a short period of time a small legion of men were after her, among them a future doctor, an investment banker, and a movie producer. My mother didn't sense a kindred spirit in the whole pack. Despite her youth and a certain naïveté, she had good instincts about men and women and the way things worked between them. She realized that men were usually after one thing, and she was bored by the idea of the usual routine—of being pursued, squired about town, then taken to bed or else home to meet Mother. Despite the number and persistence of her suitors, my mother didn't give herself away to anyone during those years. Whenever a man tried to get serious with her, she turned skittish and bolted, straight into the arms of someone else she didn't much care for.

In fact, my mother did fall in love during that period—hard, and for life—but it was with New York itself. She loved it for its energy, the thrilling sense it gave at all hours of people going places, doing things. New York gave a person the amazing ability to be part of a crowd at one moment and completely anonymous the next, an autonomy my mother could never achieve back in Antwerp, where people knew who you were going to meet for coffee before you had even stepped out your door.

My mother didn't talk to us much about her initial stay in New York. We got a story here, a story there. Mostly I imagine how she must have felt about New York from the way she talked about the city later. A lot of what I know about that era comes from *"Cher David, Chère Gisèle,"* the compilation of letters written between her brother and herself from August 1960, when my mother was living in Los Angeles, through her years in Mexico, up until August 1966, the month after she met my father. It was when she sought to have the letters published, in 1975, that she added the introduction about her childhood and adolescence.

It is from that essay, for instance, that I know her first stay in New York lasted three years, and that for the most part my mother was quite responsible, renting a series of inexpensive rooms in other people's homes until she finally found a roommate with whom to share an apartment. I also know that she tried to take the financial burden off her mother by getting decent jobs, and paying for as much as she could by herself. Probably it was the only way to get Blanca, deeply worried about her daughter's prospects, off her back. Every so often, however, my mother would have an emergency—an aching tooth that needed repairing, a dress she simply had to have—leaving her with no choice but to write home asking for money and my grandmother with no choice but to send it.

Part of the problem was that although my mother tried a variety of jobs, she couldn't quite seem to settle on a career. She ran

this way and that. Of course there wasn't a plethora of professional options for young women back then, aside from secretarial-
type posts and jobs in the service industry. My mother did her
share of both. She had the accounting job for a while, followed by
a brief stint as a night cashier in a restaurant. For a time she was
even a cigarette girl at the Copacabana. With the exception of
classes she had started taking in English language and literature,
nothing captured her attention for very long. In fact, she enjoyed
her coursework so much that she added theater classes, too, which
led her to decide she wanted to be an actress. Maybe acting appealed to her because of the personal freedom it allowed. As an actress she could be many people, live many lives instead of just one.
From that moment on, the jobs she took became secondary to her
desire to go to the theater, to read plays, to sign up for as many acting and singing and dancing classes as she could possibly afford.

In some ways acting must have reminded my mother of home.
Right up until she left Antwerp, she had been an active member of
her youth group, B'nai Akivah, a religious recreational organization that she and her friends originally joined, at least according to
one of them, in order to meet boys. In her childhood album my
mother has a photo of the group, a tight mass of smiling teenagers,
under which she wrote: "The B'nai Akivah group I belonged to
after World War II, a religious orthodox group. Marvelous times.
Shabbat, songs, learning about Israel, Jewishness." It wasn't long
before my mother was starring in a lot of the plays they put on,
which were performed on Sunday afternoons. One of her best
friends at the time told me that my mother was a real comedienne,
that just by raising her hand in a certain way, she could have
the entire audience on the floor. And I had always thought that
my mother's ability to captivate a room with a story was some-

thing she grew into, a consequence of years of interesting life experiences.

My mother began her thespian education in New York with Herbert Berghof, an acting guru of the time, but the more she learned about the discipline, the more she heard about Lee Strasberg, the founder and head of the Actor's Studio. Bracing her nerve, she applied to study with him and was accepted. Strasberg liked her. He asked her to be in his class, which was considered a great honor, as there were only about twelve students he personally taught at any one time. During that epoch, one of them was my mother, and another was Marilyn Monroe, with whom my mother was completely fascinated. As girls, my sister and I were regaled with stories of the actress's irrepressible sexiness. My mother liked to tell how each student was assigned to sing a song. According to Strasberg's "Method," you weren't supposed to move your body—all the emotion was supposed to go into your voice. Marilyn sang "Don't Worry About Me," and, as if she couldn't possibly keep her body completely still, her right shoulder sang with her, rolling about in the most suggestive way. My mother, moving her own shoulder in time with the story, took great pleasure in the idea of a woman unable to check her sexuality. At the same time, she told us how lonely Marilyn seemed. The actress often asked the other students to give her a call if they wanted to go to the movies or out for a bite. But my mother and her friends never did. They were too intimidated by the legend to befriend the girl, something my mother felt sorry about later.

Just like the song promised, New York was a wonderful town. My mother had an ideal setup: a gang of friends who shared her interests, a run of places where they liked to go, and a limitless supply of things to read and see and do. If she never quite landed the part in her theatrical career, it didn't matter. I don't know that she ever really attempted to get anywhere with it—she had terrible stage fright and hated going on auditions. I think what really appealed to her was the *idea* of acting, the ability to envision herself as an actress. Life in New York was all possibility, no disappointment. Then why did she leave? In her memoir she describes being on a visit home to Belgium and spending a few days in Paris, where, as she drove by all the tranquil buildings, she realized how much she missed such architecture, its unruffled sense of history. New York was garish, too new, she was tired of it—what she really needed was elegance and order. That's how my mother, age twenty-three, ended up in Paris, where she spent that up-and-down year that featured, in turn, her well-to-do cousins, the birdcage that had once belonged to Marie Antoinette, and, last but not least, that short but serious bout of pneumonia.

I, too, had gone to Paris at the age of twenty-three, but I hadn't been there for the architecture. I had been on a mission to find my mother, to try to relate to her as a young woman. For some reason, that year in Paris, the search to rediscover my mother, to know her in all her aspects—both as she was when I knew her and as she must have been long before I was born—took a geographical bent. In pursuit of my mother's memory, I stopped before the odd silvery green of the city's Art Nouveau Métro signs that she had admired so, went back to museum rooms to spend time with paintings we had seen together, sat for long spells at her favorite people-watching cafés, wandered down the little shopping streets in the Sixth Arrondissement where she had loved to go, all in an attempt to feel her effervescence once again coursing through me.

Sometimes it worked, and I felt an urge to laugh, her spirit a gorgeous secret known only to me. Standing before a butcher's window to watch the care with which he placed a row of frilly paper flowers on the tiny bone stalks of a prized rack of lamb, I appreciated his delicacy and patience all the more for being certain they would have charmed her. Other times the beauty of a place would turn cold on me. I could see in the site of some former or imagined happiness only my mother's absence, and I felt even more alone. Then Paris became for me like a vault to which I had no key. Instead of repositories of treasure, I had access only to a series of chill, blank exteriors.

As winter turned to spring, I began to realize that however much I loved Paris, I couldn't stay there indefinitely. Paris was a folly, a pilgrimage I had made because I had had no other choice emotionally. Being there was like living out a dream, one I cherished all the more because I had the impression (impossible to maintain in any other regard) that I was sharing it with my mother. I had no sense of permanence in Paris. I floated through the city, a fairy visitor. My job as a museum intern was a temporary post if ever there was one. Many of my friends were American and would be leaving soon, and my French friends had full lives in a way that I could never hope to in a foreign city. My future was waiting for me back in New York, at home, among family and friends.

I was scared to go back, though, scared to face New York without her. As long as I stayed away, I could fool myself into thinking she was still there, still whirling around the apartment and making our family run. Once I went home, there would be no more avoiding the fact that she was gone. Faraway and romantic, Paris was alive with her memory, but New York felt dead to me. It was her city, and without her in it, it didn't make sense, as if the tracks of its perfect geometrical grid had been picked up by a child and thrown back down in complete disarray.

After all my fear and expectations, coming home was anti-climactic. Every time my family traveled, we remarked that the apartment seemed smaller upon our return, diminished in equal proportion to the vastness of the sights we had just seen. Opening the front door after visiting the Great Wall, the Taj Mahal, or the Caribbean Sea, the bright red foyer always looked a little less vivid, less grand, than we remembered. Gradually our eyes would adjust, and our perception of the room's doll-like proportions would fade until the apartment was the same size it had always been. This time I came home and the apartment felt not just smaller, but stale.

Absolutely nothing in the place had changed since my mother had died. I had been home for brief stretches, weekends in college, entire summers even, but it had never hit me so strongly before. I don't know why I was surprised. It had so clearly been her pleasure to keep our home up to date, with flowers, the latest books, a new set of drapes. Stephanie and I were just girls. We weren't homemakers. And my father had reverted to his bachelor days, with plenty of hamburgers and steaks and not a whole lot of vegetables for dinner, a regular sending out of his shirts to the dry cleaner, and, given that he wasn't really in entertaining mode, limited concern for his home environment, as long as it was comfortable. Even with the housekeeper whom he kept on, I could tell that without my mother's eagle eye overseeing things, dust had collected on the lampshades, the high bookshelves, the tops of furniture. The idea first depressed, then overwhelmed me. My father was a man, not sensitive to these things. He was a little messier by nature, so there were more piles of papers around, especially in their bedroom. The dining room table had been completely co-opted. This used to happen every once in a while, but my mother would always be after him to clean it up, she didn't want her dining room looking that way. I didn't have such authority with my father, though. It wasn't my role to tell him what to do, and the stacks of papers grew bigger and bigger, spilling onto the chairs, the marble console, the floor, until the dining room was rendered unusable.

My sister was still in college, which meant it was just my father and me at home, and after calling in with glamorous reports from Paris, it felt weird, suddenly, to be roommates with him, to time my morning so we could have breakfast together, or remember to call in if I'd be home late. I loved my father, and he loved me, but we didn't know each other that well. While I was growing up, I now realized, my relationship with him had been completely filtered through my mother. "Your father thinks you're spending too much time on the telephone," or "Your father was very proud of your test scores," she might say. I rarely heard from him directly. This was in great contrast to my dealings with my mother, with whom (except for that one nefarious year) I spoke easily and often, about every little thing. Traditional gender roles and the fact that he was ten years older than she had contributed to his taking a slightly less active role in raising us.

When I thought about it, I saw that he and I had always had a more formal relationship. I don't mean we didn't do casual things together, like go out for pizza or to the movies, but we had been careful around each other, never really expressing how we felt, unless one of us made the exceptional effort to cross the gap of gender and years. During my childhood he had sometimes had his head in the clouds. If one of us tried to get his attention while he was reading the paper, we would have to call his name several times, loud then louder, before he responded. It's not that there was anything wrong with his hearing. I think it was his only defense against being surrounded by so many women. Now that it was just the two of us, I noticed it never happened anymore.

Sometimes I knew he felt we didn't understand him. He had had a very different kind of life, born into a Russian-Jewish immigrant family, graduating from City College at eighteen, leading a series of jazz bands as the saxophonist, earning three more degrees and an honorable discharge from the army by the time he was twenty-five. It was as a teenage student of cryptology at Hunter College that he was handpicked (along with his teacher, Rosario Candela) to be on the team that broke the first Japanese code, and in the fifties he appeared as himself—*Will the real Jerry Steiker please stand up?*—on an episode of "To Tell the Truth." He had traveled the country as a young CPA, lived in D.C. as the chief accountant for the Senate Crime Committee, and then moved to Rochester, where he was considered one of the most eligible bachelors in town and eventually became president of the First National Bank. And all this had happened before he even met my mother. My father knew we were very proud of his many accomplishments, professionally, musically, personally. But how could we appreciate where he really came from, his home life with two brothers in the Bronx, his parents' Yiddish accents, his father's butter-and-eggs business on the Lower East Side? Now that we were eating breakfast together every day, he began telling me stories of his childhood. As he rinsed our dishes (a task he had always enjoyed) he would describe how his father made hot cereal on the double boiler at 4 A.M., before going to work, and left it simmering on the stove for his sons to eat when they got up hours later. My father often had tears in his eyes as he spoke of his parents. I never met his mother, and his father passed away when I was just a baby, leaving behind only an impression of kindness. I tried to reassure him that despite our differences, I did value where he came from. I loved many of the things he loved—Benny Goodman and pickles and Jewish jokes. Mineida Street, where he grew up with his family, was just as much a part of me as De Keyserlei, Antwerp's main boulevard.

We were less father and daughter now than equals, fellow travelers on an uncharted path. I was amazed at how easily my father, having been a bachelor until his midforties, had picked up the reins of single life again. Unlike some widowers, who cease to live or do, my father was coping, keeping busy, making plans with people, going out. For a while it seemed as though he had a more active social life than I did, especially since my friends were all used to going about their business without me, and T. had gone off to India for the year, on a fellowship. The one thing that continued to upset me was the idea of my father dating. I knew it was normal, yet I couldn't get used to it. In the year after my mother died, my sister and I were shocked at how quickly my parents' friends had started calling in with the names of eligible women for my father to date. It made us realize how different it was to lose a wife than to lose a mother, most strikingly because you can never have another mother. While we knew my father had lost his great love, his rightful partner, we also were forced to acknowledge that it was healthy for him to want companionship—not in order to replace our mother, but to live more fully. I could tell that sometimes he wanted to talk about it, to tell me a funny story about a date he'd had, or maybe even ask my advice. I loved him, was trying to be happy for him, but I just didn't want to hear about it. He had had enough experience to know that his life needed to go on. I was still waiting for mine to begin.

I started sending out résumés to museums and magazines, hoping fate would take its course and I'd know what to do with myself. In the meantime, I got some freelance work, fact-checking for a home-decorating magazine. It wasn't a career, but at least I was gainfully employed. As I cast about for the next step, I seized upon what I desperately wanted to believe was a brilliant idea: I would take acting classes at Lee Strasberg's studio, exactly as my mother had done when she first came to New York.

I never imagined Strasberg's "Method" would involve crawling around on the floor making animal noises, which is what I saw a group of students doing during a tour of the school. With some misgivings I signed up for a twelve-week course. It was impossible to imagine myself, let alone my mother, engaged in such shenanigans.

Every class began the same way, with all the students, eyes closed, sitting in folding chairs scattered across the front of the auditorium. Arms dangling, heads pitched forward, we were told to get in touch with our breathing. We were encouraged to make sounds, to let the stresses of the day out in giant "ahhhhh"s, with the breaths getting louder as the warm-up went on. Students would be rotating their shoulders, stretching out their legs, hanging their heads down between their knees. Sometimes the teacher would come and stand over a fellow student, pulling on his arms to stretch them longer, rubbing his back to loosen it up.

For the first few weeks I was so self-conscious I couldn't let go. For one thing, I was completely embarrassed at the thought of making strange sounds in front of people I didn't know. I kept my "ah"s tiny, inaudible to anyone but myself. And then I wasn't used to moving my body in such odd, impolite ways. Much to my surprise, I got used to it. As the weeks went on, I began to take up more space, until I was no longer afraid to let the room resound with my voice or to reach my arms above my head and circle them slowly and widely in the air. I loved finding out that without any external aid I could rid myself of my own tension, find the knots and work at them until my body had no choice but to release.

The relaxation techniques were followed by sense-memory exercises, in which you were supposed to re-create a physical experience down to the minutest detail. I was instructed to begin with an imaginary cup of hot coffee. For the first couple of times I wasn't even allowed to taste it. The teacher told me I just had to concentrate on the physical reality of holding that cup in my hand. I took turns, variously, smelling the aroma, seeing the steam rise up, sensing the heat of the liquid through the mug, feeling the weight of it in my hand. Only after those qualities were real to me could I go on to take that first sip. Using my imagination to such single-minded purpose was dull at first, than gradually rewarding, like meditation.

As the weeks went on, the exercises became more and more complicated. From coffee I moved on to peeling and eating an orange, taking a bath, and from there to working on emotional memories. We were told to choose a place or item from childhood, whether it was a room or a doll or a letter, and then to conjure it as accurately as we could, with all its attending emotions, the idea being that we would then bring that kind of richness and emotional specificity to the stage. I decided to return to my childhood room, to its peach wallpaper and ruffled curtains. I was living in the same room now, of course, but it had been redone, and looked and felt much different than it had then. I imagined myself as a child lying in my old bed at night, surrounded by all my stuffed animals, watching the changing scaffolds of light against the ceiling, an effect produced nightly by the fluorescent-lit buses rolling up Madison Avenue below my windows. It didn't bring up any untoward emotions, as far as I could tell.

After these exercises, it was time to become animals. The room was transformed. Wherever you looked you saw cats stretching against the wall, snakes wiggling on the floor, dogs nuzzling chair legs, even the occasional ape (always a guy) careening in circles. This was what I had seen on my tour, but by now I understood it better, having learned that Strasberg had famously coached Marlon Brando to play Stanley in *A Streetcar Named Desire* as a gorilla. I loved hearing about Strasberg's instructions to his actors, especially knowing that my mother had been among them. Once he advised an actress who had to be terrified in a scene to pretend the furniture in the room was out to get her. It was amazing what that kind of imagining could do to you. It made you come alive, and therein lay the crux of his theory, that acting was about being in the moment, and letting the audience share in the realness of that.

Just as you were feeling particularly snakelike or whatever, the teacher would announce a break. It was funny to see students rupture their brute poses and become human again, walking to get their things. Everyone would go outside, to the street in front of the building, to have a smoke or something to drink. When we came back in, after twenty minutes or so, students in pairs presented scenes that they had rehearsed on their own time.

I liked doing scene work. That was the kind of acting I was used to, not all this pretend-to-be-cold, be-an-animal stuff. I preferred having lines, a script, something to work with besides my own body and voice. I especially enjoyed the more formal roles, the ones in which you could wear a costume, preferably period. At some point I did a scene with an older woman from *Mrs. Warren's Profession*. The woman was very kind. We'd meet a little before class, to practice in one of the empty hallways or, if the school was too crowded, outside, on the sidewalk. She had a strong Spanish accent. You might have thought that this, in combination with the fact that she was playing my mother, would have dredged something up, but the well-written words, coming out of my mouth at a dynamic clip, prevented me from feeling anything too personal.

I got a lot from the classes, though maybe not what I was expecting. I wasn't "discovered," nor did I decide to abandon everything to become an actress. And yet I felt myself loosening up in important ways. I had always been the straitlaced first child, a good girl. If I was never going to be the grooviest kid on the block, at least having to perform in front of other people regularly helped me become a little less inhibited. I felt freer in my body, less constrained by the reserve that natural shyness and years of ballet lessons had instilled in me. I spoke up more, became friendly with a few people in my class. My mother had written to me in my high-school yearbook, "I love all the yous in you." I sensed myself expanding, felt for the first time the possibility of becoming other mes.

From the beginning I hadn't given much credence to the emotional memory exercises, which struck me as an artificial way to access the past. I was surprised out of my skepticism, though, the second or third time I "went back" to my childhood room. While nestling into that specific time and place, I found myself recalling a terrifying night, during which I was awakened by a gleam on my brass doorknob, which had never shone so brightly. My eyes traveled that night from the doorknob to the lamp above my bed, which also happened to be a music box, with a little wooden lion that, when you pulled the knob at the top of its head, would pivot in its cage to a lullaby. As I glanced up, I noticed the lion was poised to strike, and felt with fear that it had every intention of tearing down the flimsy brass bars of its prison and breaking free. Then the shade fluttered and I saw the orange-pink of the street-lamp outside my window, whose rays were casting the strange gleam on my doorknob, where my eyes inevitably went next. For what seemed like hours my eyes performed an exhaustive dance among those three points: the shining doorknob, whose role in letting me out of my room I had always taken for granted; the taut whiskers of the lion, ready to pounce; and the surreal glowing egg of light outside my window, belonging to the world outside but now a component, foreign and unwelcome, of my room. I felt trapped, mesmerized by the inarguable logic of following the same visual trail. It wasn't that I thought anything bad was going to happen necessarily, but that I was gripped by utter paralysis. I prayed for my mother that night to somehow sense that I couldn't move— only her coming through the door would break the spell, remove the glow from the doorknob, and free me from this nightmarish triangle. But she never came, and sleep must finally have released me.

I awoke and was puzzled to find myself lying on the floor

under a set of bright fluorescent lights, surrounded by other acting students, all, like me, lost in a world of their own making. Until that moment I had completely forgotten about the incident, a seemingly inconsequential moment of childhood terror. Reaching out to me across the years was the remembered dread of feeling stuck, an invisible yoke from which I longed to shake free.

It was with only a couple of classes left in my twelve-week acting course that I found myself, one late December afternoon, standing at the border of Central Park, waiting for the bus to take me down Fifth Avenue to my new job in publishing. The trees were bare, their twisting armature the same dull gray as the stone wall enclosing the park, and yet my heart was humming. The day felt fresh and important, like the beginning of a new chapter.

When the call had come from the literary magazine, saying I had the position after all, I couldn't have been more surprised. I had been dying to work there, partly because I loved the tradition of it, and partly, I am not ashamed to admit, because a controversial editor had just taken over, to much scandal, and it seemed like the most exciting game in town. I had sent my résumé there three months earlier, and received a polite rejection note. They really did keep my résumé on file, however, and when an opening came up I was called in for an interview. I had been granted a post in the word-processing department. It was only freelance, and a night job at that, but the way I saw it, it was a foot in the door of a great institution. As I boarded the bus that would take me to my new office, I said to myself, "O.K., Valerie, here we go . . ."

My first night there was a reeling experience. The magazine's longtime beloved former editor had passed away the day before, and the phones were ringing off the hook with writers calling in their reminiscences. Along with the other word processors (who seemed like a cool bunch), I spent all night glued to my computer, typing up these pieces, which were coming in by phone, fax, and messenger. It was a good feeling to be part of a team all of a sudden, even if I barely had time to figure out what I was doing, let alone to admire the look of that famous font enlarged on my computer screen. As I got caught up in what I was typing, the person being described became more and more vivid, his elegance as an editor, his unflappable reserve, his meticulous intelligence, and even his odd habit of eating cereal for meals besides breakfast and his hatred of elevators. I smiled to myself as I worked, laughed out loud a few times, and at moments found myself almost in tears over a man I had never met. I was typing about loss, and about things being different than they used to be—all too familiar territory to me. Despite my being a recent arrival and my feeling that the new editor was glamorous, many of the friends I eventually made at the magazine, the assistants and editors and writers to whom I was drawn, were from the old order, those who cherished and believed in what the magazine had always stood for. We fell in together naturally. Although I had never known what it was like in the glory days, it was easy to mourn with them for a lost paradise. (It took me longer to appreciate that most of them weren't content merely to live in the past but were making every effort to move forward with the new regime.)

I came in every day at 5 P.M. and left around midnight. I liked the word-processing department, often called "WP," which was made up of young people like me with vague writerly aspirations. It felt like an old-fashioned apprenticeship. Without ever getting to know or rely on any one of us too much, the magazine harnessed our energy, our enthusiasm, our curiosity. In return, it taught us to pay attention to words. Over the years an increasingly elaborate editorial process had evolved, which had every piece winding its way through the copyediting, fact-checking, legal, and proofreading departments, all the while being under the care of a specific editor. There was an entire department whose job it was to collate all those changes onto one proof, which would be passed along to us for inputting. Sometimes mistakes would get through, and it was thrilling if you caught one and got to go up and interrupt a closing session, in which writer, editor, fact-checker, legal adviser, and page-O.K.'er sat in an office trying to put a piece to bed. The ten of us were broken into day and night shifts that changed week to week, which to some extent guaranteed that we remained interchangeable. We didn't have undue amounts of responsibility, but what we did do we had to do well, and writers and editors trusted us, occasionally coming down and hanging around with us on a break, other times relying on us to move their text quickly and expertly through the system.

Partly because they could count on one another in a crunch, the group in WP had developed a friendly working rhythm, with lots of bad puns and good-natured ribbing flying back and forth, which made for a convivial environment. I joined right in. We had all been hired by the same person, a woman just a few years older than we were with an almost unerring sense of what made for a close-knit crew. She was bright and kind and a little bit motherly, chiding us if we were lazy or late, encouraging us in our own writing. I noticed we all shared certain qualities: youth, a passion for words and the *Times* crossword puzzle, a deluded confidence in our own wit. With so many shared hours, and everyone being a little bit too smart for their own good, we always had some kind of dopey experiment going on. Some I liked more than others, like the bulletin board of infamy with the worst sentences we could find taken out of context from the magazine, or the bowl of live Sea-Monkeys, whose ads I remembered from the backs of comic books, kept on top of the file cabinets in the middle of the room. (I was less fond of the "nipple count," held in honor of the magazine's first fashion issue, which, much to my surprise, writers and editors alike came in to bet on.) Whenever two of my favorite guys in the department had to turn in their overtime memos, they used it as an occasion for comic relief, parodying Shakespeare, Melville, Chaucer, the Constitution. I laughed so much and so often I almost didn't know what to do with myself.

I started hanging out with the group after hours, going to bars after a late shift to have a few beers. As time went on, and we got to know one another better, we went out more and more frequently. We had a lot of fun, playing incessantly—fierce late-night games of hearts or poker in the office, pool and darts and the jukebox outside it, in a run of downtown dives. Let loose on the streeted plains of New York, we were a little wild, full of our own muscle and sting and this illusion we had of utter freedom. I felt good with them, strong and funny and stylish and on the right track. I wasn't afraid to wear crazy outfits (I had developed a real penchant for vintage clothing), or to stay out late with the boys. T. was in India, writing letters regularly that warned of the dangers of mixing business with pleasure. I ignored his advice, and concentrated instead on the gratifying feeling of being with people with whom I had common interests. I was happy to see that my sister liked my new friends, easily falling in with them whenever she was in town. And if my father was a little annoyed at my late schedule, which often meant that he went off to work in the morn-

ing while I stayed in my pajamas watching TV in the library, I
didn't let it get to me too much. Maybe it wasn't the most serious
job in the world, but I wasn't going to do it forever, and for now it
felt just right.

That February, I went to India to visit T., for six tempestuous
weeks, and when I got back, I gladly relinquished my freelance status and joined the staff as a full-blooded member of the department. It was immeasurably comforting to be around people my
own age who were both directed (that is, working for a remarkable
magazine) and a little stalled (because we had no real accountability, it was hard not to feel like cogs). Although I now worked days,
too, I still preferred the nights, for the weird feeling of being in
midtown after dark, cozy with a job to do and good companionship. There were usually four or five of us on the late shift, and we
made it a point to stop work and eat dinner together every night,
pizza or Chinese or Mexican takeout. The food was greasy and
mediocre, but it was fun to sit around a table, part of a mock
family whose members and dynamic changed nightly. It was a lot
more lively than having dinner alone with my dad, where we were
two down from four around the kitchen table. At work, hunched
over my take-out carton like everyone else, I didn't have to think
about such things, I was too busy trading stories and quips. I got
teased a lot, which made me feel loved. There was one guy, handsome and quick, with whom I especially liked to trade barbs. My
intellect and his were well matched, our words zinging across the
room as if we were stars in a forties comedy. We had other things
in common besides a love of bantering. He had lost his father to
cancer while he was in college. We spent a lot of time talking about
that unforgiving sadness, and because he was smart and talented
and, like me, had been hugely encouraged by his parents while

growing up, we also talked about what it was like to be told on a regular basis that you can do anything. We came to the conclusion that it was highly agreeable, but also slightly daunting. The problem with thinking you can do anything is that a lot of times you end up doing nothing. You can't go anywhere in life if you don't choose a direction, but taking that first step feels too limiting. It requires a mental letting go of all those other intangible possibilities. So as long as you don't make a decision, you stay free—a freedom that, because it prevents you from moving on, quickly becomes its own kind of prison.

It wasn't by accident that I was having this kind of conversation. During the three and a half years I was in that department, I remained perfectly poised to take my next step but somehow I never did. I didn't completely stay still. I started writing a little bit for the first time, small humorous pieces at the beginning, and then more serious personal essays, and showing them to my friends in the department. They gave me suggestions back, as well as their own writing to comment on. It was like being part of an informal workshop. I began to think that maybe I could call myself a writer, although I wasn't sure exactly what such a declaration would involve. More concretely, I started writing short, unsigned art reviews of gallery shows, and became the research assistant to the fashion and photography writer. Going to the library to do research for her in old issues of *Harper's Bazaar* from the seventies, I began to wonder why I wasn't working on my own projects. I was getting too old to be behind the scenes and at the same time felt mired by a strange lassitude.

As time went on, my friendships in the department and my

connection to the place deepened, but so did my fears about the future, and what I would do with the rest of my life. I was twenty-four, then twenty-five, then twenty-six, then twenty-seven, and I still didn't have any real responsibility or a career to speak of. I knew I should leave WP, and yet I couldn't drag myself away. I would wake up in the middle of the night in a cold sweat, thinking, *What am I doing with my life?* I began to have dreams that my mother came back and was terribly disappointed in me. After all her pride in me, these dreams were very hard to take. On the one hand, I was so happy to see her, to have her back, to discover as I had always hoped that her death had been a terrible mistake. On the other hand, she was so angry and cold with me that I almost didn't recognize her as my mother. Whenever I woke up, I felt pressure to change, to move forward, in a way that I could never acknowledge with my dad at the breakfast table, when he'd try to ask me casually and supportively where I saw things going in word processing.

Perhaps to relieve some of this tension, I started going bicycle riding several mornings a week with a friend of my mother's in Central Park. We met early, at around 7 A.M. or so, unless there was snow or rain or she was out of town. We weren't too rigorous about getting exercise, preferring to go fast enough to flush our cheeks and slow enough to keep a steady conversation going. Moving around the loop a few times a week allowed me to admire the majestic spectacle of the changing seasons without going anywhere from year to year. I learned the landscape by heart, from the flat baseball fields high on the west side to the bend at the base of the park just before the old merry-go-round comes into view. Every time I biked past those painted wooden horses I rode as a child, I began humming "The Circle Game," a Joni Mitchell song

I learned at camp. My sister and I would sing it for my mother in the back of the car when my parents picked us up from the bus station at the end of the summer. We never remembered all the lyrics, only the chorus, which was about being "captive on the carousel of time." We loved it without knowing what it meant.

In the trajectory of grief, this was my most passive period. I was waiting for something, for my life to start, for things to make sense again. I didn't realize it at the time, but I was making progress. It was during this period, for example, that my father and I became friends. We settled into a comfortable routine, having French toast in the morning, sharing a cab to work. We made a good team, running the apartment together. Sometimes he might ask me to take care of something, like call a repairman, other times he handled things himself. If things didn't go as smoothly as they had under my mother's reign, we nevertheless managed pretty well. I was surprised by what good talks we started having. One night we went out to dinner and had an entire conversation about his dating other people. We both cried. I could tell it was a relief to him to be able to talk about it. From then on I did my best to have a sense of humor toward his dating life, to be supportive. My sister did, too. For my part, I went from never wanting him to know a thing about my private life to talking to him about almost everything. He even knew when I had cramps, and would fix me a hot toddy to help relieve them.

My father and sister and I were fortunate. In the gap left by my mother's death, the three of us stepped toward one another, forging something new out of the remains of the old dynamic. Without my mother as an intermediary, we had to learn to speak to one another directly, and we did. After a time my father joked that if Stephanie and I got *him* to open up, anything was possible.

My second December back at home, Stephanie and I, with our father's enthusiastic support, decided to throw a holiday party. She and I got down on our knees and scrubbed every inch of the apartment, waxing the floors, polishing the silver, Windexing the mirrors. We reclaimed the space, replenishing it with our energy, until the place sparkled as it had in the old days. We filled it with flowers, and candlelight, and savory food, and hired the pianist from Elaine's, one of my parents' favorite hangouts, to come regale the guests with jazzy holiday tunes. My friends from the magazine came, and I was proud for them to see my home looking its best, the papers from the dining room removed to my father's den where they belonged. The party was a huge success, and it became a new tradition. Slowly I started to feel like I was making New York—the apartment, my life there without her, the city itself—my own.

Looking back now, I wouldn't trade that going-nowhere time for anything. I needed to be stuck, at home, with my dad, in WP. The not knowing what I was doing was what allowed me to gather my resources for the next step, so that eventually I was able to break the spell of inertia. After about three years at home, I found my own apartment and moved out, leaving my dad (perhaps to his relief) to fend for himself again. Around the same time, I applied for an assistant editor job at the magazine and was transferred upstairs, to a whole new arena of work and responsibility. I also broke up with T., whose assertive ways had felt more and more alien to me the further away I got from my mother's death, and started going out with my soul mate from WP, who in the meantime had realized that what he really wanted to do was be a doctor and had left for medical school.

One day while I was still in the word-processing department, I had lunch with a Swiss couple, friends of my parents who were in from Geneva. I met them at Café Un, Deux, Trois, a large French brasserie near my office that my mother used to love. After I walked across the crowded, red-velvet-draped room and sat down to join them, the wife looked at me, and said, "You know, Valerie, you walked through the restaurant just now with such confidence. Your shoulders were pressed back, your head was held high—it was a pleasure to see. For a long time you weren't walking so tall." It was true. My mother had always worried about our posture. We had a little thing we used to do. Whenever we were in public, we used to give each other a discreet thumbs-up sign, to remind each other to sit up straight. Without her around to remind me, I had been hunched over, caved in, as if to protect my heart from being exposed to the world. But things were changing. I was opening up.

I loved this couple, for their warmth, their humor, their intelligence about life. Along with their daughter, they were like family. The summer after my mother died, my father and sister and I had visited them in Geneva. Sitting up late one night with the daughter, who was between me and Stephanie in age and had been like a sister to us for many years, I was struck by something she observed. "Don't worry," she said to me, "you'll get to know your mother more as you go through the different phases of your life."

Her observation, given in friendship over a glass of wine, filled me with hope. My relationship with my mother had been interrupted too early, before I could connect with her woman to woman. My friend was suggesting that the very course of life would allow me to continue to understand my mother. Sure enough, being at loose ends in New York a few years later, I unwittingly got a glimpse of my mother's younger untamed self, maybe even more so than she would have liked, in the sense that I wasn't as directed or responsible as she probably would have wanted me to be at that age. The more I discovered who I was and what drove me, the more I related to the passionate young woman she had been then. I, too, knew what it was to be full of fear and excitement and bravado, surrounded by friends but also alone, with all of life lying, like the unseen path beckoning the female rider forward on that long-ago elevator plaque, perpetually just out of reach.

Driving the Deer

For most of my life, I never questioned why we keep things. I took it for granted that if someone wrote you a letter, you stashed it in your desk drawer, that when you went on a trip, you took pictures and put them in an album, that somewhere in the house your parents had stored all your report cards. I was my mother's daughter, the slender tine of a strong antler, and like her I kept letters, photographs, old Playbills (although I stopped short of scribbling "loved it" or "very moving" or "Jerry fell asleep" on their covers, as my mother had). I had mementos of travel, of school, of summer, of love. My desire to keep was never merely for the physical. I wanted to retain whatever had happened to me, as if I could hold on to the events of my life like so many receipts, thereby keeping a purchase on the past. Even after my mother died, my faith in saving life's memorabilia remained unshaken. If anything, the preserving of such tokens became even more important, allowing me the illusion that I was still connected to her somehow.

Growing up, I had been surrounded not just by objects but by stories. My parents were born raconteurs, telling anecdotes about their childhoods, their families, their youth, their day. There was even a story behind the story about their meeting. A year and a half earlier, they had both been invited to another party, also in New York. They figured this out later because it was the night of the blackout of 1965. My mother went to the gathering, which was in the penthouse of a high-rise, and once the power went out, she was stranded there along with the other guests until morning. My father didn't make it. When he got home from work, he lay down on his living room couch for a snooze—he was expecting a friend to arrive from out of town before heading to the party. Well, the friend came, and rang the bell a few times, but the buzzer was shorted out like everything else, and so my father slept until morning. As a result my parents didn't meet that night after all. (At least one person got lucky that evening. My father's friend went to the hotel next door and met a woman at the bar.) Every time I heard it, this story taunted me with its near success in redesigning history as I knew it.

The best tales, however, came back with my parents from their trips, as eagerly awaited by me and Stephanie as their suitcases full of souvenirs. Every adventure they had was transformed into an amusing anecdote whose very telling was a means not only of holding on to what had occurred but of making the past a shared affair. Once they found themselves in a small indoor market in Morocco, and my mother, who loved everything she saw, kept saying to my father, "Buy something! Buy something!" when in fact (they discovered later) they were inside a bordello. Then there was the time my parents and another couple got lost trying to enter Rome in a rental car and, after driving around the autostrada for hours (the city eluding them the whole while), began cheerfully hollering at each turn, "We're surrounding it!" That little phrase became a part of our family's vernacular—a useful response to getting lost or otherwise frustrated.

Retold around the dinner table, these stories became increasingly pleasurable to hear over time, as easy familiarity gradually replaced the anecdote's original punch. More than mere listeners, my sister and I were often active participants in their formation, either as the main subject, or as crucial eyewitnesses. As the years went on, our supply of lore grew, becoming as much a part of the familial fabric as my mother's hats or my father's flutes.

When I got back from my year in Paris, I had been away from the household for so long that on some level it was a comfort to be back among my parents' keepsakes—the intricately inlaid chess set from Spain, a dappled-leather frame I remembered my mother picking out in a Cairo market—and all the stories they brought to mind. My father and I told many of our old favorites over breakfast or dinner in the kitchen. Something would remind him of one, and even if I had heard it a million times, I let it unfold, indulging my father's pleasure in repeating it, and reveling in the humor that I knew was waiting just around the bend, a little farther down the well-trodden path.

As an adolescent I had liked to envision my life in chapters, each of which corresponded exactly to my age. There was my fifteenth year, my sixteenth year, and so on (as if life could ever be divided so neatly). When I broke up with my high-school boyfriend, I wrote a letter to him that began, preciously, "In this, the summer of my nineteenth year . . ." I hoped that all those chapters and incidents were going to add up to something, that the curve of my life would be well drawn and meaningful. When my mother died, the idea of those silly chapters dropped away. Instead everything deftly fell into one of two categories: Before and After. Now, a few years past her death, in the course of spending time with my father and retelling our stories, I began to feel as if my life might be of a single piece after all.

Along with the customary stories, I was also grateful to be back around the hundreds of photographs we had amassed as a family. Separated from them for too long, I began perusing the albums regularly, fairly amazed by all the rooms and places we had been together. Some days, when my father was at the office and I didn't have to go into work until late afternoon, I'd dump out a couple of drawers of loose photos, the ones my mother hadn't gotten around to sorting, and sift through them for glimpses of the past. With no one watching, I'd bring prints to my lips, kissing my mother's glossy image, as if to let her know I still loved her. When I was little I used to pore over a big black Hollywood directory my parents had, its pages filled with small black-and-white photographs of the stars (whose individual traits had been rendered almost uniform by the deluge of images), going over the almost imperceptible—but to my mind crucial—differences between the vivacious eyes, upturned mouths, and shellacked hair of the various beauties. Now I was captivated by only one countenance, the particular combination of light and shadow that made up the planes of my mother's face, confounded by the idea that those angles had once held the miracle of her soul inside them.

This rooting for my mother in photographs became part of a general desire to find my bearings in the apartment. It wasn't like I was going to touch or change anything; it went without saying among my father, my sister, and me that my mother's placement of our furnishings was almost holy. I wouldn't have had it any other way. In your own house you take the presence of things as a given. Objects stay in the same place for so long you can't see them anymore. You don't stop to wonder how they got there. That purple glass salt shaker has always been on the kitchen table, same for the African baskets lining the walls. For years we had a certain pepper grinder, a kitschy gift to my mother from her brother, with an old-fashioned wooden crank and a carved brass hog's head mounted on top like a miniature hunting trophy. When we had people over, it took on the guise of a slapstick prop, as each guest, expecting the pepper to come out the bottom, would hold the mill over his plate and grind away, all the while a pile of freshly ground pepper, having spewed out the snout, would be collecting on his place mat. Aside from those incidents (which seldom failed to amuse me), I took no notice of the grinder. It was just part of our family's everyday scenery—its ugliness didn't pierce my consciousness. That's what happens: the strangeness of things is dulled by dint of repetition.

Once I was over my initial dismay that nothing had changed since my mother died, I didn't want to look at anything with new eyes, as if I had been transformed by distance and time. Instead I began to appreciate the sense of permanence that emanates from things when they stay where they belong, like the dozens of liquor bottles standing in rows on their shelves in the library, dusty and foreign-labeled and filled with malodorous brown-hued liquids whose levels stayed the same from year to year (my parents weren't drinkers but liked to keep a fully stocked bar for guests). It was a solace to know that my father's formal velvet-collared coats continued to hang flat against the wall, as usual, on their hooks behind the heavy mirrored door of the foyer closet, even if, unintentionally topped by a few of my mother's feathered hats on the shelf above, they sometimes frightened me a little, emerging from the shadows like a crowd of urbane scarecrows.

It wasn't long before I got quite upset if anything in the apartment was altered in the slightest. This happened, of course. A delicate armchair in the library broke beyond repair and had to be thrown out. The juicer that we used to make fresh carrot juice for our mother when she was sick became inoperable—or maybe was just too sad to look at—and was given away. If at all possible my father, with his practical frame of mind and innate dexterity, had no compunction about jury-rigging something back together. I knew he derived great satisfaction from his workaday solutions (he was a businessman, but still enjoyed the opportunity to put his engineering degree into play), and so when the out-of-print wallpaper in the hallway buckled a little and my father got it to stay on the wall with black electrical tape that my mother wouldn't have stood the sight of, I held my tongue, not wanting to hurt his feelings. Such a small thing wasn't worth arguing about.

There were other changes I didn't let pass, however, like the first time I walked into the library and realized that my parents' silver-framed wedding picture, which showed them dancing and smiling into each other's eyes, had been turned facedown on the console where it usually presided. It struck me unpleasantly that my father had probably had a date over the night before, and out of some kind of delicacy (I wasn't exactly sure whom he was protecting—himself, his date, or my mother) didn't want to be faced with that image. Over breakfast the next morning, I let my father know how much this upset me, both on my mother's behalf and my own. I didn't want him to renounce the past. I wanted him to acknowledge that his twenty-three-year marriage was still a vital part of his life. I was soon crying so hard my father couldn't respond. He finished his coffee, got up, and left the kitchen, leaving me alone, weeping into my cereal. It didn't occur to me at the time that five years after her death, it might actually be quite painful for him to have so many reminders of his wife around.

I began to see that in order for my father to function, he could not have things remain exactly as they had been. When I thought about it, I realized this had been true right from the beginning. The night after my mother died, he had moved to her side of the bed, the side closest to the telephone and the unacknowledged center of operations for our family, as if to announce, to himself and to us, that from now on he was in charge. Moments after they took my mother's body away, he had also taken off his wedding ring, and I had never seen him wear it again. Watching him go about his life now, I was starting to understand the extent to which that gold band had moored him to my mother, to see that his continuing to wear it once she was gone would have imperiled his ability to live.

Having no choice, I had gotten used to these modifications. I no longer thought twice about it when I walked into their bedroom and saw my father on my mother's side of the bed. When he tried to make more sweeping changes, however, I resented him for it. One day, for instance, out of nowhere, he gathered up the photographs of my grandmother (my mother's mother) and gave them to me in a pile. He said he didn't want to see them around the house: she wasn't part of his family, and without my mother there, it didn't feel right. Without a word, I took them all into my room and placed them across my bookshelves, where they looked kind of crowded and funny until I got used to seeing them there. The wedding photograph stayed in the library, faceup most of the time, on occasion conspicuously down. I didn't bring the subject up with my father again. Whenever I saw it lying prone on the console, I just righted it, at the same time removing a fleck or two of dust from the glass-protected whiteness of my mother's dress.

A short time after I moved back in, my father started in on me and my sister to clean out my mother's closets (still so jam-packed that no matter how many times I went in to plunder, I was invariably rewarded for my efforts, turning up a little skirt, or a striped vest I hadn't noticed before). This had been a sore point with him for years. He understood that Stephanie and I might want to hold on to a few things, but he disliked having every single one of my mother's personal effects about, as if she might walk in any moment or as if we were maintaining a shrine. It's true we had kept everything. Aside from the natural erosion caused by our regular raiding of her closets, four years later my mother's earthly possessions were almost intact, from the red-lacquered chest of drawers in the foyer, swarming with fawn-colored gloves and gossamer scarves and sequined hair accessories, to the piles of lotions and lipsticks in her bathroom, which hadn't been touched. Behind the russet-colored wall cabinet in their bedroom, the rack of her brilliantly colored silk shirts hung undisturbed, littered underneath with assorted evening bags, crumpled tissues, old receipts, and plastic baggies of foreign currency, all exactly as she had left them.

Despite our father's insistence, my sister and I had so far managed to put off the task. The fact is, we couldn't bring ourselves to do it. We were still too attached. There was something wildly consoling about being able to walk into the deep hall closet, searching for something to wear, and rifle through the velvety coats and beaded evening dresses and ostrich-feather stoles my mother had worn, still wondrously redolent of her scent. Sometimes without thinking I'd walk in there, grab an armful of dresses, and press myself into them. I couldn't really pretend I was hugging my mother as the hangers banged up against my forehead, but I did it anyway, breathing in deep the quaint odor of beautiful, slightly faded fabrics invisibly soured by perspiration and perfume, and finding in that mustiness a thrilling residue, like the faintest heartbeat, of the vibrant essence of my mother.

I began to have a recurring dream. As a child, one of my favorite pastimes had been to go around the house looking for treasure. The building we lived in was almost a hundred years old, and our apartment featured all kinds of architectural nooks and crannies: decorative panels, froufrou moldings, recessed corners. I used to spend hours walking around the house, tapping the walls, waiting to hear a telltale hollowness. (I knew from television that that was how you could tell a wall was fake.) I imagined finding such a spot and discovering a safe behind it filled with old jewels, to my parents' surprised delight. My hunts were fruitless, of course, but for a long time I remained convinced that there was more to the place than met the eye.

In the dream, it is as if all those childish searches have at last paid off. I do find a hidden compartment. Sometimes I enter it through an existing closet, pushing aside a set of familiar clothing and opening a secret door; other times I don't even know how I've gotten inside, only that I'm somewhere in our apartment, in a room I haven't been to before and never even knew existed. The room is the same every time: a giant vault, with large, square dimensions, its walls, ceiling, and floors painted entirely in black. Cleanly suspended in the darkness are a series of chrome racks, like the kind found in department stores, with spacious aisles between them. The racks themselves are full of clothing. When I see the clothes, I feel like crying. I know without asking (there is no one to ask, anyway) that the garments belonged to my mother and grandmother, that they are heirlooms that have been lovingly passed down.

The clothing, as if appearing in one of the colossal costume exhibits my mother used to take me to at the Met, is laid out chronologically. There are saucy suits from the forties that I recognize from photos like old friends; generous skirts with dainty frilled blouses from the fifties that I sense my mother wore as a young woman; kaleidoscope-patterned loungewear from the sixties of the kind she proudly made by hand when she first married my father; and things I haven't caught sight of in years, half-remembered raiments my mother wore in the seventies, when I was just a child. In the dream I walk all around the room at a leisurely pace, filled with an enchanted sense of well-being. Not once do I attempt to put anything on, or take anything out of the room. Fingering the glorious fabrics, I pay homage to each well-cut piece, their collective beauty a rich legacy of femininity for me to revel in and enjoy. I am overwhelmed with relief to have found this room, this marvelous place for which I have longed since my mother's death, and which I have no desire to leave.

With its sensation of discovery, its promise of perfect preservation, its offer of maternal things not lost but merely waiting to be found, the dream closet splendidly counteracted what was happening in real life, where, as the years went on, my mother's dresses were slowly but surely going out of style, their colors little by little losing their luster. Solidly black dresses were taking on a reddish-brown tint, white scarves and blouses a grayish hue. My mother had been dead for four years. We had kept everything, but we couldn't keep everything still. Velvet hats were wearing away in places, the felt showing through, while the beads on her beloved antique gowns were unthreading and falling off. We wanted to hang on to all that we had of hers, but an undeniable gap was widening between the time when she—and by extension her clothing—had been alive, and the present, in which she was gone, and her adornments had grown dilapidated.

It was around this time that, despite the massive stock of old garments already at my disposal, I began to collect vintage clothing. I liked to go to flea markets, to specialty antique stores, even to the Salvation Army (to which as a family we had given hundreds of pounds of clothing over the years), and rummage through the racks until I found the dress or hat or bag that spoke to me. It was unexpectedly gratifying to buy a one-of-a-kind outfit that looked good on me, that no one else had, that reminded me of my mother, like going hunting and discovering you have a good eye and steady aim. I had a knack for finding things, the perfect cherry-red velvet dress to wear to a party on a boat, a

Jackie O–style shift with a cool cell-like pattern. One sunny day at the flea market, feeling a bit low, I spotted a jangly jet bracelet almost exactly like one of my mother's to which my sister and I both felt attached. My mood changed instantly. Seeing it glinting on the crowded table made me feel practically euphoric, as if my mother had left it there for me on purpose so Stephanie and I could have one each.

To my growing stockpile of vintage apparel, I added new clothing purchases as well. Like any young woman, I wanted to be of the moment, to take part in the world. But I had mixed feelings about this obligation to constantly renew myself, which at times seemed to be hastening away the past itself. My anxiety manifested itself in a bizarre way. Every time I left the house, I mentally tallied what I was wearing, counting what was new versus the number of items my mother would have been familiar with, as if to reassure myself that she would still recognize me. As time went on, the minutes taking me further and further away from her, the number dwindled, of course. Shoes wore out, sweaters grew pilled or moth-eaten, pants and skirts became passé. I finally got down to one item—my watch, steely and elegant, her last birthday present to me, an irreducibility that forced me to stop counting.

If my sister and I couldn't bear to lose a single button of my mother's clothing, I soon made it a mission to gain control of my own closet. I wanted to streamline, to let go, but it was hard, almost everything I had was fraught. In the course of cleaning I'd be unnerved by certain juxtapositions, like the contrast between the last pair of shoes my mother got for me and the first pair I bought for myself after she died. The former were a pair of green suede flats, square-toed, with Mary Jane–like straps held in place by little black rosettes. They were a last stand for girlhood, those shoes, and I remembered being in the store downstairs with my mother, her glazed disinterest in the whole process because she wasn't feeling well, my urgent desire to have them anyway, to reinject the simple act of shopping with all the verve and splash that it had had for us over the years. A few weeks after she died, I walked by a little shoe store on 66th Street, midway between the synagogue and our house, and saw a pair of black suede stilettos, with a flap that lay across the top of the foot like a tongue. They were ridiculously high-heeled, but I bought them anyway. As soon as I got home, I realized I couldn't walk more than a few steps in them—the height of the heels made my legs go gangly—and so the shoes stayed in their box, unworn. Now, four years later, I gave both pairs away, conscious that neither had ever been quite right.

Thanks to my late-shift schedule at the magazine, I had a lot of time on my hands, and it wasn't long before I went from cleaning my closet to tackling the rest of my room. I passed entire days in its dusky-pink confines, trying to get a handle on my desk, awash with papers, or consolidate my books. While the rest of the city went to work, I'd pull things off shelves and out of drawers and from closets until I was knee-deep in my own stuff, and our house-keeper, Miss Millie, would just walk by, shaking her head. I had this idea that if I could only make order, everything would be O.K. She thought that what I was doing was somehow unhealthy, that I should just live my life and let things be. It's true that the task often seemed oppressive. It was the same room I had grown up in, its bulletin board covered with old party invitations and dated posters of rock stars. I'd choose an area, the low bookcase where my records and tapes sat dappled with dust, the shelved closet out of which my travel memorabilia—airline tickets, museum passes, restaurant matchbooks, a red gelati spoon from Florence shaped like a Lilliputian shovel—threatened to pour. I was only twenty-four years old, already drowning in the quicksand of my own past.

When I wasn't throwing things out, I reread my mother's letters. As a break from the mess around me, I would pull out the box in which they were stored, and leaf through them one by one, reliving the various stages of my childhood and adolescence. It was a guilty pleasure to go over everything she had written, finding in her chatty, intimate missives and funny notes to me over the years renewed confirmation of her love. There'd be a letter I had forgotten about, one she had written when I was eight years old, happily at camp for the summer, mildly scolding me for my frequent requests for candy, or a little note in which she had written jokily that she'd be home at noon and then "free for you, you, and you." It was painful to bear witness to the gradually diminishing series of cards she had sent me in college, as her cancer slowly robbed her of the energy to write, but often her very words, by allowing me to feel again what had been, gave me strength. From May 16, 1988, after I had come home from college for a brief visit, I have a card that begins: "Dearest Valerie, I truly understand the feeling that went into the song 'You are my sunshine.' You came like a whirlwind *fée* to our home for one evening, and spread love, goodwill, intelligence, joie de vivre, and filled our hearts and minds with *été*." She really knew how to make me feel appreciated, my mother.

I reread these letters so many times that on occasion, if I wasn't in the right frame of mind, they lost their power to move me. It was like the stack of prewritten postcards that my mother would give to the doorman every summer we were at camp, instructing him to mail us one a day while she and my father went to Europe. My mother had tried to guarantee that there would be no interruption in her correspondence, that we would know she was thinking of us without having to wait for her letters from abroad to wind their way to the Adirondacks. I remember the good feeling of hearing my name called by the camp counselor distributing the day's post, and the disappointment if it turned out to be one of those prefabricated postcards, which meant well but were already obsolete. *By this time we are in St. Tropez*, my mother would write, *hopefully having a marvelous time.*

Stuck in my room years later, with the shades drawn and papers everywhere, I had the same uncomfortable feeling. Though it was soothing to reread her letters, it was also depressing. There I was, in my midtwenties, trying to hold on to my mother's presence in my life. It made me feel estranged from my peers, none of whom, I was sure, were spending their days like this, surrounded by old papers, like so many shrouds.

A little more than two years after I returned home, my father, sister, and I came to the unavoidable conclusion that the apartment needed repainting. It was time. There were cracks in the ceilings and a kind of unpleasant blackening around the edges of the walls and doors. We were loath to do it, though, and not only because it was going to be a lot of work. Painting and decorating had been my mother's domain. What did we know about it? I vaguely remembered my mother saying that the living room walls were *strié*, but what that meant I didn't have a clue. Unfortunately I would have to figure it out, because it was understood that the painting operation was going to be, for the most part, under my charge, as

I was the one home most during the day thanks to my frequent late shifts. My sister, who had moved back in after graduating from college, was luckily working nearby, so she could come home to check on things at lunchtime.

In order for the painters to do their job, we would have to dismantle absolutely everything. This was an intimidating prospect. It's not that I was worried about the furniture. I knew, down to the last footstool, what piece went where. What troubled me were the smaller items, the tchotchkes that bordered the library shelves, the array of antique French boxes on one table, of gilded Czech and Hungarian glass on another. If we took everything apart, how would we remember where it all went when it came time to put it back together? My mind kept turning to the unfortunate case of Humpty Dumpty.

Daunted by the possibility of inadvertently altering my mother's much-loved decor, I was equally reluctant to challenge her vision of how the apartment should work, since, alongside cultivating the appearance of our home, she had also organized its inner workings, the configuration of the minutiae of living. Clandestine objects like cans of soup and paper doilies each had their ordained spot in kitchen cupboards and pantry drawers. Her blueprint for these tangibles was so entrenched that the mere thought of change seemed tantamount to questioning how life should be lived. At the same time, it seemed likely that cleaning and clearing out and reorganizing our house would be beneficial to our emotional and physical well-being, especially in the kitchen, where I was pretty sure some of the jars had been around since the early Carter administration.

Going from room to room in a not quite methodical fashion, Miss Millie, my father, Stephanie, and I took it all down—

paintings, wall hangings, sconces, window treatments. We rolled up the carpets, except in the living room, where we tried to make sure that my mother's cherished Aubusson, securely nailed to the floor, stayed protected under old sheets. In the library we packed all the knickknacks and books and musical instruments into dozens of boxes and shoved them into the center of the room along with the furniture. We covered the whole jumble with drop cloths, which produced an ominous impression, as if we were trying to conceal a large, recently deceased circus animal.

Stephanie and I were on a mission to throw out, get rid of, pare down, although in some sense we were only scratching the surface. One afternoon we took down the African baskets hanging high up on the kitchen walls only to discover years of grime imbedded in their fibers. Since we thought it impossible to clean them properly, we set them out with the garbage. That night my father found the baskets piled casually by the back elevator, and came into the kitchen holding them in his hands, furious. "What are you doing? You have no right to throw these away. They're not yours. Your mother and I bought them together on one of our early trips. I can't believe you'd throw them out without taking my feelings into account." We apologized profusely. He was right. This had been their home together. Who were we to alter anything without asking? It was reassuring to see him get so emotional about objects he and my mother had chosen long ago, even if it forced me to acknowledge how inaccessible their relationship was—how separate in some ways from our communal life as a family. The truth is, I had no idea what meant a lot to him where my mother was concerned. The miscellany that moved him was so much less obvious than wedding rings or pictures, so unlike the scraps of the past that I held dear.

Of all the rooms we tackled before the painters arrived, it was the library that really got to me. The most crowded room in the house, it took hours to pack up. I thought I'd never see those bookshelves empty, especially as they were home to so many things besides books: framed photographs, hookahs from India, the black-and-white clapper board from my mother's film production days, all the professional medals and plaques awarded to my father over the years. One corner housed our entire collection of photo albums, which had to be treated gingerly; their spines were fracturing, the glue holding image to page, and page to binding almost completely dried out, so if you moved too quickly, individual prints would break out and flutter to the floor.

As I handled each of these items in turn—climbing up a ladder to retrieve something, bringing it down, dusting it off, and laying it carefully in a box—it occurred to me, for the first time, how completely bizarre it is that we keep things. Almost all families do, and no one gives it a second thought. You walk into someone's house and you see high-school trophies, wedding albums, perhaps on the mantel a pair of bronzed baby shoes—every form of remembrance. Suddenly it struck me as unbelievable that we bring all and sundry back to where we live, surrounding ourselves with reflections of our journeys, past achievements, and personal taste, loading our walls, our shelves, our drawers with objects we love or that suggest to the world that we ourselves are loved (or at least were once appreciated), even though we know the fate of things, which is to fade with age and ultimately wither away. As I had learned all too well from having lost my mother and seen her belongings begin to disintegrate, nothing on this earth is permanent. In the face of this, I hadn't considered before how much faith it takes to create a home—to save your child's first scrawls, to come

back from a trip and frame an especially good shot. The thought
of all that senseless effort going on all over the place made me
momentarily dizzy. I sat down for a while amid the packing debris
to collect myself. After a few minutes of this I shook my head
and realized I had to keep going—the painters were coming any
minute—and so I climbed up the ladder again, continuing piece by
piece the task of undoing my mother's handiwork.

Soon enough the painters arrived and took over the apartment, tracking paint and plaster in their wake. Drop cloths rendered everything uniformly mottled and indistinct, and in place of
my mother's pretty bric-a-brac were dozens of used coffee cups.
Reduced to its most rudimentary self—walls, ceiling, floors, bare
lightbulbs—for weeks the civilized landscape of our apartment
hung on to its status as a home by a mere thread.

And then one day it was over. The paint on the walls was declared officially dry, the moldings and doors and window frames
glowed a lustrous white. We began putting things back, rehanging
paintings and curtains, unrolling rugs across newly waxed floors.
The house started feeling like itself again, as everything went
back, more or less, to where it had been. The tones were slightly
revised, sometimes on purpose, sometimes not. If the orange in
the dining room came out a bit more crayonlike than its previously
majestic shade, we convinced ourselves we liked it better. For
some reason, the painters had had the most trouble matching the
color of the library, a jewel-like hunter green. Their version possessed a grayish cast, forest leaves leached of color on a cloudy
day. But we got used to it. It was kind of liberating to realize that
nothing bad was going to happen if things were a little bit different this time around.

Taking everything down and then putting it back up gave an

almost buoyant feel to the apartment. In the library, two shelves of now-gleaming liquor bottles had been streamlined into one, the newly empty shelf the setting for a little tableau designed by Stephanie and me; in the kitchen, drawers and cupboards were lighter; everywhere surfaces were scrubbed, objects shiny, freed of the dust of the past. Heaving a huge sigh of collective relief, my father, sister, and I resumed our routines, with the elated sense that we had somehow managed to infuse my mother's vision with new life.

During this same period, a similar process of appropriation had been occurring at our house in Easthampton, where our family traditionally went for weekends from early spring through Labor Day. At first I had hated going there just the three of us. Intellectually I knew I was lucky even to have such a place to go to, but I just didn't feel it. Without my mother's warmth and spirit, the setting had soured. The decor was a lot less formal and cluttered than our apartment in New York—a smattering of seashells decorated one table surface; a bamboo card table was permanently set up in the living room for games of boraco or rummikub—and yet once she had died, the house made me feel more claustrophobic, as if the air was as tired as the five- or ten-year-old fashion magazines still laying about. Wherever I looked I saw signs of decrepitude: crusted-over guest soaps, expired bottles of aspirin, flat cans of soda in the pantry. For the first few years after she was gone, whenever we went out there, I gave my father a hard time about how dead the house felt. I was acting like a child, wanting him to fix everything, which left him saddened, not knowing how to address my frustration. It took me a long time to accept that the dejected state of things out there wasn't his fault, or even, on some level, his responsibility to fix. After all, it had never been a man's job in our family to make a home come alive.

One day (my first summer back from Paris; I was twenty-five years old) I wandered into a store near our apartment in New York and saw a pretty pair of gardening gloves. They reminded me out of the blue that my mother had liked to put small bunches of flowers from our backyard in each room (a tradition that had completely ceased with her death), and so I bought them. The next time we arrived at our country house for the weekend, I put the gloves on, and went out into the garden with a pair of shears. I wasn't exactly sure what I was doing, but I just started snipping, trying to pick a good assortment without overly depleting any one area of its blooms. While my father and sister looked on in surprise, I came back into the kitchen and laid my booty across the kitchen counter. In our motley collection of vases, I made little arrangements, and then brought them to every room in the house. From then on this flower-cutting ritual became the first thing I did when we arrived. I loved it. I was surprised to realize that more even than reminding me of my mother, the enterprise was satisfying entirely on its own merits. Every time I opened the door to my room, the bouquet on my dressing table greeted me happily. It was funny how quickly having flowers everywhere (even if from a purely critical standpoint they were occasionally mismatched or droll-looking) changed the mood of the house.

Stephanie and I started sprucing up the place in other ways, too, bringing in art and objects and little pieces of furniture we liked. Mostly we picked up tchotchkes at yard sales, which had become a passion for us. We would take out our father's treasured (if slightly unreliable) old car, a 1964 Mercedes, and, using the local paper as our guide, ferret around all kinds of unfamiliar neighbor-hoods. The ignition would hardly be turned off before we had both raced out of the car to examine the goods. There would be mostly rubbish on offer: broken-down lawnmower equipment, worn Parcheesi boards with half the pieces missing. It was amazing what people tried to sell, and even more amazing what we actually bought. For not much more than a few dollars we picked up baskets, vintage jewelry, iron wine racks, and unusual glassware, bringing these things back to our house like trophies for our father to ooh and aah over. Sometimes we asked ourselves why we were so into it. There was something a little depressing, after all, about walking through houses that had been stripped of their belongings. You had to think that people were closing these houses for a reason, and it was probably a sad one—a grandparent had died, or a couple was getting a divorce. And there we were, merrily picking over the remains. Yet it often felt as if, in salvaging an item from such dismal surroundings, we were renewing its spirit. Stephanie found, burgeoning from one rickety table full of junk, a whimsical trumpet-shaped wine decanter, which quickly assumed the coveted spot over the fireplace in the living room.

Another shift took place on the food front. For the first time since my mother had died, Stephanie and I dusted off the grill and the grease-spotted cookbooks and began experimenting, much to our father's delight. Instead of eating takeout all the time, we started keeping the kitchen stocked with fresh produce, making sure to get the best tomatoes, the sweetest summer corn. Over time we began inviting a few friends over for Saturday-night get-togethers, which, though more casual, seemed reminiscent of our parents' weekly dinner parties. Stephanie and I were new at being hostesses, and everything wasn't always perfect (our timing left something to be desired—dinner often wasn't ready until 11 P.M.), but we had a lot of fun in the doing.

My sister and I discovered that despite our differences we worked well together. Each of us was at once fiercely bossy and willing to concede immediately if she realized the other person was right. It sometimes took us hours to get the food shopping done, because we'd argue over little things like what kind of bread to buy, or whether we should go with the nectarines or the white peaches. We weren't deciding the fate of nations but, working in tandem, we took our newfound duties seriously. At the end of my first summer at home, with Stephanie's warm encouragement, I invited my friends from the magazine—the entire word-processing department—to the house for the weekend after Labor Day. There were fourteen of us in all, and from the basement to the room over the garage, every corner of the house was full. With Stephanie's help I put flowers in all the rooms, made the beds with clean sheets, tried my best to match the towels, and bought every tasty thing to eat I could think of. To my relief, the weekend was a success. We played charades until three in the morning, took midnight dips in the pool, sat around singing and playing guitar, and ate to bursting at every meal. The house buzzed with people and activity.

Stephanie and I joked that we had become like a couple of Victorian sisters: we cooked, we hosted intimate dinner parties, we arranged flowers, we collected antiques. She took up archery; I played darts. My father wandered around the house playing the saxophone as he had in the old days. I came to my senses and apologized to him for having acted like a spoiled brat where the house was concerned. I told him how grateful I was that we were together, that we had such a wonderful place to go to, that we were enjoying our time there to the fullest. Secretly I felt that at long last we must be making my mother proud, and I could hardly believe it had ever been any other way. At the end of my second summer back in New York, a little over five years after my mother's death, I wrote in my journal: "In my mind . . . I thanked Mommy for creating that beautiful environment and for teaching us how to enjoy the simple, true pleasures of friends and food and flowers. I am only sorry it took me so long. I hardly recognize myself, so different is my attitude toward that house. And it feels so much more healthy and natural and right. I hope we enjoy it for many years to come."

A few years later, when these rhythms of life were well on their way to feeling permanent, I went to France on vacation. I was twenty-nine years old, living on my own by then but still seeing my father regularly. My plan was to stop in Paris for a couple of days before going to visit a friend whose family had a house in Corsica. I had just spent the previous weekend in Easthampton with my father and sister (our last weekend together for a while because Stephanie and I were going away), and we had had a great time together there, fixing an especially memorable lunch, playing cards, renting a few good movies. I was so filled with love for them and for the reconstituted sense of family and family life we had created that the Sunday morning of that weekend—in the midst of making French toast and coffee and setting the table for breakfast— I insisted that we all stop what we were doing and hug for a minute. They thought me a bit silly but they did it anyway, and as I held first my father and then my sister in my arms I cried a little at the thought that it was going to be a long time before the three of us were together again.

I left that Wednesday night for Paris, arriving the next morning, so happy to be there. I was staying with friends in the Marais, a neighborhood I loved. After having breakfast in one of my favorite cafés in the Place des Vosges, I went to the Pompidou to see an exhibit of Ferdinand Léger, whose gleaming painted vistas of man-meets-machine my mother had adored. In the museum shop I bought a postcard of one of his still lifes—a kaleidoscope of hats and jazz instruments and umbrellas—to send to my father. Later I went to my mother's friend Julia's house for dinner, and as we talked I briefly sketched out my plans for the next couple of days.

The next morning, Friday the 13th, I set out early. I walked all over the city and ended up in the Tuileries gardens, sitting in the sun and writing giddy notes in my journal while watching the clouds roll in. That night I had dinner plans with Hélène and Richard, a couple I had known since she and I had worked for the uncompromising P.R. woman. Richard was the one who had helped me with the mouse when I lived there, and the three of us had remained close. They invited me to have a drink before dinner at his showroom and, because he was a fashion designer, I chose to wear a new dress—it was long, with spaghetti straps, and a brilliant red. (My mother, I knew, would have approved.) After half an hour or so of being at their office I realized with dismay that my new dress felt tight around the chest, and I was having trouble breathing properly. I kept having to cover my mouth with my hand to yawn. We left for the restaurant, an Italian place around the corner, and I hoped the suffocating feeling would go away in the fresh, rain-sliced air.

Moments after we got inside—I believe we had just ordered our main courses, but I can't really say for sure—the waiter came over to our table and told me I had a phone call. In the few seconds it took me to walk to the bar, I did a quick calculation. The only person who knew where I was having dinner was Julia. Why would she be calling me? When I put the receiver to my ear, her voice sounded leaden. "Valerie, I have bad news. It's your daddy," she said, and at that point I hung up on her, not wanting to hear anything else in that bright busy place. The restaurant was only a few blocks from where I was staying, so I excused myself incoherently to Hélène and Richard and rushed out. I felt the rain spotting my dress as I tore down the narrow sidewalks, a figure in red darting past glowing streetlamps and perplexed pedestrians alike. As I ran, I prayed frantically under my breath, *Please let him be O.K. Please let him be O.K.* I couldn't wait to get off the dark wet streets, to be safely inside, to find out what was happening, to hear my sister's voice.

When I got to the house the phone was ringing and it was Julia again. My father had had a heart attack in his office. His secretary had found him slumped over his chair, and had called 911. The medics had managed to get his heart pumping again, but my father still hadn't woken up. He was in a coma in the hospital. Stephanie was with him, as were my aunt and uncle (my father's brother and sister-in-law). Other family was on the way. After talking and crying with Stephanie, I arranged to come home the next day.

I lay awake all night, my mind racing with everything this meant, my body charged with a terrible, unrelenting electricity. I prayed nonstop for my father to wake up, to do one last magic trick and surprise us all with a big smile and one of his hearty hellos. I sobbed the entire flight home, terrified my father would die before

I had a chance to see him again. One kind flight attendant asked me what was wrong. When I told her, she knelt in front of me, took my hands in hers, and looked me straight in the eyes. "He will wait for you," she said, and something in the intensity of her dark eyes made me believe her.

For the next five days we lived at the hospital. There was a heat wave. The city was stifling, unbearable. Stephanie and I stood over our father's bed, kissing his broad, still hands, stroking his wide forehead, and talking to him about everything we could think of. We thanked him for being a wonderful father and friend, recalled all the adventures we had had together as a family, and told many of his old jokes, even the bad ones. We sang all the songs he had ever taught us. We remembered how when we were little, every night he put each of us to bed, separately, with a story, a joke, a discussion, or a song. If it was a story we wanted, we could choose the characters and the setting, if a discussion, we had only to pick the topic, if a song, we had our choice of four or five standards—a motley selection that included "Russian Lullaby," "Wabash Moon," and (though none of us were Irish) a highly sentimental song about Ireland that began, "A little bit of heaven fell from out the sky one day . . ." For years he had teased us that we only ever knew the first half of any of these songs, because we had usually fallen asleep by the end. Now we realized we knew them all, every word.

Despite our prayers for his recovery, my father never woke up. On the fifth day, a Wednesday, a strangely misted sky greeted us as we left the hospital, fatherless. There was much to do, a service to prepare, the apartment to get ready for the Jewish custom of shiva, decisions to make about what we were going to do with everything. For my sister and me it was all too familiar, but it also felt markedly different. We were twenty-six and twenty-nine years old this time, adults really, and loss didn't have the same power to knock us down. That happens only once. From then on, you always know on some level that it could happen again. My father's death filled me with immense, at times overwhelming, sadness, but it didn't completely shatter my confidence in the world as my mother's death had.

That night Stephanie and I went into our parents' room together knowing that an era had ended. From now on it would be just the two of us. Outside a thunderstorm broke the heat. It was so vigorous—the rain was practically whipping our windows— that, only half joking, we decided it was a last declarative burst from our father, signifying the love he had had for us, the passion he had had for life, and his final reunion with our mother, his wife. As we lay side by side in our parents' bed, Stephanie and I talked and cried about what had happened. Our father was seventy-five years old when he died, and he died in the middle of doing what he loved to do. We were thankful he hadn't suffered, and consoled ourselves with the thought of his long, full, and rewarding life. We were filled with gratitude for having had him as a father, for his unflagging spirit. It was incredible to think that he hadn't ever admitted to having had a bad day. Every time I ever asked him how his day was, he replied, "Splendid."

Devastated to suddenly be in the world without our parents, Stephanie and I nonetheless realized how lucky we were to have had two such extraordinary individuals as our mother and father. I wished that things could have been different, that my mother could have known her grandchildren, that my father could someday have walked me down the aisle, but I also knew I wouldn't trade who they were—or for that matter, one iota of the warmth and wonder of my childhood—for anything.

Within weeks of our father's death we decided we weren't going to keep our parents' homes. They were too big to keep afloat, in both emotional and practical ways, looming large in our imaginations as our childhood settings, on the one hand, and representing a major financial commitment on the other. Stephanie and I had our whole lives before us; we might want to make other choices than the ones our parents had made.

With heavy hearts and a sense of déjà vu we began dismantling the apartment for good. Things had to happen quickly, quickly, the going through of a family's lifetime of belongings, the lifting up of one thing after another to deliberate: do we keep it, throw it away, save it for later? Anything that we found either remotely sentimental or beautiful we decided would be tucked into our tiny apartments or sent into storage. At the same time, we were forced to recognize that if we were going to embark on our own journeys through life, we couldn't be bogged down with absolutely everything my parents had ever acquired. Certain items had definite albatross potential—our mother's prized twelve-piece Gothic dining room set among them—and so after debating back and forth we eventually opted to put such things up for auction.

As Stephanie and I distilled the apartment's vast contents, we cried a lot, our sorrow at times giving way to bouts of almost uncontrollable (bordering on lunatic) laughter. There was no one else in the world I wanted to be with more, no one who understood so well what this all meant, who could feel the joy and sadness of it so intertwined. In the kitchen or library or one of the bedrooms we spent our days, together, packing up whatever we had any kind of attachment to, and for the rest, shouting, at times with a kind of maniacal glee, "Out!" Sometimes she'd have to bring me to my senses, if I wanted to keep something absurd like my mother's crumbling stamp collection (which I later retrieved from the garbage and kept anyway—I couldn't help it); sometimes I'd do the same with her. Finally, as my father had long wanted, we attacked my mother's closets, dividing the pieces we loved from the duds we were ready to give away. But we had to do his, too, and it rent my heart to take down all those serious, heavy suits, to scatter the brilliant ties, to watch all those dapper pairs of shoes be swallowed up by crackling black garbage bags. We called the Salvation Army. As they started to remove the bags, which covered the entire floor of the foyer, I remembered a gray wool top from the sixties of my mother's that I suddenly couldn't bear to lose. I plunged my hand into a bag (don't ask me how I knew which one), and pulled the top out, pieces of clothing spilling out like entrails. The Salvation Army men looked on, bemused by the last-minute frenzy.

Although I had always known they were keepers, I was nonetheless astounded by all the things my parents had held on to. In one afternoon we'd manage to unearth our childhood collection of tutus, our father's box of penny magic tricks (seemingly untouched since boyhood), and a stack of our mother's old sewing patterns from *McCall's*.

The most astonishing thing about going on an archeological dig in your own household is that almost everything you find is linked to the development of you. (I even found the assembly instructions for the cardboard playhouse I had loved to play in as a child.) Throughout my growing up my mother had left me notes telling me where she was on a given afternoon, or simply that she loved me. Now I found a note in my own handwriting that said:

To: Mommy
Will you please
Write too me
If your out when
I come home
From school
Every day that your
Out I want to see
(on my bed) a letter
of love.

at the bottom of which my mother had written "Valerie 1975?" With a shock I realized that my mother's routine note leaving had occurred as a result of a request I had made to her at the age of seven. It made me think about the startling symbiosis that exists between mothers and daughters. I had continually felt her molding me as a daughter, but it hadn't occurred to me that this process went both ways, that I had also been shaping her as a mother.

Another day, flipping through one of her scrapbooks, I found—next to a clipping of an early photo of her as Miss UJA—the words: "After my mother's death, I went through her papers, pictures. I was moved by all the memorabilia she had kept of me during all those years, pictures sent by me from wherever I happened to be." And so my mother's voice came back to me as I

worked, assuring me that, even in this, I was following in her footsteps, going through a rite of passage as a daughter that she had
experienced herself.

Whenever we went on vacation as a family, on the last morning my mother would come into Stephanie's and my room while
we were packing and get after us to make sure that we weren't
leaving anything behind. She had us look under the beds, behind wardrobes, on top of closet shelves we hadn't used in the
first place. Sometimes she even started opening emptied dresser
drawers herself. *You don't want to forget anything!* she would cry. I
thought of her frantic admonishments as Stephanie and I finished
withdrawing from our home, scouring one last time the kitchen
cabinets, pulling up a stepladder to double-check a final closet
shelf. Despite our thoroughness, we did encounter a few surprises.
In one of the secret compartments of my mother's desk, I found a
giant petrified moth, its sere white scaffolding a metaphor of strip-
ping away. And on a high dusty shelf in my father's den was a
faded, somewhat melancholy photograph I had never seen, of my
mother, seated on a pale green velvet sofa in an evening gown, her
loveliness an elegy to a lost time.

On our last day in the apartment on 66th Street, once it was
completely empty and we knew we wouldn't step within its walls
again, Stephanie and I walked through the space, spookily bare of
my mother's imprint except for the still-vivid colors of the walls
and ceilings. As we moved in and out of each room to say goodbye, we called out a motley list of beloved and mundane reminiscences, recalling for each other the French toast we had eaten in
the kitchen, the dance recitals we had put on as children in the li-

brary, my mother's hands circling the Sabbath candles in the dining room. It was a game only the two of us could play. And when, for the last time, we closed the front door behind us (all the nights my father would announce himself in three short happy rings flashing through my mind), I knew that from then on I would have to carry the familiar warmth and beauty of that bright red foyer inside me, like an extra heart.

Within a few months we embarked on emptying the house in Easthampton, too, knowing that the sooner we unburdened everything, the sooner the rest of our lives could begin. My mother had stored a lot of things out there, the clothing she had saved "for the children," our earliest drawings, our elementary-school cahiers. Stephanie and I sifted through things warily, a little tired by now of this whole process, once again keeping what we felt some kind of kinship to (often choosing one example of something to stand in for many), and letting the rest go. Seeing our kitchen cart stacked against my father's old blue wardrobe—two pieces that hadn't ever been in the same vicinity—reminded me of all those yard sales Stephanie and I had enjoyed, and I remembered wryly that old saying about what goes around comes around.

For some reason the most painful departure (even though we had consciously decided we didn't want them) was a pair of end tables from my parents' bedroom, a room whose walls were covered with flowered fabric, which produced the delightful feeling that you were sleeping in a bower. My mother had had the night tables lacquered a deep Chinese red, and the wire-woven doors backed by the same flowered fabric as the walls. The legs of the end tables were delicate and spindly, and when the moving man sent by the antique dealer picked the first one up, one of the doors, with a large blue tulip carefully sewn behind it, swung open in a small goodbye bleat. Later I thought about those things—my mother's dressing table, the wicker chair with the jesterlike spirals—like dozens of amputated limbs. Although I knew they had to go, I felt each piece of missing furniture as a bodily ache—something that had always been there was gone, and could never be retrieved.

A few days later, after finishing a few errands around town, I found myself headed back to the house in my father's old Mercedes on the same twisty back road where I had first learned to drive. I was thirteen years old when Julianna, our mother's helper for that summer, had put me in the driver's seat as a joke, and I still remembered the crazy feeling of being behind the wheel and going up and down that curving, tree-flanked road, hardly believing I was in control. Now—so many years and unforeseeable events later—for no good reason (there was no one behind me, egging me on) I found myself speeding up, taking the turns faster and faster, my heart about to explode in my chest when suddenly I saw her, she was galloping in front of me on the side of the road, as if she had been flushed out of the woods by hunters. For a few minutes we rode in tandem, cantering forward together, my heart keeping time to the rhythm of her legs, the lighter-than-light running of her hooves. I was mesmerized by the graceful striving of her head as she pushed her body onward, until I slowed the car down and let her go, my heart pounding in my ears as I watched her run away, back into the thicket of trees, a dream vision, half seen, half imagined. Like time itself she was destined to slip away. Nothing was safe against such fleetingness, not people, not things. I leaned my head against the wheel and sobbed. I had let go of so much—everything, it felt like everything—what would be left?

The Elephant's Back

When the time came for me to leave my twenties, I decided that instead of lamenting the passing of my youth, I would treat the occasion as a beginning and throw myself a party. I had always liked to mark my birthday in some fashion. As I was the first to admit, I was still looking for that feeling of love-dazzled well-being I used to feel at the age of seven or eight, the moment the rose-festooned cake arrived before me, radiant with candles and topped by a colorfully striped circus tent—or, better yet, a perfect corps of graceful plastic ballerinas—and, with all eyes riveted and my mother's arm dangling casually over the back of my chair, I blew out the flames and made a wish. Ever since my mother died, it felt as though I had lost the one other person for whom the date May 1st signified not the International Workers' Holiday or the pagan festival of spring but, on a more modest level, the day I made my entrance into the world. Sure, other people were happy to have me around, but no one else could appreciate the anniversary of that event—not even my father, who after all had been relegated to the status of enthused bystander on that long-ago Wednesday morning, racing to the hospital pay phone a little after 6 A.M. with a pocketful of change and then realizing it was so early he could call only his father and two brothers to share the news, and would have to wait until a more reasonable hour to call everyone else.

I spent some time thinking about the kind of party I wanted to give, where it should be, what kind of mood it should have. It had been a year since my father died, and my friends had been so supportive in the aftermath that I wanted to thank them in some way, to bring everyone in my life together for celebratory rather than mournful reasons. With Stephanie's help I settled on a small French bistro downtown. The food was quite good, the room charming and intimate, and best of all, I knew I could pack the place with friends. Things started falling into place—the date, the menu. My Belgian aunt, the one with a talent for flowers, offered to go with me to the 28th Street flower market and make a bouquet to put on the bar, for atmosphere.

In going to friends' thirtieth-birthday parties I had been struck by how their parents had integrated photographs of them as kids into the general party decor, using funny shots for place mats, posters, and the like. I didn't want to go overboard in that direction, but on the other hand, just because I didn't have my parents around didn't mean I couldn't raid the past a little myself. After poking around I found a somewhat capricious photograph of myself as a five-year-old, seated on my father's desk with my legs crossed and my hands folded in my lap, looking at the camera with a knowing smile. (What I could have known at that age frankly escapes me.) I decided to use it as a frontispiece for the invitation, pasting the image onto the front of bright red folding cards. As I worked I thought about what made birthday parties great as a child. First and foremost was the feeling of being loved by my family, who would wake me up that morning with a chorus of "Happy Birthday." The three of them would have worked like elves to transform our home overnight into a birthday Shangri-la, secretly blowing up balloons in the kitchen and pulling open the flat, accordionlike orange-and-pink crepe-paper streamers my mother bought at the party store to drape across every available doorway and mantelpiece in the apartment. After getting out of bed to admire their work, I would join them in the kitchen for a breakfast of my mother's French toast, whose buttery bites I could scarcely swallow in my impatience. Then there was the excitement of getting dressed for the day, the promise of presents and cake, and later the way each ring of the doorbell heralded the arrival of another friend.

Going to other people's birthday parties was also fun. Amid the comforting din of high-pitched voices you'd be showered with sweets and subject to all kinds of familiar entertainment. There'd be running around and singing with the lights out, followed by manic efforts to get the piece with the biggest rose or the most icing, and the playing of increasingly rowdy games. Afterward your mother would come to pick you up (commiserating for a few minutes with the hapless hostess, who'd be exhausted by then from all the unscripted madness), and you'd float away on a tide of goodwill, clutching your treat-filled party bag. It's true that during the actual event there might be disappointing moments— overly made-up clowns whose tricks you guessed the secret of, occasional flaps over sharing toys, somewhat hairy spikes and dips in everyone's blood-sugar levels, all punctuated by the periodic shrieks of balloons bursting. But in those days a birthday party, any birthday party, had the striking ability to fill up more than its allotted time, to spread its buttercream sweetness over the hours leading up to it with anticipation, and after, to grace the rest of the day with jollity, as if all bets were off when you had experienced such delirium.

As I mulled over these lost pleasures, I realized I wanted to give out party favors at this birthday party of mine, a little something to make everyone feel more festive. It occurred to me that rhinestone tiaras would be just the thing (for the women, anyway; I hadn't yet figured out what to give the men). I had a vision of the women in my life looking extra ravishing, their heads glittering in the candlelight. I looked everywhere, scouring party stores and cosmetics emporiums alike, but to no avail. I couldn't find a single fifties prom-girl tiara, let alone the slew of them that I needed.

In the meantime I was also trying to determine what I should wear, whether it should be an outfit I already had, or something bought for the big night. After going through my closet a couple of times, my eyes kept falling on the red dress, the one I had worn on that fateful Paris night. I ignored the sight, convinced that the sadness of that occasion made it impossible for me to wear it, that to put that dress on my body again would be grotesque. And yet as the event drew closer, the dress, hanging gracefully in my closet, became a silent dare. The more I thought about it, the more I thought that in another light, it could be a beautiful gesture to wear that same dress—not to be macabre, but to try to reclaim it from the past. By bringing out the dress for a happy gathering, I might save it from being forever emblematic of a horrible moment in my life. I wouldn't change its essence completely—grief was woven into its very threads for me—but maybe other shades could be added also, tints of gratitude, perhaps even of joy. My father had complimented me on the dress when I had originally brought it home from the store, and I liked thinking that if he couldn't actually be at the party, at least he'd know what I was wearing, he who had always been so sweet about giving compliments and advice to my mother, and then later to us, about how we looked before we went out. Then, too, I couldn't help feeling that, optimistic magician that he was, he might applaud the feat I was attempting, that of turning the spirit of a thing around.

Perhaps it was silly that I thought so much about a dress, but the question seemed to me at the time to be about something more: how I would take the past, how I would admit the facts of it into my life, whether from then on I would take pains to avoid, endlessly mourn, or try to integrate all that had happened. It occurred to me that Indian brides typically wear red on their wedding day. Not that I was getting married, but still, on a symbolic level, this event, with all my friends as witnesses, would be in its way a kind of marriage—of where I had come from with where I was going, of all that I had lost with all that I still had to be grateful for, of the daughter I had been with the woman I finally felt I was becoming.

When I was twenty-four years old, I up and went to India for six weeks. It was kind of a crazy thing to do—I had to take a leave of absence from the magazine, and jobs like those were hard to come by—but T. was spending the year in New Delhi on a fellowship, and I hadn't seen him in six months. I was very excited about going, and also nervous. Although we'd been dating for almost four years, this had been our longest time apart, and I wasn't convinced we would still know each other.

The truth is, we didn't know each other that well to begin with. From the beginning we'd had an unspoken agreement: I idealized him, and he idealized me. In broad strokes: I was supposed to be beautiful and strong and upbeat; he was supposed to be handsome and just and intelligent. We never attempted to shake these majestic illusions, or at least to flesh them out with other, more realistic nuances. Partly this was an issue of time. Of the four years we had been together, only one had been spent in the same place. No matter. I remained very stoic about our perpetual long-distance status. My mother had taught me that it was important not to have any regrets in life. "There is nothing I regret more than regret," she wrote in one of her letters, and I tried to live up to the notion. If I had to go to Paris, I had to go to Paris. If he wanted to go to India, he should go. I didn't think either one of us should hang around simply for the other person and then later bemoan the fact that we had let an opportunity slip by. Who knew whether we would really end up together?

I hadn't always been so philosophical. The day I went to college, I cried and cried during the car ride up to Boston at the unfairness of being wrenched apart from my high-school sweetheart, who was remaining in New York. I remember my mother was very gentle with me, putting up with my tears on what should have been a great day. I must have reminded her of herself as a young woman, when she went to the South of France with her mother and brother and wasn't able to enjoy a thing, for missing her boyfriend. Losing her broke something inside me. Ever since, I had been a lot more detached. Each time I went away for the summer and left a boyfriend behind, I missed him, but not enough to stop me from doing my thing.

From the beginning, my going out with T. had allowed me to put my grief on hold, and not only because I had been completely caught up in our narrative. He hadn't liked to hear stories about my childhood—he said it made him feel like I had been happier in those days than I was with him. Of course I was touched by how much he wanted me to be fulfilled in the present. At the same time this ban on my family history hurt, especially at first, when I was only a few months past my mother's death and wanted more than anything to savor my childhood. It was as if all the memories I cherished were a pile of precious coins my mother had left for me. What good was it to feel their heft and value privately? I needed to share these treasures, to know that I could transport into the somewhat lackluster present the gleaming richness of the past.

Before leaving for India, I did exactly what my mother might have done. I was still living on 66th Street then, which somehow made it easier to envision her plan of attack. First I found a doctor to give me the requisite shots and the advice I needed to outfit myself pharmaceutically, with everything from aspirin to malaria pills. Wanting to be ready for all contingencies, I bought loads of sunscreen in the highest SPF, extra pairs of contact lenses in anticipation of the dry, dusty air, and enough Band-Aids to cover a hundred blisters. Then I planned my travel wardrobe, covering my bed with all the clothes I wanted to take. I laid down practical, long-sleeved shirts, several pairs of khakis, and my father's multi-pocketed beige safari jacket, which, after my begging long enough, he had graciously allowed me to borrow. It was far too large for me, but it fell in with my romantic idea of traveling through India. For the finishing touch, I found a pair of mirrored aviator sun-glasses, which made me feel at once glamorous and tough. I looked over everything. I had T-shirts and breathable cotton button-downs, canvas sneakers and suede driving shoes with good treads, delicately ribbed socks and sturdy cotton sweaters, and all of it was beige and white and light, to deflect the glare of the sun. What I was bringing didn't feel entirely like me. I needed to shake it up a little, and so, at the last minute, I threw in my favorite pair of open-toed black suede platform sandals. They were highly im-practical and took up valuable space in my backpack, but I had a vision of myself as a kind of dark-haired Catherine Deneuve, as she appeared in *Indochine*, which I had just seen and loved. It didn't occur to me that the colonial look was way past its heyday.

Actually, buying a backpack was the one thing I did for the trip that my mother never would have done. I myself hadn't ever trav-eled that way, sticking with the large, boxy suitcases I had grown up with, but I knew that on this trip there would be no porters to help with the luggage. I would have to carry everything myself, and the truth is, I liked the idea of being self-sufficient.

Once I completed making provisions for my physical well-being, I turned to internal preparations. In the weeks before I left I read as much India-related fiction and nonfiction as I could, tak-ing in the disturbing world of E. M. Forster's *A Passage to India*, and the wild ride of Salman Rushdie's *Midnight's Children*. I filled my head with books of political essays like Elisabeth Bumiller's *May You Be the Mother of a Hundred Sons,* works by the Indian journalist Khushwant Singh (my favorite being *Train to Pakistan,* his thrilling novel about Partition), and everything I could find by Ruth Prawer Jhabvala, whose quirky yet even-keeled fiction I quickly grew to love. For kicks I read *A Princess Remembers,* the Maharani of Jaipur's memoir of her colorful, pampered life; and for a challenge I began Vikram Seth's *A Suitable Boy,* a massive tome of over a thousand shimmering pages. I thought that with all this reading I would be mentally primed for India, but of course nothing I read or did—not even the fact that I had been there once before, as a child, with my parents—prepared me as an adult for the place itself.

We had gone to India as a family in December 1979. I was eleven and a half years old. Why India? My father had been stationed in Calcutta for two years during World War II, and remained sentimental about his time there, telling us stories about learning magic tricks from the local snake charmer, and going to Fleury's, a tea salon where they served the most delightful lemon tarts, and taking the trolly-train up its looping, vertiginous tracks to Darjeeling on holiday. For all his official-sounding military duties—he was in the China-India-Burma theater of operations and went on reconnaissance missions across East Asia—my father had been an impressionable young man of twenty then, away from home, family, and country for the first time. It had been an important period for him, scary and exhilarating, and all these years later he still loved to eat Indian food, to explain how many paise went into a rupee, to laugh over the time he and a friend went to a Chinese restaurant in Calcutta and, in an expansive mood, ordered the entire menu, at the princely cost of six dollars apiece. He often reminisced about the Friday-night dinners he had there with a Jewish family who'd befriended him. As long as I had known him, my father had made a concerted effort to try every single lemon dessert that came his way, and although he declared many of them quite fine, he swore that not one came close to the sharp sweet taste of the lemon tarts he had feasted on as a young soldier in Calcutta. (My father often displayed a sort of Proustian desire to reconnect with his past through food, though he might not have described it that way.)

Thirty-five years after he left military service, my father, age fifty-six, decided he wanted to return to India with his family, to show us the sights and sounds that had struck him so forcefully in his youth. My mother was worried about taking us; we were only children. What convinced her in the end was the way my father felt about it. In one of her notebooks she wrote: "He moved me most of all when he told me he'd like to share the experience with Valerie (10 1/2) and Stephanie (7 1/2) now because 'let's face it I am not getting any younger, and it's not a trip one repeats easily and who knows if we'll ever get there together in years to come.'"

All growing up, I never knew my parents' real ages. A year before my mother died, I was at home one day, rifling through some papers in her room when I came across a stack of expired passports. I flipped them open to look at the photos, curious to see us all again in earlier versions. I quickly realized it was the first time I had ever seen my parents' official birth dates. Typed in black, the numbers informed me—impersonally, irrefutably—that my parents were five years older than I thought they were. With a chill I realized they had been lying to us about it. I hadn't ever questioned their ages. Why would I? I assumed that my parents always told me the truth. I decided it had most likely been my mother's idea. Knowing her, she probably hadn't wanted Stephanie and me to feel badly about having older parents, to worry that they would be less there for us in any way. My mother called me that night from the restaurant where she and my father were having dinner, and I could tell she heard something in my voice, but I didn't say anything about what I had learned, the discovery too unsettling for me to share. Privately I set about revising my conception of my parents. It was the first time I realized that memory is a flexible thing, that it will incorporate whatever you ask it to.

For our trip to India, my parents, bringing all of their talents to bear, produced a three-week-long extravaganza that was like a fairy tale come to life. Through business connections, my father knew the owner of a group of luxury hotels, ensuring that not only would our accommodations be first-rate, but that even within those parameters our experience would be over the top. Everywhere we went we were met by the fantastical, garlands of flowers draped around our necks, rose petals thrown at our feet. We slept in canopied beds dripping with mirrored fabrics and tiny silver bells, set into beautifully appointed rooms through the windows of which we watched iridescent-feathered peacocks stroll about manicured gardens as if for our pleasure alone. Our first night in Delhi we were treated to a private banquet followed by a magic show in my father's honor. In Agra, we trotted to the Taj Mahal in an open carriage, drawn by four white-plumed horses. In Jaipur, an elaborately costumed camel and elephant waited outside the hotel all day on the off chance that Stephanie and I might want to ride them. We did, once, for the photo opportunity, both of us looking vaguely uncomfortable up there. I had never been so close to an elephant before, my experiences of them having been limited to zoos and circuses. Unlike any of the cheerful miniature ones in my sister's porcelain collection, this elephant had many more whiskers than I was expecting, its eyes were more sad, its face more wizened. But the truth is, I didn't think twice about the harnessing of such a noble beast for our amusement. I took it for granted, along with so many other things.

My father was dashing in his safari jacket and crisp Panama hat, and he smiled through everything, taking huge pleasure in this pilgrimage to the past. I think the highlight for him, aside from the general enjoyment of showing his family the sights, was returning to that tea salon in Calcutta, where he explained to the new owner (grandson of the original proprietor) how often he had longed for one of their famous lemon tarts. With grand ceremony they brought a fresh one to our table. I watched my father take a bite of that gluey phosphorescence, and then his face broke into a grin. "It's just as I remembered it!" he exclaimed. (But that was my father—he wasn't the type to let himself be disappointed by the passage of time.) The new owner sent a box of tarts to our hotel as an expression of his goodwill. Aside from the lemon-tart episode, I didn't take to Calcutta. I was frightened by all the people, saddened and confused by the poverty visible everywhere on the teeming streets. In the other places we visited, we were protected from reality by the mere fact of being tourists, going to well-established sites where signs of destitution had been carefully removed. In Calcutta, there were no such boundaries, no way to avoid being confronted with the cruelty of life.

As a complement to our tour of India, my mother organized a jaunt to Nepal, where we spent a few days in Kathmandu and another few days on a trek, which she had been reluctant to commit to at first, nature not exactly being her thing. But, after concluding it would be good for the family, she did the requisite research, and we were off.

From the moment the nine-seater plane landed in the middle of nowhere and we descended its wobbly stairs to see a makeshift tent under which dozens of locals had gathered to gawk at the arrival of such strange-looking cargo (namely, us), it was clear that as a family we were on completely foreign ground. Imagine my mother's surprise when we were told that we had to take a four-hour elephant ride to get to the campsite. An unadorned elephant knelt down while his mahout, the young boy who drove and cared for him, helped us climb aboard the howdah, a square platform with a railing secured on the animal's back. Each of us put our legs around one of the posts, four explorers bravely facing the four corners of the earth.

And so we pushed off, the elephant beneath us loping along through the dry, grassy landscape. After an hour or so we found ourselves on the banks of a wide river, and it became clear that we were about to cross it. I think my mother would have given anything to be in Paris right about then. The river wasn't very deep (we were nowhere near monsoon season), but still the elephant labored across it slowly, weighted down by his load of five. Stephanie and I were still young enough that my father could make us laugh simply by turning our attention to a series of brown balls, the size of large cantaloupes, bobbing past us down the river, and making the keen observation that—who would have guessed it— elephant dung floats.

Not five minutes after we had safely crossed the river, we saw a rhinoceros grazing on the other side, its horn thankfully facing the other way. Hearing us approach, it charged away, its huge leathery flanks shivering, and before we knew it, our mahout had dug his knees behind our elephant's gargantuan ears, at the same time hitting its forehead with a medieval-looking spike, and we were after the rhino, hot on its trail. Once my mother realized what was happening, she began screaming. "We just want to look!" she yelled, but our guide, thinking he was providing his visitors with a better experience, egged his charge on, and for the next twenty minutes or so you could have sworn we were on a sea-tossed raft instead of the placid back of an elephant.

Soon after we settled back down to a normal pace, it started raining, and by the time we got to the camp we were completely drenched, sore-bottomed, and exhausted, glad when after a quick bite it was already time to retire to our tents. Right before I was about to jump into bed, I noticed there was a strange bulge in the center of it. I was terrified. My father grabbed a stick from outside and poked the lump, which jiggled in response. Emboldened, he lifted the white goosedown comforter and revealed a hot-water bottle. I slept fitfully.

In the middle of the night, a guide came to the door of our tent and whispered for us to get up and, without putting on our shoes, follow him. We did as he instructed, following the other sleepy guests to a long sheet of canvas tacked up across the trees.

Through a pin-size hole I watched as a picture-perfect leopard ate a bloody piece of meat that had been left out for him as a lure. He seemed incredibly far away until I realized that someone had handed me the binoculars backward. The guides made a big deal of it, saying in hushed tones how dangerous he was, and my eyes grew wide as I watched him slink away—he had been so close, just on the other side of the canvas. Once he was gone, we were all shepherded back to bed. In the morning, I wasn't sure if I had dreamed the experience or if it had really happened.

In the end the four of us enjoyed our foray into the wild. Trekking was less "cultural" than what we usually did on vacation, but it was no less interesting (or, for that matter, contrived). The best part was the chance it gave us to make fun of ourselves for being so steeped in city ways.

My second trip to India took place with much less fanfare. I flew to Delhi alone, arriving at two o'clock in the morning to an all but deserted airport. T. was waiting for me outside customs, but we didn't have much of a reunion because there was some kind of road strike going on, and he was eager to get us on our way. It was a hellish ride. Our cab couldn't get ten feet without being stopped by policemen, who shone big flashlights in our faces, as if we were fugitives on the run. By the time we got to his place, I was completely unnerved, too tense to sleep, wondering if the person next to me was anything like the idea I had been carrying around in my head.

For the first couple of weeks, I got acclimated to life in New Delhi, the nightly lighting of an electric coil to induce torpor in the ubiquitous mosquitoes, the unbelievable crowds swarming the streets, the fact that traffic regularly ground to a halt because of a meandering cow, the brilliant flowers blooming from the oddest places. Having been there for six months, T. had made lots of friends and gained an impressive knowledge of the ins and outs of the city. I was glad for him that he had made a life for himself there, but it was strange not to be a part of it. On the other hand, I, too, was forging my own routine back in New York, one that naturally included him less and less.

Both because he was spending time in India as a young man and because he was tall and dark and handsome, with a knack for making things happen, T. reminded me a lot of my father. But he was a lot more anxious and wound up than my father was, shilly-shallying over every decision. I had been away from him for such a long time—a year and a half, if you included my year in Paris—that I had forgotten how stressful it could be to be around such worry. I tried to take it in stride, because the alternative would have been to question the idealized view of him that had been se-curely established in my mind from the start. As he took me to task for not being open enough, or for not understanding that things were done differently in Delhi, I'm sure he refrained from revising his opinion of me, too. After all, holding each other up to impos-sibly high standards allowed us to see not just one another but our-selves in the best light.

In a way, my being in India put him back in the driver's seat, where he had been at the very beginning of our relationship. He had a tendency to be bossy, to have firm ideas about where we should go, what we should eat, and so on. When I had first lost my mother, I had been very attracted to that quality. It made me feel I was doing what I was supposed to be doing. (It didn't occur to me that I had just switched authority figures.) The longer I had been away from him, the more I'd become used to making my own decisions, living life at my own pace. Now we clashed more frequently.

But in India, he knew the ropes, and I let myself be led by his decisions. I followed him to dance parties, to clubs and restaurants off the beaten track. He introduced me to many of his new friends, whom I liked for the most part. I saw that they had a proprietary affection toward him, which was nice, yet on some level made me feel like an intruder instead of his girlfriend of four years. I also couldn't stop contrasting my appearance with that of the Indian girls I met, admiring the bangles snaking up their arms, their nonchalantly draped saris next to which my button-down shirts and pants seemed clunky and unfeminine. The more I observed their lissome figures and easygoing ways, the more uncomfortable I felt in my own body. One of my mother's favorite expressions had been the phrase "with it." She used it when she was feeling jazzed up about a party, a person, or occasionally herself. I kept thinking about her saying it, how she would smile and snap her fingers to convey the full force of the phrase, and sadly realized I was, for the time being anyway, feeling distinctly "without it."

I couldn't help but be reminded that I was *forenghi*, foreign, even to myself, with my blistered feet and skin blotchy from the heat. Each time I went out, I was catcalled as I walked in the streets, mocked for my whiteness and my strange green eyes. Being outside the caste system and not protected by the privileges of traveling first-class, I was an especially easy target for local cabdrivers, who would start making kissing noises once they figured out my traveling companion and I were mere boyfriend and girl-friend. The fact that they had no compunction about deriding my status as a proper young lady bugged me. Sometimes I'd insist T. say we were brother and sister, to avoid the rude comments. All these incidents reminded me that I was no longer a child, safe in the company of my parents.

We were going to be covering a lot of the same ground in our travels as I had with my family. But we would be visiting other places, too, sites that would have been inappropriate for children to visit, among them Varanasi, the city of burning ghats along the Ganges River, and Khajuraho, whose temples are covered with erotic carvings. We would begin with a tour of Rajasthan, from Agra and Jaipur, where I had already been, all the way to Udaipur, the famous city on a lake, where I hadn't. Our first stop would be Vrindavan, a small town full of temples, as T. thought it would be interesting to be there during the festival of Holi, a religious holiday in which children traditionally sprinkle delicately scented flower water on one another.

As we set off on our tour, I dressed accordingly, or so I thought. It was hot, but I wore my father's safari jacket anyway, belted tightly around my waist, along with my new aviator sun-glasses, and one of my mother's silk scarves tied around my neck. I felt like the very picture of chic as we got off the train in Mathura and hopped into our three-wheeled open scooter, which would take us to the ashram where we'd be staying for the next couple of days. We hadn't gotten more than twenty yards from the sta-tion when we realized that Holi had begun. But the little children with their flower water were nowhere in sight. Instead, we were stopped by a crowd of about twenty laughing, feral teenagers holding spray bottles of neon-colored dye. "Don't be scary!" they said leeringly, jostling to get a closer look at us. T. was reaching into his wallet when the first splatter hit. The smile I had been wearing disappeared as I watched turquoise dye streak my father's beloved safari jacket, while a spurt of hot pink liquid hit my cheek and ran down my mother's Parisian scarf in a spidery splotch. I tried to duck, and when that proved hopeless I just put my hands over my face, but it didn't help—the color even permeated the clear plastic nosepads of my sunglasses. They finally let us go (not before T. paid out ten rupees), adding insult to injury by squirting us from behind as we drove away. When we got to the ashram, we went to our room. I was a little trembly as I took off my clothes and hung them up to dry, noting that my father's jacket was ruined. I felt like the whole country of India had just told me off. It would no longer put up with anything colonial, least of all colonial chic. I got the message. Putting away that vision for good, I slipped on a pair of fresh white kurta pajamas that I had bought in Delhi.

Later that afternoon we took a walk through the town, passing many temples, Buddhist, Hindu, South Indian, set one after another along winding streets medieval in feeling. Still a little shaken by our earlier experience, I loved retreating into the sun-warmed courtyards, and then into the temples themselves, which I found eerie with their candlelit shadows, the odor of incense rising up from cool dark floors stained pink from Holi. It was a relief from the mood outside, where there was a feeling of anything goes, as if everyone had agreed that all decorum would be set aside for the day in favor of sheer anarchy. We continued getting sprayed by youngsters, until my crisp white duds were as spattered as my face. I tried to be more relaxed about it, to go with the crazy flow of the day. Adding to the mayhem were all the creatures of the non-human variety. I had never seen so many animals running wild. Horses, donkeys, cows, goats, bulls, and stray dogs flooded the narrow streets. It was far different from the carefully orchestrated meeting with the animal kingdom I had had with my parents in Nepal, watching a leopard as if he were part of a live panorama. Now, on the river, snapping turtles guarded the banks and, in a nearby field, a horde of vultures stood around like a bunch of tired, hunchbacked old men. As if to heighten the aura of truancy in the air, in the course of our walk a monkey snatched a bunch of bananas right out of my hand, and I recoiled in horror at the lack of boundaries between inquisitive, greedy nature and my physical being, which I was increasingly dismayed to realize was less than sacrosanct. It made me aware that I had always held nature in abeyance, as if it were something that could be contained and controlled. My father had loved zoos and circuses, had been happy to see animals behind bars or performing for their audience in well-designed habitats. My mother had washed her hands of animals altogether. I saw now that I had grown up thinking nature in all its glory was somehow inappropriate.

When we got back to the ashram, T. and I joined the other guests in an outdoor pavilion where chants were being conducted, and as we sat listening we took snapshots of each other, to commemorate our recent attack. It's one of my favorite photographs of myself. My face is psychedelic pink, silver, green, blue, and I'm smiling, my gaze relaxed, as if I've conceded defeat to the fact that I am soiled and human. These were perhaps the most honest pictures of each other we ever took, the pristine vision we usually held of one another plainly marred.

It occurred to me that I was tougher than I thought. I didn't need everything to be arranged for me, to have hot-water bottles and white goosedown comforters or their warm-weather equivalent. (I didn't even need plates—the ashram served every meal on individual banana leaves.) That said, I was really looking forward to our next stop, Agra, chiefly because we would be staying at the same hotel where I had stayed with my parents. But right away things weren't as they had been. The contrast was depressing at first. No one greeted us with garlands, or took notice of our arrival in any way. And then the hotel itself wasn't half as grand as I had remembered, the rooms a little run-down, the food in the dining room average at best.

Then I realized maybe it was a good thing that we repeated a step I had taken with my parents right at the beginning of our trip. It dashed any expectations that this new journey was going to be in any way similar to the old, and made me in fact lose the desire for it to be so. I valued the time I had had with my family, but I had been a child then. I was grown up, ready for a different experience of the country, for the possibility of having another view of it than the one afforded by the windows of five-star hotels. It wasn't just because we were on a budget this time. Both of us had the desire to encounter the country in a real way, to try to overcome being mere tourists. Although we didn't ride to the Taj Mahal in a horse-drawn carriage, I noticed that this in no way diminished the ultimate splendor of the sight, which was as stupendous as I had remembered. Posing for a photograph on the same white stone bench I had sat on with my family long ago, I mused on the fact that in travel, as in life, there is often more than one way to approach the same destination.

We continued our journey, stopping first in Jaipur, where we stayed in a lovely, slightly dilapidated hotel that used to be a maharajah's palace. I liked it so much that thoughts of my earlier experience began to recede. And then we went on to Udaipur, where we spent a few days in a hotel on one side of the lake, and then a few days on the other, to experience the view from both sides. By this time I was more into the swing of things. I had grown accustomed to the heat, the food, even to the teasing of the cabdrivers. When fellow guests came down and said they had seen a cockroach in their room the size of a small dog, I laughed with them, and was just grateful that such a creature hadn't seen fit to pay us a visit. T. and I were feeling more comfortable with each other, narrowing the space that had opened between us in our time apart. There were many things I no longer knew about him, many things he no longer knew about me, but at least we were enjoying the sights and each other's company more with each passing day. Together we walked the streets of Udaipur—I loved the white city, the way you constantly came upon the lake at the center of it from yet another angle. Not once did I ride an elephant or a camel. My feet planted firmly on the ground, I had an altogether different perspective, looking up as they lumbered past, not suited up for touristic purposes but bearing huge loads, fulfilling their fates as beasts of burden.

It was in Udaipur that I got my parasite, as if India wouldn't be content until it infiltrated not just my skin but the very core of my body. I can pinpoint the meal. The restaurant had a groovy feel, its clientele a medley of backpack-carrying kids who weren't all that different from the two of us. I liked the apricot-colored walls and the pop music playing in the background, but my appetite wasn't exactly piqued by our tabletop, which offered an assortment of Rorschach-like grease stains and a suspicious-looking plate of yellowy-orange butter. Flies, meanwhile, circled above our heads warily, as if they had already tried the food and been put off. But the rest of the customers looked satisfied, and so despite my misgivings I ate everything put in front of me, the end result being that I spent the next two days running from my bed to the bathroom, which was situated down the hall. In a funny way, getting sick took the pressure off. Once you've been laid that low, you figure you've seen the worst of it and have no choice but to take it easy.

So I relinquished control, and took pleasure in details, like the ritual of buying tea from a vendor when you arrived in a train station, the steaming sweet liquid passed up to you in a hard clay cup that you smashed on the floor of the platform when you'd finished, dust to dust. I marveled at the explosion of vegetables and fruits cascading over one another in the markets, the bazaars showcasing textiles of every imaginable hue. I even got used to the steady intrusions of nature, saying nothing when a mouse practically ran across my foot at a local tailor, not flinching at the sight of the occasional garden lizard climbing up our bedroom wall.

An Indian friend of my mother's from New York was in town visiting her sister, and I spent a few afternoons with her. It was good to get away from my boyfriend a little bit, to enjoy the womanly pleasures of shopping and talking, to feel that a part of my experience in India was mine alone. I went to the old city with her, and we wolfed down some deep-fried sweets from a street vendor (I knew T. would have declared such delicacies off-limits). We went to an outdoor market, where she taught me to bargain with the sellers, saying that they wouldn't respect me if I accepted the first price, that I shouldn't forgo the pleasure of haggling. I loved looking at the lustrous fabrics, the way a store owner would take a tall stack of shawls and shake them out one by one, until my eyes got lost in the waves of color and pattern and shine.

A few days later we visited a museum to see a show of Indian miniatures. As I peered in to admire each flawless detail, the gilded elephants and minutely bejeweled thrones, I thought about how gemlike these paintings were, how they offered up a bird's-eye vision of India that was exotic yet unthreatening. I began to see that in that first trip the whole vast spectrum of India—its masses of people and terrifying poverty and resounding culture—had had for me and my family the very aspect of a miniature painting. In our going from five-star hotel to five-star hotel, eating spaghetti bolognese and seeing the requisite sights, a process of pictorialization had occurred. India had become something to marvel over, an assemblage of facts and pain and history that was moving, like art could be, yet able to be held in the palm of your hand and set aside.

During the second trip, I lost a sense of my body's invincibility, but more importantly, I lost the conviction that my childhood had expressed at all times the only point of view, the only experience of a place. Going back involved seeing other sides. I needed to realize that life with my parents had been one way, but that it wasn't necessarily the only way—there were wonderful things about it, but also things I missed out on. Of course, this was partly because I had been so young. But still, the return taught me not to be afraid to learn things on my own. It was like the story my mother used to tell about my nanny. One day, my mother was cooking artichokes, and asked her if she wanted one, too. "Oh, no," she said. "I don't like artichokes." "Really?" my mother said. "But they're so delicious, how can you not love them?" "Well," the woman admitted, "actually, I've never tried one. It's just that my mother told me I wouldn't like them." The story became an example of how not to be, a reminder that I should never take my mother's word for something in place of experiencing it myself.

My mother always used to say that until she met my father, she thought love meant suffering. I had never known such anguish personally, but soon enough I felt the truth of her words. A year after my trip to India, when T. and I were both finally living in the same country, I found out that he was having an affair. A friend of mine was kind enough to tell me about it. I couldn't believe it— that someone I loved and whom I thought loved me could hurt me that way, that the reality I had understood was so completely wrong. It was very strange to go back over the preceding months and rewrite them, having thought things were one way and being forced to acknowledge otherwise. At first I could hardly take the shock of it. What he had done was so at odds with the actions of the noble personage I had so sorely needed at the time of my mother's death, the image of whom I had held dear for five years. I began to see it had been a cinch to maintain the fictitious perfection of our love in the letters we wrote to each other faithfully during our separations, to adore the picture I had of him, goodlooking and clever. It was much harder to admit that I had never quite felt like myself when we were together, that I had never found it easy to talk to him. The truth is, if I had really been able to see him, warts and all, I wouldn't have stayed with him for so long. When it came down to it, our interests were too unlike, our personalities too contrary. The real him, with his good qualities and his shortcomings, was of no use to me.

It was one thing to have lost my mother. That was no one's

fault. It was quite another to have someone whom I had trusted betray me. I lost confidence in my own judgment, in my ability to love or choose a person to love. Going out with him had been the first big decision I made after my mother died. For a long time I didn't want to think it had been a mistake, and so, holding on to the abstract idea of what we had, I remained in a kind of self-imposed trance. It took him cheating on me to snap me out of it and force me to act. My heart broken, I ended it by phone the same day I found out, and told him I never wanted to see him again. I knew it was the right thing to do, that we never would have made each other happy in the long run, but it took me a long time to get over it. I found myself in mourning, for the person I thought he had been (who as far as I was concerned no longer existed), for the relationship I thought we had had, for my own innocence.

With the abrupt end of this period of my life, I began to consider the fact that unlike most young women, whose early twenties are a time of differentiation from their mothers, I had been desperately trying to hold on to my mother, not to lose any part of her, and that this had happened somewhat at the expense of my growing more fully into myself. It struck me that idealizing anything—the past, a man, myself, my mother—could also be a way of being hard on it, of holding it up to standards that are impossible to meet. And, finally, because in my early hopes for this love that had come so swiftly following my mother's death, I had hidden much pain, the end of our relationship also served as a time-release capsule, unleashing torrents of sadness I was hardly aware had been stored away.

✳   ✳   ✳

A month or so before my thirtieth-birthday party—I had all but given up my hope of finding tiaras—I went out to do a few errands in my neighborhood, around the corner from the 26th Street flea market. It was the end of the day, the vendors were packing up as I walked by, but my eye was caught by a heap of twinkling objects. I stopped in my tracks. There before me were dozens of vintage tiaras, each one with a distinct rhinestone design set on a lightly carved band. I asked the woman how much, and she gave me the price of one. "No," I said. "I want them all!" She didn't believe me at first, but finally I convinced her I was serious, and we agreed on a fair price. When I got home I couldn't stop smiling, thrilled that the universe had provided and I now had a slew of tiaras on my hands.

When the day of the party arrived, I put on the red dress. I chose the biggest tiara of them all and stuck it on my head, and then strapped on a pair of red patent-leather open-toed heels with clusters of plastic fruit on them. "But Valerie," my sister said, "you can't do the Audrey Hepburn thing and be the Chiquita banana lady at the same time. You have to choose!" "No, I don't," I said, weirdly confident it was all going to work together somehow.

The moment the evening began it was pure magic, from the magnificent bouquet of deep burgundy peonies on the bar to the sultry sound of Edith Piaf wafting through the air. As my friends arrived, they exclaimed about my tiara and with great pleasure I told them that they each had one waiting for them at their place setting. (The men, it turned out, had to make do with cigars.) It was a spring night, so the restaurant owner flung open the French doors to the street, and as the breezes danced through the room, I felt as if we had been transported to Havana—the men with their cigars, the women sparklingly animated.

It was wonderful to have all my friends in the same room, laughing and enjoying themselves. As I groped for the reason why the night felt so special, why its romance moved me so, I realized that to create something meaningful as an adult is all the more precious because you know how ephemeral life is, how painful and difficult and even ugly it can be. In planning that trip to India so long ago, my father had been aware that he wouldn't be around forever, my mother nervous about taking such young children along, but they made it happen anyway, wanting to give us, as a family, an experience we would never forget. And they had. As I thought of all they had given me over the years, I felt borne along by their spirits, as if the room was filled, along with the invigorating air and the smiling, familiar faces, with all the trumpeting force of their energy and love. Toward the end of the night, the cake was brought out, and as I blew out the candles, my sister took a picture of me. I look happy.

A couple of years later I was going through some boxes when I found a letter that my mother had written to me when I was seven, one that she had never given me. "Today you are 7," she wrote, "and we'll have candles, cake, children, and presents. You and your sister will glow from happiness at all the love that will surround you. I will smile at the parents and children alike. I will organize it all, but something in me will cry and remember my own birthday in Antwerp, Belgium, 1940. I remember hearing sirens in the middle of the night behind closed curtains. I remember being huddled with other children in the cellar while our parents, wearing the Jewish star, whispered nearby. I remember being bewildered and afraid, more of their fear than of the airplanes dropping their bombs over our heads."

And so what had seemed one way was actually another. The happiness I felt all those times was the offspring of her terrible pain, and at the same time a testament to the strength of her will.

I was reminded of the story of the blind men and the elephant that my father used to tell Stephanie and me when we were little. Each man goes up to a different part of the elephant and, taking the measure of the tusk, the foot, the ear, the tail, declares with certainty that he knows exactly what the creature is. The funny thing is, that while each of them is absolutely correct in describing what they have in hand, not one of them grasps the whole. And so it is with the past, the memory of which forever changes shape according to what we are holding in the present.

A Conclusion
About Lovebirds

A few months after my thirtieth birthday, I took a new job as an editor at an art magazine. I was excited about it, though not in a high-flying sort of way. I loved the idea that I would be immersed in the world of culture, as if the opportunity had blossomed from seeds instilled in me early on by my mother's passionate museum-going, but my eagerness was tempered by a very real dose of fear. Becoming an editor represented a big jump in my career. It was the first time in my professional life that I was going to have account-ability, the first time a section of a magazine ran the risk of putting out blank pages unless I had commissioned and edited the right number of pieces. For once I would have, directly under my aegis, a group of writers turning to me for advice, discipline, support, and clarity. This was something of a frightening prospect.

Even more daunting was the thought of leaving the safety and comfort of the literary magazine where I had been for so many years. On the one hand, I was more than ready, having grown out of the role of assistant editor that I had held for two years. I admired the senior editors for whom I worked, and was happy to come in each day, but it was increasingly frustrating not to have any actual responsibility. On the other hand, I was loath to leave such a supportive environment. It was like being one of many children in a large, indulgent family. I felt adored and cosseted, and yet I knew I was in danger of being forever perceived as a junior.

In theory I was all for the idea of spreading my wings. In reality I had no idea what I was in for. I was going from the supposed chaos of a weekly to what I imagined would be the relative calm of a monthly but fast observed that the pressure at a monthly simply had that much more time to build up. I soon realized I had been used to something of a luxury-liner approach toward putting out a magazine. My former place of employ had been a titanic enterprise, characterized by gleaming headquarters and highly individualized ranks, all of which made for a fairly smooth production process. Even when things got down to the wire, as they often did, there were always enough hands on deck to push the issue through. On the whole, people were polite, even generous toward one another. If a colleague went on vacation, it didn't make your life miserable, so you wished them a bon voyage. Suddenly I had joined the small, harried crew of a rugged schooner, whose ability to launch a magazine each month was contingent on every person on board pulling his or her weight and then some. You couldn't even take a long lunch without your absence being felt.

One of the greatest shocks was the number of hours I was required to spend at my new job. In a matter of days I had gone from sailing out every evening at six with hardly a care in the world to never leaving my desk. The offices were high above Lafayette Street, and luckily I loved the view from my chair, the low tracts of buildings spreading east, the variegated rooftops, the occasional glittering glimpses of the far-off river. I never tired of watching the sky turn colors each evening as it grew dark, the mad crescendo of pink and orange streaks followed by that strange quiet moment when the entire city seemed drenched in blue, as if submerged underwater, until finally the glow of my desk lamp, like a lone-burning taper, would overcome the day's last light, and instead of the city below I would see only my own reflection, a weary young woman leaning over a manuscript with a pencil.

Occupying a large loftlike space on the thirteenth floor, the offices had the feel of a garret. Our individual cubicles were created, hodgepodge, using wooden dividers and bookcases of various heights, and there was just one set of bathroom stalls, which meant you had to knock before entering to make sure that any occupants were of the same sex. I had fallen in love with the setting immediately, despite the lack of amenities. Between the profusion of art books and the hundreds of past magazine covers held in thin black frames that lined the walls, the place had a warm, edgy glamour, like a woman whose charm resides in the fact that she never looks completely put together.

One fall Saturday, about two months into my job—I had taken

to regularly replenishing my underwear supply by then, no longer having time to do laundry—I was at my desk, lost in the theoretical intricacies of a recalcitrant review, when I heard a squeak, and a persistent one at that. At first I told myself it was just the usual clanging of the pipes overhead or a vibration in one of the ineffectual radiators. But this sound was different. Small and shrill, it seemed to be coming from the other side of my bookshelf. Strangely paralyzed from investigating any further, I kept wondering to myself what it was, until finally an editor whose desk area was next to mine stood up and said, with a grand flourish of his pencil, "O.K. Where's the rat?" I prayed that it wasn't a rat. The two of us rounded the corner cautiously. Sitting on a table next to an open window and eyeing us calmly was a small bird. It was beautiful, with pale green feathers that ended in a deep blue tail, a soft yellow face, and, above its beak, a stain of peach. Its eyes were dark, shining dots, surrounded by a miniature fringe of what looked like carefully drawn Betty Boop lashes. As lovely as it was, there was something comedic about it, too. It took to walking around on the pipes up near the ceiling, and every time we tried to approach it, it would do a quick sidestep, like a feathered incarnation of Buster Keaton.

While I kept my eye on the moving target, my colleague ran out to get supplies, returning a half hour later with a bag of sunflower seeds and a plastic cage. By Marie Antoinette's standards it wasn't anything grand, but the bird didn't seem to mind. As soon as we put it down, our little friend hopped right in. For the rest of the day I kept getting up from my desk to go look at the creature, admiring its form, so graceful and light. I wasn't quite superstitious enough to think that my mother had sent it to me as a sign, but still, it struck me as a pretty magical thing, to have a bird fly in the window like that.

On Monday morning, word of the new arrival spread quickly around the office. Everyone came and paid their respects before the cage, oohing and aahing over the beauty of the bird and the bizarre story of its appearance. One of the publishers called in an expert, who told us we had a peach-faced lovebird on our hands. Without analyzing its DNA she couldn't tell us if it was male or female, but she said that lovebirds have a need to bond—we had to hold it in our hands every day or else get it a companion (of either sex, it didn't matter). She scooped it up easily, stroking its belly and the crown of its head, and then clipped its wings so it wouldn't be able to fly away. After she left, several people tried to reach in and pick it up, but it batted around frantically every time someone put their hand in the cage. I decided to try it, sensing that at the first wing flutter I would lose my courage. As if to mock me for my cowardice, the bird, in a wild flurry of dashing around, bit me, leaving a red pinpoint of blood on my left index finger. We decided we would probably have to get it a mate.

I wanted to believe that the bird didn't need any company. I liked picturing it as a solitary creature, probably because I had just ended a relationship. I was trying to feel exhilarated about being on my own, and so I found myself identifying with the bird, seeing in its lone trajectory an uncanny reflection of my own circumstances. I, too, had serendipitously landed at the magazine, I, too, was unsure of how long the place would be able to hold me.

I wasn't the only one who took to the bird. Almost overnight, the entire staff grew very attached to the little thing, which spent every afternoon chirping away the hours. It became a point of pride that we had acquired a bird in such a fashion. Visitors to the office were brought to see it straightaway. Though at first all the fuss made it somewhat hard to concentrate, people gradually got used to having a pet on the premises. After an officewide vote, we decided, for the sake of convenience, that we would think of the bird as a male, and we named him Verdi.

It was incredible how swiftly Verdi brought the whole office together, as if he were a baby, with everyone offering advice and various forms of affection. And as is often the case with newborns, it was the women (I couldn't help noticing) who took charge of the cleaning and feeding, fashioning a weekly schedule. Though we reproached them repeatedly with jokes and threats, the men on staff washed their hands of taking care of our communal charge in any practical sense.

Though his cage was on the other side of my area, I could spy Verdi from my desk through a narrow crack between the book-shelf and the wall. I had only to shift my head slightly to see what he was doing, his feather-rustled body a small prize, an unexpected consolation amid the workaday grind. Sometimes, thinking of all the freedom he had given up, I felt claustrophobic looking at him in that little cage, where he had no room even to flap his clipped wings.

As for me, I had wanted responsibility, and now I had it. The job was incredibly demanding, with work piling up nonstop. While I felt I was holding my own, I was also exhausted most of the time, my inner resources strained. I came to the conclusion that if the literary magazine had played a parental role in my life, the new office was like high school all over again, with a similar sink-or-swim atmosphere. Working long hours was just another part of proving my cool (and my editing mettle) to my sharp, somewhat intimidating peers. I often found myself wearing a tiger-striped skirt I had, to make me feel more fierce. Silly as it was, I believed it gave me what my mother called *koyech*, the Yiddish word for strength.

At least I was developing good relationships with the writers under my care, an interesting cast of art historians, critics, professors, and graduate students. Though a few of the older ones gave me a hard time at first for being young and inexperienced, for the most part everyone accepted my authority as an editor, and I took pleasure in the back-and-forth of honing each piece. I had the feeling that every time the phone rang, I had to put on another hat. I was alternately taskmaster, cheerleader, psychiatrist, judge. Most often I felt like the mother hen of a particularly bright and anxious brood, toward whom I felt in turn affectionate, protective, and exasperated. As I cajoled one of them into accepting a drastic but necessary change, or scolded another for being delinquent with a piece, it was a relief to lean over and watch Verdi preening himself, softly oblivious to editorial egos and the unrelenting crush of deadlines.

One day I asked the senior editor if he thought the bird was happy. "Would you be happy if you were locked up in a little cage?" he asked. "How am I not in a cage?" I replied, laughing, thinking of my cubiclelike space, the piles of manuscripts that kept me bound to my desk late nights and weekends. I shocked us both with my answer, which had burst forth from me before I could censor it.

Perhaps being in a cage was putting it too strongly. I was enjoying many things about the job—the growing sense of camaraderie with my colleagues, the huge feeling of accomplishment at the finish of each issue. With several closings under my belt, I was finding the workload more manageable. At the same time, it was obvious that the general volume of work far exceeded the capacities of the tiny staff. We were perpetually behind, every issue in danger of falling apart at the last minute, and once it was thankfully sent to press, we were without fail already behind on the next. No matter how many people were brought in, this way of doing things wasn't going to change; it was part of the institutional makeup of the magazine.

It occurred to me that though I couldn't do anything about my own situation for a while—I had to earn my stripes as an editor before I even thought of changing jobs—I could at least do something about Verdi's. The plastic cage was clearly inadequate. Over the next couple of weeks I made a few quick trips to the flea market but found nothing. Finally, as I was passing by the window of an antique store on my way to meet a friend for dinner, my eye was caught by a big, square cage whose floor had been covered with autumn leaves. I went inside to inspect it more closely, noting with satisfaction the evenly spaced bars that met at the top, at a plaque on which the imprint of a brass star was visible. The cage, which had two fat wooden perches, handsomely carved corners, and the requisite swing, was tarnished and battered, but strangely appealing, with the aura of a surrealist *objet*. When I asked about it, the owner said he would give it to me for a hundred dollars, exactly the amount I had been told I could spend.

I brought it back excitedly to the office. Everyone agreed that Verdi looked very good in his new home; his vivid coloring stood out splendidly against the old, dull metal. I was so glad. That same evening—I was alone in the office, working late to meet yet another deadline—I leaned over my desk at one point to peek at the bird, and couldn't see him. I walked around the corner to get a better view, and my heart sank. The cage was empty. How Verdi had gotten out was a mystery—the door was securely shut. I glanced up and saw him walking overhead on one of the pipes. This time I was not amused by his sashaying. After an hour of chasing him around (I was anxious to catch him, but also, being my mother's daughter, terrified at the thought), I finally cornered him and shooed him back inside.

The next day, when I told everyone what had happened, we convinced ourselves that he had shimmied through a small opening near the cage door, so we wired that part shut, sure the problem had been solved. But Verdi kept escaping. To walk over and find the bird sitting on top of his cage was deeply unsettling. It just felt wrong. People began muttering that he could probably fit through the bars. He seemed too big to make it through, but I had to admit it was possible.

Over the next few days, Verdi pretty much stopped chirping. His body seemed more elongated than usual, and he looked fearful and forlorn, not the relaxed, puffed-out ball of feathers we had grown used to. Checking on him more and more frequently, one afternoon I rounded the corner and watched as he neatly hoisted himself back into the cage, pulling himself through two bars and gliding in like a diver into water. The cage, despite its beauty, was revealed to have a major flaw. We all agreed it had to go, so I returned it myself, slightly teary, feeling as if I had failed.

As I lugged it back to the store, I thought about a lot of things. I thought about my old job, and how strangely hard it had been not to have any accountability, as if I had been a child. I thought about my new job, and how hard it was to have so much, to be the grown-up finally. Having too much freedom or being too squeezed wasn't good for the bird, and it wasn't good for me either, not in terms of a job, not in terms of life.

Soon after the cage debacle there was a groundswell to find Verdi a companion. I had to agree. He certainly wasn't getting any physical affection from us. Although I was considered something of a bird expert by this point—because I had been there the day he arrived and was strongly linked in everyone's mind with his con- . tinued presence—I had never been able to bring myself to hold him, preferring to admire him from afar, much in the same way my mother might have, she who had always claimed she loved birds. Inculcated with her distaste, I couldn't help feeling a tinge of re-vulsion at the thought of getting any closer.

But it was difficult to find a single lovebird in the city. The species is traditionally sold in pairs. After much research, we lo-cated a source. One afternoon I ventured there, along with three other members of the staff (all women, of course). It was a spe-cialty store in Tribeca, where they were selling off a small brood of lovebirds one by one. At the entrance, there was a sign saying we had to disinfect our hands. As I rubbed on the disinfectant, I laughed to myself, thinking how the instructions were a complete inversion of my mother's worldview. Rather than being worried that we might catch something from the birds, the store owners were worried that the birds might catch something from us.

Finished with these preparations, we walked in to find our-selves surrounded on all sides by a dazzling ornithological array. There were birds everywhere, of every color and size, hanging from every conceivable perch. They created a remarkable din, flapping and squawking and talking to one another. It was almost too much for me, what with dodging the droppings being launched from overhead and avoiding the large, gaudy parrot by the door, who seemed ready to bite all newcomers with his fearsome beak.

The group of us approached the front desk gingerly, only to see three unbelievably tiny lovebirds hopping around on the counter. We told the guy what we were looking for, and he picked one of them up. "This is the one for you," he said. The little bird was a faded green, a muddier tone than Verdi's, with a blue tail, a black beak, and bright black eyes. Because I was standing closest, the guy offered me the chance to hold him.

My fingers were trembling as I reached out to touch him, and in those seconds I felt myself to be equally attracted and afraid. As my hand drew closer, my heart started beating faster in my chest, while sweat formed on my temples and in the hollows of my arms. Drawn to the smallness, the sweetness, before me, I nevertheless had to fight every instinct in order not to pull away. I felt I was moving in slow motion, breaking through the invisible bars that my mother had established in my childhood to keep me at a remove from any flesh-and-blood manifestation of the animal world. Next thing I knew I was holding him. He was so jittery in my hands, his minuscule bones tangible just underneath his feathers, which brushed against my skin in little fluttery kisses. I felt a kind of joy surging through me. In the taxi back to the office, I carefully held the perforated cardboard box. It was like holding air. I couldn't believe there was life within.

We named the new bird Omar. He was only two months old, still a baby, and so we were instructed to wait a few weeks before introducing him to Verdi. In the meantime, he got a lot of attention from all of us. I for one went constantly to his cage to pet him. I had never known that a bird could be so loving. This bird liked being held. He called out to me when I passed his cage, pacing back and forth excitedly until I went over and opened the door, at which point he'd jump right onto my waiting hand. It amazed me each time that he recognized me, that he wanted me around. I took so many breaks that I was worried I would get in trouble, but I couldn't stop myself. It satisfied a deep need, to hold and to love this creature so much smaller than myself. I had thought Verdi exquisite, and he was, but Omar spoke to me. I held him, fed him, bathed him. I knew the exact spot beside his beak where he liked to be caressed, and when I rubbed it he would shut his eyes and make a little clucking sound that let me know he was happy. Sometimes he inadvertently shat on me, but I was surprised to find this didn't fill me with horror as it once might have.

We were all a little sorrowful at the thought of losing Omar to Verdi, but we geared ourselves up for the task and ordered a fancy new cage from a catalogue for the occasion. If the first cage had been too small, and the second too big, this third one was just right. Spacious and white, it was like a luxury condo, with multilevel perches, a swing, and twin containers for food and water. An officemate asked a friend of hers, a young woman who was studying to be a veterinarian, to come in and advise us on the merger. Lovebirds mate for life and are very territorial, she told us. It was important that neither one of them feel overly proprietary about their soon to be shared space. For that reason, they should start out with a chaperoned date, and then, when the moment of truth arrived, be put in the new cage at the exact same time.

To our surprise Omar and Verdi didn't take to each other immediately. They pecked and screeched until we were forced to cover the cage with a sheet to calm them down. Sometimes they just sat placidly side by side, seemingly ignoring each other. The best, of course, was when they nestled close, leaning in, eyes half closed, feathers fluffed, not caring a fig for anyone or anything else, a state of bliss we witnessed more and more frequently as the weeks passed.

At the beginning, Omar had been much more physical than Verdi, very much a baby who needed attention. In reaching adult size, he began to look more and more like his companion. His face took on a similar peach hue; his beak lost its black and became the same fissured yellow. As they became harder to tell apart, Omar increasingly bonded with Verdi, becoming less and less attached to me. Soon he wasn't so quick to jump on my hand; he was more likely to bite it. As they became a pair, I was forced to let go.

It occurred to me that in transferring my affections from Verdi to Omar I had begun to renounce, too, a vision of myself as the heroine of my own adventures. I had moved away from identifying with the first bird to wanting to extend myself over the second one, to hold his fragile being near and safe. This felt like a big change for me—I had never thought of myself in a maternal way. Five years past the age my mother had always wanted me to marry, I was starting to see how I might be good at nurturing and protecting those I loved, that I might even derive great pleasure from doing so, as she had. My mother hadn't taught me to care for animals, but she certainly had given me an inspiring example of how to take care of one's own.

A few months after I left the magazine to go on to other things, I accepted an invitation to attend the wedding of my second cousin in Antwerp. I was looking forward to going, especially for the chance to be with the grandmother of the bride, my *tante* Roszi, the only *tante* I had left since Bella had passed away a few years earlier. I enjoyed visiting my mother's family, but I didn't go that often because it was hard, too, to be in Antwerp without her. It stirred up so many things—the trips we used to take when I was a child, her vulnerability during the war, the stunning lack of a mother, or a grandmother, in my life.

I usually had a lively time with my uncle David, who still lived in Antwerp. Whenever I visited, he would take me to little jazz bars and stylish cafés where he would smoke and I would ask him questions about the past. Sometimes he spoke to me so frankly about his love life that it made me uncomfortable. I would have to remind myself that in losing my mother he had lost one of his best friends—I thought about how open I was in conversation with my own sister—and I would try to respond as she might have, giving advice or sympathy as needed. In many ways my uncle reminded me of my mother, in his knowledge of art and literature, his sense of humor, his gift for storytelling, but at the end of the day I was struck even more by the differences. He had a more pessimistic view of life than my mother had had, and on occasion being with him made me miss her lifting spirit all the more.

The best thing about going to Antwerp was the chance to stay with a *tante*. I would feel as if I had turned into a child again, acquiescing meekly as one of them fed me sweets or suggested I take an afternoon nap. Now that Bella was gone, I stayed with Roszi. We had fun together, playing cards, looking at old photographs, cooking (me watching, her doing), and always, once I had been with her a few days, and we had gotten used to each other's company, she would ask me why I wasn't married yet. Knowing she was asking out of love, I didn't get angry. I just tried to reassure her that I was happy with my life, that I didn't feel ready yet to settle down, that there were certain things I wanted to do first. She would shake her head at me. I would laugh and say, "Look, my mother didn't marry until she was thirty-four. I still have time!" But we never reached a satisfying conclusion. In her world, women were meant to marry young. Her four granddaughters were each being married off as they turned eighteen.

In my mother's time, Jewish men and women still danced together at parties, married women didn't necessarily wear wigs, and young people got to know each other a little bit before getting engaged. In the years since the war, the Jewish community in Antwerp had become increasingly religious. My second cousins were raised orthodox, observing the Sabbath, keeping strictly kosher, and following other rules I didn't even know about. Their father, Roszi's son, was a successful businessman, a pillar of the community who was sought out constantly for his opinion or his blessing. He and my mother had always gotten along. I found him frustratingly old-fashioned and a bit gruff sometimes, but he was also charismatic, and I appreciated being welcome in his home for Shabbat dinner, to visit with his wife and their four sweet-tempered girls. Each daughter had her role in the family: the eldest was the beauty, the second soulful and wise, the third a natural comedienne, and the youngest the apple of everyone's eye. It was the third one who was getting married now. The older two, ages twenty-five and twenty-three, were wives already, with several children apiece. The first time I met their young husbands, each one kissed the air around my face, making a joke of the custom dictating that a man not touch any woman but his wife. I liked my cousins, and I think they liked me, but we were strangers to one another, our ways of life so divergent they could have been taking place in different centuries.

* * *

Two months before the wedding, *Tante* Roszi died. She had been ill for several years but was still so energetic that, though she herself was in her eighties, she had gone every week to a retirement home to help feed "the old people." (No one knew her exact age since Blanca had made her change it when she arrived in Antwerp after the war.) My uncle told me that hundreds of people had gone to her son's house to pay their respects, all saying what an outstanding woman she had been. Greatly saddened at the thought of being in Antwerp without Roszi, it hit me anew how important it was to keep relations with the family alive.

The closer the time came, the more nervous I got. I was going to be such an odd duck there, a thirty-two-year-old writer and editor, not religious, not married, not even accompanied by anyone. The wedding was going to be a huge black-tie event, and men and women would be separated, according to orthodox custom. I wasn't sure what to expect. My uncle had already passed along a message from the father of the bride, saying they were very much looking forward to my coming but would I please wear something that covered my décolleté. I decided not to take offense, and ran around New York looking for something to cover me chin to toe.

And so it was that on the Saturday before the wedding I found myself in Antwerp, going to the synagogue with my uncle to pay respects to the family of the bride. I was in black, wearing a Panama hat at a rakish angle, the way I had often seen my mother wear one of my father's. (It seemed appropriate to cover my head,

311

as I knew that all the women my age, without exception, would be married, and wearing wigs or hats or both.) I felt very alone as I walked up the stairs to where the women, in candy-colored suits with matching confections on their heads, were holding court, acutely aware that I was dressed wrong, making the fact that I didn't belong all the more obvious. I was relieved when I saw my second cousins, so grown up I hardly recognized them. We spoke about Roszi, grieving a little together. But this was their day, and they had so many people to talk to that I soon found myself shunted about by the growing tide of women. Though I was comforted by the sound of their voices, gossiping in snippets of French, Yiddish, and English, I also felt quite alienated from the scene. I started humming "And the Band Played On" under my breath, which only heightened the carnivalesque feeling I had of seeing myself in a funhouse mirror, grotesquely off compared to everyone else, who without question knew where they were supposed to go, what they were supposed to say.

I wanted to do my mother proud, but in her absence it was hard to feel like a part of things. On some level I wondered why I had come, and was relieved when I met my uncle back outside and we went on with the rest of our day, going to a couple of galleries, a movie, and then out for *moules frites* and a good glass of beer. Kosher living it wasn't, but it was much more akin to life as I knew it.

The next day we had a break from the wedding activities, and so I arranged to have coffee with one of my mother's best friends. We met at Fouquet's, the obvious place for a rendezvous, and she recognized me instantly as my mother's daughter even though we had never met, which was weirdly reassuring. (If my mother's friend recognized me so easily, then surely my mother would still know me, too?) The first thing the woman said to me was *"Elle avait les doigts les plus sensuels que j'ai jamais vus"* (She had the most sensual fingers I've ever seen). I thought of my mother's hands, of their charm, as her friend went on to talk about my mother's crushes when she was young, how all the boys had been madly in love with her. She mused, *"Elle avait une magie."* It was true, my mother possessed a magic, the kind a woman can't fake or hide.

In the course of our conversation, she kept interrupting to say how like I was to my mother in my gestures, in my way of talking with my hands. I had always noticed with friends of mine how much they reminded me of their mothers, in their way of express-ing themselves, their laughs. It was marvelous to realize that I, too, had taken on some of my mother's mannerisms, that this was un-conscious but inevitable. It made me feel good, not that I had be-come my mother—as her friend said, *"Il n'y a pas une deuxième"* (which is the French way of saying "they broke the mold")—but that I had inherited a few of her less ineffable qualities.

The following afternoon more than five hundred people came together in a large reception hall at the Antwerp Hilton for the *chu-pah*, the marriage ceremony. I hadn't brought any formal daytime wear, and the contents of my suitcase were being stretched to their limits. Each time I saw my family, I had to be dressed in heels, with a skirt going below my knees and my arms covered. This wasn't exactly the sort of thing I was traveling with for a trip to Europe in July, especially since I had planned to dress up only once in

Antwerp, for the actual wedding. Back in New York, I knew what to wear to almost any occasion. Here, without any female points of reference, I was completely at sea.

Just as I was realizing I was dressed inappropriately again— all the ladies were once more in fancy day suits—I was taken in hand by an elderly woman, who introduced herself as a friend of Bella and Roszi's. Holding my hand in hers, she told me she had been like a sister to them, and in her waved dark hair, her erect carriage, the softness of her skin, I sensed something of Roszi. She knew all about me, that I had lived in Paris, that I was interested in art, that I had a sister—the obvious result of my *tantes* talking proudly about us over the years. She was so inviting and affectionate with me, it almost gave me the feeling of being with one of my real *tantes*.

I sat next to her during the ceremony, among the women. The men were sitting on the other side of the raised aisle leading up to the flower-festooned *chupah*. As I waited for it to begin, I couldn't stop thinking about how many differences there were between this event and the type of wedding I usually went to. For one thing, the eighteen- and nineteen-year-old bride and groom were practically children. Then there was the fact that they hardly knew each other. They had met maybe a couple of times, under heavy supervision. This was the way things were done in the community. Matches were arranged by the fathers of the involved parties, through letters of introduction or a marriage broker. My mother's cousin was considered quite liberal. His daughters were allowed to meet their intendeds and express their approval before being given away.

The room hushed as the young groom walked up to the *chupah* at a deliberate pace, as if he bore on his slender frame the weight of the ages. He was flanked by his father and soon-to-be father-in-law, all wearing tallises and solemn, almost mournful expressions. The rabbi and the cantor waited for them under the *chupah*, where the groom and his retinue stopped and turned around to face us. As the rabbi began praying, accompanied by the cantor's plaintive song, the young man seemed to enter into a trance. He was davening as he waited for his bride, his lips moving silently and incessantly, and after several minutes I saw that he had tears running down his face.

Moments later the bride arrived, standing at the head of the aisle, her face so heavily veiled it was erased completely, a wall of white. As she passed by me, practically held up by her quietly weeping mother and mother-in-law, I saw her chest convulse with sobs, and only then did I grasp how terrified she was. She circled the groom seven times, in accordance with Jewish custom, and in her somber steady steps we seemed to be witnessing her passage from girlhood to womanhood, part of the inevitable cycle of life. The atmosphere in the room was more than somber. It was funereal. I thought about what was coming to an end with the marriage of these two young people. It was their innocence, their untroubled childhood existence. From this day on the two of them, joined for life, would assume the responsibilities of adulthood in the community. Did I envy them that certainty about how their lives should be lived? Yes, a little.

Once the ceremonial glass was smashed under the foot of the groom, the mood became much more lighthearted. The newlyweds, clasping hands and grinning, ran back down the aisle, while the rest of us, moving more slowly, drifted back into the entrance hall and milled about. The bride and groom were nowhere in sight, and when I asked my uncle why, he explained that they had disappeared to be alone together in a room for ten minutes. Guarded by two witnesses outside the door, during that time they would eat something and speak to each other for the first time as husband and wife. My uncle said that this moment of privacy was very important, that it was a symbol of their married status. Before I knew it, the couple had returned, and there was a burst of dancing right there in the hall, with the men surrounding the groom, the women the bride. I looked at my cousin's face and was relieved to see her smiling. Women kept coming up to her to kiss her and say mazel tov. Her laughter could be heard throughout the room. I felt happy for her, but separate from the joyful throng, and after a few minutes of watching, I found my uncle and we left. We had a few hours before the evening celebration, but I was tired from the strain of trying to understand everything, and we didn't go out. I just went to my hotel room to rest.

I took my time getting ready for the evening, drawing a bath, pinning my hair back with a sequined clasp. I had chosen a dove-gray silk skirt that ballooned from the waist, a black silk top with peasant sleeves, a beaded black shawl, and a small black lizard-skin clutch of my mother's. I slipped on a pair of square-toed black satin heels and started to feel, if not exactly right, at least passable.

I was meeting my uncle back at the Hilton for the reception, and so anxious was I about being late that I was literally the first guest to arrive. The staff was still setting up, rolling tables into the same vast room where the ceremony had taken place. My mother's cousin, the father of the bride, was walking around in a tuxedo, giving last-minute instructions. He teased me for being so prompt as he said hello, and I was slightly embarrassed. Then again, I figured I'd be lucky if being early was my worst faux pas of the evening.

Guests began to arrive, elegantly dressed, the men in black suits, the women bedecked and bejeweled. They reminded me of my mother, with the Deco jewelry they wore, their brilliant plumage. Even their wigs made me think of her; she wore one at the end of her life because of the chemo. I was struck by how many successive generations of families there were—children, parents, relatively young grandparents—and by the way everyone seemed to know one another.

After twenty minutes or so I found my uncle, and we went to the bar to get a drink. He reminded me not to lift my hand to shake any man's hand, but to wait to see if he made a gesture first. He introduced me to a couple and the woman eyed me kindly, saying she had known my grandmother. I excused myself for a moment, and when I returned, my uncle told me that she had been embarrassed to say that my grandmother had come to Antwerp as a maid. "But I knew that already!" I said to him, and we chuckled about her sense of delicacy.

I was a visitor from another realm, and yet as I met more and more people who had known my mother and my grandmother, I began to see that I had as much a right to be there as anyone. Within moments of making my acquaintance the sparkling, gossiping women would be clasping my hands, smiling at me, telling me things in their accented English as they looked me up and down, nodding. *Your grandmother was a beauty, too . . . She had legs to here . . . I knew your mother . . . I knew Gisèle . . . I lived next to your grandmother when I was a child . . . You are the exact picture of your mother.* (Of course this last pleased me most of all.) I saw that though she had left so young, my mother had made quite an impact. Everyone knew who she was, that she had lived in New York, that my father wore hats, even that my parents regularly took the *tantes* on trips with them. I really felt like my mother's daughter, my grandmother's granddaughter, felt my kinship to them.

My uncle kept telling everyone I was engaged. I got really mad the first time, since I wasn't, and it didn't strike me that you should lie about such a thing, but then he asked, "Do you want prospective suitors to start arriving at your table?" Balking at the thought, I told him to say whatever he had to, he would hear no further objections from me.

After an hour or so I went to take my seat. I was expecting to be stuck in Siberia, but as I wended my way through the tables I saw that I had been seated in the heart of the room, at the table of my second cousins, the two older sisters of the bride. I chatted with the oldest one, the twenty-five-year-old, serene in an upswept wig dotted with pearls. I told her about my life, and asked about her three sons. She spoke about them proudly but matter-of-factly. I struck up a conversation with the girl sitting on my other side, a friend of theirs, also a young wife and mother (I think she was twenty-three), who by coincidence was the daughter of the gracious woman I had sat with earlier. When I admitted I wasn't kosher, she said, in a gentle way, "Oh, I'm sorry," as if I had suffered a loss, and seeing how sure she was of herself and her place in the world, I almost felt as though I had. She mentioned she was interested in interior design, and I asked her what period she liked best. "Modern," she said. "What's the point of being in the past? But not too modern, it has to be able to last." And for her, it was true. Today is the same as yesterday which will hopefully (*Mirtsishem*) be the same as tomorrow, and I felt lulled by the comforting continuity of it, so different from life in New York, with its governing principle that anything can happen.

At the head table, their family members spreading out on either side of them according to gender, the bride and groom sat next to each other, symbolically joining the two halves of the room. Before the meal began the bride's father stood up and made a toast, a *simcha*, to acknowledge the spiritual presence of the loved ones who were no longer with us. Everyone was thinking of Roszi, of course, but I thought of my mother and my grandmother, too. As I looked out at the hundreds of people in the room, I thought about destiny. In a sense we were all gathered—for this occasion, in this place—because Blanca had run away at the age of eighteen to Antwerp, where Bella and Roszi had joined her after the war. The spectacular gala being held that evening was the flowering of roots that had been set down long ago. I was proud, thinking of Blanca's bravery, Roszi's heart, Bella's goodness, moved by the loving relationship between the sisters, wanting to be together after the devastation of the war. It was thanks to their strength as women that the family had survived to celebrate on this day.

In between courses, the men and women danced, separated by a row of palms. I was content to be like one of those trees, observing everything, not on one side, not on the other. But then, despite my feeble protests, my oldest cousin took me by the hand and led me onto the floor. I was laughing nervously, relieved when the steps came easily. For a few brief heady moments I was pushed into the center to dance with the bride, our leaping feet moving us toward and away from each other as we held hands high above our heads and spun.

Just when I was really feeling like a part of things, holding hands with strangers in an ever widening circle of women, enjoying the mindlessness of the dance, I noticed an attractive darkhaired woman across from me say to her well-heeled daughter, "Isn't she lovely?" I knew they were talking about me, and I started to repress a smile. Suddenly everything else in the room— the bride popping balloons, the subsequent spray of glitter, the young girls tossing candies across the barrier—faded for a moment, and all I could see was the condescending shake of the daughter's head and her lips mouthing the question: "Yes, but how old is she?" The words resounded in my ears. I flushed red, and left the circle.

As I went to sit down, I realized that despite people's civility, for every woman there, my unmarried status was a *shanda* (a scandal). Trying to have a sense of humor about it was hard. Although I appreciated the warmth with which I was embraced each time I met someone, as the evening progressed I had started to dread these meetings a little, finding it tiring to be questioned always about the same thing, as if marriage were the ultimate criterion by which a woman should be judged. *But what's wrong, you're still pretty, where is the problem?* each one would invariably ask. It was uncanny how quickly the women deduced this information from my ringless fingers, like hungry birds pecking sharply for a worm. Each time my heart sank a little at their nosiness, however well meant. I would have to remind myself not to take it personally, and just smile and bow my head a little and move away.

It occurred to me that if I was getting upset about the ceaseless questions after one night, it was nothing compared to how draining it must have been for my mother, who actually came from within the fold. Earlier in the evening I had been idealizing the safety of having a rightful place in this close-knit society, but by the end I had started to see that it was a little claustrophobic to be so known, to have your every action (or inaction) judged. Never before had I truly understood the type of discomfort my mother must have felt on a regular basis, first living here, then returning for visits as a single woman—the pressure that must have come to her not just from her mother but from the entire community. I remembered her wanting me to swear I would get married young, and began to appreciate in an almost visceral way where her insistence had come from.

For the first time, I found a poignancy in my mother's trips back to Antwerp, seeing in them not only the desire to visit family that I had always known of but the desire to prove that she had made good in the world, which I had never fully suspected. I felt embarrassed for her, moved. It was like growing up and realizing the rest of my mother's drawings weren't as graceful as her renditions of birds. Though she was candid in her efforts, she drew too quickly. Whenever I saw her sketches, which were a little raw and messy but also sweetly true to their subjects, my heart would fill with love for her. The vulnerability of those drawings, their slight awkwardness, made me want to protect her, though from what I was never sure.

The following morning I called the mother of the bride to thank her. I told her I would never forget such a wedding, that I was leaving Belgium with my heart full. She said that her oldest daughter, my cousin, had enjoyed talking to me, had appreciated knowing that the family is moving in different directions, having different life experiences. I thanked her for seating me with my cousins, saying she had given me a lot of honor. She said, "But of course, Valerie. *Blit blaybt blit.* Blood remains blood. You're family."

When I left to return to Paris later that afternoon, I was drained. At the same time, as I sat on the train and watched the flat green landscape of Belgium go by, I also had an unexpected feeling of accomplishment. I had set out to pay respects to my mother's family, to renew those bonds, but in so doing I had also reaffirmed my own identity. I was one in a line of dynamic women. I had felt for a long time that they were a part of me. Now I saw that I was equally a part of them, of their legacy, which meant that no matter what happened next, I belonged to a trajectory. My grandmother would always be the difficult one with the great legs, my mother the fantastic one who got away, and I would always be her daughter, even if I didn't have her in my life anymore. I didn't have to hold on so tightly. I was forever going to be connected to them, to the past, even as I went forward with my life. The story would continue. I felt free.

In that spring almost a year earlier, before I left the art magazine, I became involved in a debate about the cover of the May issue. The choice was between a large-scale abstract work, filled with cell-like shapes in swimming-pool blues, and a minor painting, a sketch almost, of a delicate little bird, all off-green lines on a pale bluish-pink background. I desperately wanted the editor in chief to go with the bird. "It's gorgeous—people will buy it even if they've never read the magazine before, just to have it in their living room," I argued. And then, "How perfect for May, the month of the birds and the bees." I pointed out that we had just had an abstract cover the previous month, that it was good to have something figurative now and again. My strongest argument, however, was that the bird would be a little inside joke

for the magazine, one that everyone who knew us would appreciate. People listened, but they teased me, too, calling me a bird
lady, saying I had grown obsessed. I was holding my ground, until
the editor in chief said, "How do we know this isn't just an attempt on your part to thematize this era?" Spooked by how well
he understood the way my mind works, I thought to myself, *If
he only knew.* Outwardly I backed off, though I was delighted in
the end when they went with the bird painting after all, its lines
floating—like the birds my mother had taught me to draw as a
child, like the patterns through which I tried to make sense of my
life after her death—between illegibility and a kind of spare, bracing elegance.

Acknowledgments

There are many people who have been invaluable in the process of writing this book. I would like to thank Matthew Lane for being there every step of the way. I am indebted to him and to Justine Cook for the intuition and care with which they read each chapter. My deepest thanks to Deb Garrison, my editor and friend, and Tina Bennett, my agent, for their insight and dedication. I am also obliged to John Bennet and Dan Menaker, whose encouragement early on meant so much.

Thanks to all those who passed through the pages of this book in friendship. In particular, I take my hat off to Peter Hirsch, the real-life mastermind behind the Secret Santa episode. For their sustaining faith and support, I thank Daphne Beal, Nathalie Farman-Farma, Elisabeth Frankel, Stephanie Ittleson, and Maurie Samuels. I am grateful to David Neiman for his generosity in revisiting the past and wanting to get it right. Special thanks to Judy and David Steiker, Francine Steiker, Carol Steiker and Paul Holtzman, and Sylvain and Michèle Ferdman, for always opening their homes and their hearts. And, of course, to Stephanie, without whom none of this would have been possible.

About the Author

Valerie Steiker's writing has appeared in *The New Yorker, Vogue, ARTnews, The Forward,* and *The New York Times Book Review.* Before becoming an editor at *Artforum* and, more recently, at *Vogue,* she was on the editorial staff of *The New Yorker.* She lives in Manhattan.